URBAN INDIGENOUS ASSEMBLAGES

Urban Indigenous Assemblages

Qom Mobilities and the Remaking of White Buenos Aires

ANA VIVALDI

VANDERBILT UNIVERSITY PRESS
Nashville, Tennessee

Library of Congress Cataloging-in-Publication Data on file

LCCN: 2025020129
ISBNs:
978-0-8265-0835-5 Paperback
978-0-8265-0836-2 Hardcover
978-0-8265-0837-9 ePub
978-0-8265-0838-6 PDF Ebook

Front cover images: Buenos Aires and the Puerto Madero Neighborhood, photo by eli medeiros/Shutterstock.com; and countryside around Bermejito, photo by Ana Vivaldi.

This book will be made open access within three years of publication thanks to Path to Open, a program developed in partnership between JSTOR, the American Council of Learned Societies (ACLS), University of Michigan Press, and the University of North Carolina Press to bring about equitable access and impact for the entire scholarly community, including authors, researchers, libraries, and university presses around the world. Learn more at https://about.jstor.org/path-to-open/.

CONTENTS

Acknowledgments *vii*

INTRODUCTION. "Welcome Indigenous Brothers": Indigenous Subaltern Assemblages and the Challenge to White European Buenos Aires 1

1. **"Ending Up in Buenos Aires":** Histories of Movement from the Chaco 23

2. **The Villas:** The Spatiality of Race in Buenos Aires 54

3. **Making a Barrio Qom in Buenos Aires:** Space and the Politics of Recognition 87

4. **"Encountering the Indigenous":** Middle-Class Humanitarianism 117

5. **Subaltern Assemblages:** Extending Spatial Control Through Multiple Associations 146

CONCLUSION. Assemblages and Rethinking Indigenous Territorialities 185

Notes *195*

Bibliography *225*

Index *245*

ACKNOWLEDGMENTS

This book was the result of multiple encounters. I was fortunate to receive support beyond reason from many people. I met with the people who have shaped these pages in Buenos Aires and the Chaco, in Vancouver, and a few other places. I am deeply grateful to all the people who shared their time, life, and ideas with me.

I am in enormous gratitude to the people in the Barrio Qom for their hospitality and friendship, for their teachings, and for guiding me across the places you have courageously created. (I keep your surnames away for issues of confidentiality). In particular, I thank Mauro, José, and Cecilia and family; Jorge; Valentín and family; Ana and Roque and family; Clemente and Audelina; Ramón, Sandra, Lili, Nelly, Anahí, Belén, Ángel, and Carmen; Marcela and Pablo; Vivi, Ofelia, Celeste; Felipe and family; Virgilio; Bernardo and family, Hilda; Brian, Leonel, Germán, Miguel, and Walter; and Camachi. Different families who did not know me hosted me in the Chaco province and in Rosario during my trips. I thank them for their hospitality; they hosted and showed us around even when we arrived unannounced and at bad timings. In Rosario: Juan and Lorena, Javier and Luisa, and María. In Chaco: Julio, Cecilio, Viyen, Luis, Ana's family, and Cecilia. I am thankful to many more people whose names I did not record and who offered me a seat and a mate as I walked around their communities. I am also thankful to the Qom in the Toba barrio in Formosa with whom I worked earlier; they were the main reason for starting this project. The enduring strength, deep forms of reciprocity, the collective intelligence, and the complex forms of collaboration are some of the many things I will be always learning from you. Thank you.

In Vancouver, and at the University of British Columbia, I was incredibly lucky to meet people who were simultaneously intellectually sharp and challenging, personally generous and supportive, and mostly a lot of fun to work with. I am particularly grateful to Gastón Gordillo, my supervisor and a central interlocutor, a never-ending source of support, challenge, and inspiration. Juanita Sundberg offered key insight and was a generous reader of every chapter's version. Jon Beasley-Murray accompanied me during my research and the process of turning this work into a book, providing a weekly routine and multiple readings, with a loving dedication I am overwhelmed by. I thank my reading group family for continuing to share ideas and life through the years: Bonar Buffam, Mikki Stelder, and Ewen MacArthur—a most unexpected travel companion—alongside the "aunties" Renisa Mawani and Tom Kemple, all equally sharp, a joy to meet, and an endless source of power. I give enormous thanks to my friends and colleagues at UBC for their generous readings and formative conversations: the late Susan Hicks, Marie-Eve Carrier-Moisan, Sandra Youssef, Sungsook Lim, Sanjeev Routray, Tal Nitsan, Lainie Schultz, Solen Roth, Dan Harper, Fabricio Tocco, as well as Alexia Bloch, Alejandra Bronfman, and Alec Dawson. My friend Chisu Teresa Ko was a starting point in my thinking about racialization in Argentina, what became a turning point in this analysis. The Department of Sociology has been a stable home since graduation and a welcoming community for developing this work, particularly Becky Ross, Amanda Cheong and Sean Lauer; and in particular all the students I had the honor to learn and teach alongside with; among them Tea Rawsthorne Eckmyn, who gave me invaluable assistance in the submission process. Furthermore, this work has benefited from the financial support of the International Development Research Centre, the Liu Institute for Global Issues, and UBC Graduate Fellowships.

As part of Cultures of Anti-Racism in Latin America (CARLA) at the University of Manchester, a project that redefined for me how far collaborative research can go, I was enriched by the exchanges with Peter Wade, Ignacio Aguiló, Lúcia Sá, Jamille Pinheiro Dias, and especially Carlos Correa Angulo. At Vanderbilt University, I thank editors Zachary Gresham, Gianna Mosser, and Steven Rodriguez, and the comments of the two anonymous readers for the generous and dedicated reading all of which made the best version of this work.

I am grateful to mentors, friends, and colleagues at the University of Buenos Aires, where this project originated, and the National University of Río Negro, where much of it was developed. I am grateful to friends and colleagues Mariana Gómez, Soledad Torres Agüero, Carlos Salamanca, Valeria Iñigo Carrera, Nicolás Fernández Bravo, Mariana Sirimarco, Cristina

Messineo, Claudia Briones, and Morita Carrasco, and Florencia Tola, who guided part of this project, and to Axel Lazzari, who was one the readers. For their friendship, hospitality, and comradeship through the years, I thank Laura Kropff, Lorena Cañuqueo, Miriam Álvarez, and Brenda Canelo, Carola Goldberg, Marian D'Agostino. I thank Guido Korman for challenging me to submit this manuscript, and Erika Kiki La Douce and Chang for keeping me as healthy as I can be.

I thank my family of origin, Florencia Ure, Octavio Frassoni, Julia, Catalina and Miguel Szejnblum, Clara y Agustin Frassoni, Daniel Low, Horacio Vivaldi and Estela Goldschläger, and Nicolás and Clara Vivaldi; and my Vancouver family, Hanna Cho, Natalia Bercovich, Marco Todesco, Julie Talerico and Dan Manson, Meghan Toal, Christina Moth, Silja Hund, Colin Ferster, Brandon Burke, Anna Hyden, Oralia Gómez-Ramírez, and Maayaa Quist-Adade for keeping me grounded and nourished in so many more ways than I can count. I thank my family of choice for being patient and loving throughout this project, but mostly, for making me rediscover the world every second I am with them—gracias infinitas, Rafa, Franka, and Ramona.

INTRODUCTION

"Welcome Indigenous Brothers"

Indigenous Subaltern Assemblages and the Challenge to White European Buenos Aires

Indigenous People March

On May 20, 2010, four days before the bicentennial celebration of Argentina's independence from Spain, I was at a central intersection in downtown Buenos Aires, waiting for what was expected to be a historic event. For the first time since the 1940s, when a march dubbed the Malón de la Paz (peaceful raid) came to Buenos Aires, there would be a rally of Indigenous people in the country's capital. In the 1940s, Indigenous people from Argentina's Northwest walked to the capital to ask President Perón to intercede in their land claims. Seventy years later, a massive contingent from different provinces was due to turn up for a countercelebration of the bicentenary.[1] The capital of a country that has long presented itself as "white European" would be experiencing an irruption of Indigenous peoples claiming to have been part of the nation since its constitution.

This march sought to make Indigenous people present in the celebration of the bicentennial anniversary and to remind the government that they were representatives of nations that had preexisted the Argentine state. The bicentenary was not a celebration for them: Independence had marked the onset of state violence and land expropriation that continues in the present. But they wanted to show that they were "still alive," challenging dominant narratives that Indigenous people had disappeared and that Argentina was racially homogeneous, composed solely of descendants of white European immigrants who had arrived in the late nineteenth century, thereby "dissolving" Indigenous and Afro blood.[2] The government itself supported the march as part of a broader effort by the Peronist president Cristina Fernández de Kirchner to redefine Argentine national identity as multiethnic and to bring the country closer to the rest of Latin America. In this moment of "refounding," the government redefined "the people" as culturally plural and racially diverse.[3]

An unprecedented number of social organizations had gathered to welcome the Indigenous contingent marching to the city's central square, Plaza de Mayo. I stood awaiting the march's arrival alongside other non-Indigenous local supporters: representatives of various unions, leftist political parties, and the *piqueteros*, the movement of the unemployed based in Buenos Aires Metropolitan Area, in the city's mostly working-class and poor periphery. Yet I noticed a significant absence: There were no representatives of any *local* Indigenous organizations based in Buenos Aires. I saw no sign of the city's several barrios of the Toba or Qom people, one of which had been my fieldwork site for over a year. There was nothing to signal the presence of the urban Indigenous people who had been living in Buenos Aires since its constitution. This absence revealed a clear separation between the urban Indigenous on the one hand and, on the other hand, non-Indigenous local social organizations and the march's protagonists, who were rural (or imagined to be rural) Indigenous participants coming from distant parts of the country. I knew that the people in the Barrio Qom where I worked had been awaiting an invitation to join the march. A few days earlier, I had taken the train with Lorenzo, a barrio elder, to visit the downtown offices of the National Institute for Indigenous Affairs (the Instituto Nacional de Asuntos Indígenas, or INAI) and inquire about the bicentennial activities. We received a warm welcome but a vague reply. INAI had made no arrangements to support urban Indigenous participation. Urban Indigenous people living in the city of La Plata were also in the office that day, complaining that they had not been invited either. It was clear that this moment of Indigenous recognition in the nation's capital did not include them.

The day of the march I attended the event with a group of close friends, anthropologists from the University of Buenos Aires, where I had studied and worked. We are mostly middle class and of European descent (though not only), and we employ collaborative and politically engaged methodologies. We were hoping to meet some of our collaborators and friends there. I was also a student from a Canadian university returning "home" to conduct fieldwork with the people of an Indigenous nation I have been in touch with since the early 2000s.[4]

Soon, we saw a large group advancing, with Indigenous leaders at the front wearing colorful "traditional" clothing. We moved to the side to make space for the march. A large block of people led the way, dressed in brown woolen ponchos, carrying flags that contrasted with the European architecture of the buildings around them. There was an air of excitement. Some of the marchers began singing, unpacking *erkes* (musical instruments from the Andean region) and *bombos* (drums), and playing carnival songs. Local supporters responded with enthusiasm, cheering on their "Hermanos Indígenas" (no mention of sisters), as some of the signs they held put it. To accommodate the march, the downtown was closed to traffic on a workday. In contrast to the response to street *piquetes* (pickets) by the unemployed, this march was met with an enthusiastic welcome by *porteños*, the "average" middle-class inhabitants of the city who identify as white and as Argentines of European descent.[5] Office workers, who regularly appear in the media blaming the *piqueteros* (who they often call "negros," which refers in Argentina to all non-whites in urban areas) for stopping traffic and taking over the city center, were cheering and welcoming the similarly nonwhite bodies of Indigenous people coming from afar.

An hour later, we arrived at the Plaza de Mayo, and from the stage, a man welcomed the Indigenous people coming to Buenos Aires "for the first time" and "after a long trip." Milagros Sala, from the Kolla nation, one of the march organizers, took to the stage alongside progressive journalist Sandra Russo, who welcomed the marchers.[6] Russo urged us to rethink who we are as Argentines. Recognizing Indigenous people, she said, was "as an internal debt with ourselves, to recover our honor and dignity." Later, another organizer concluded in a refoundational tone: "We do not only welcome you to the city; we welcome you to a new country, in which you are no longer exotic, *but wise*."[7] I was touched by this recognition and welcome, yet I also felt uneasy. Statements about "us" (progressive intellectuals) welcoming "them" (the colorful Indigenous peoples) implied that "we" were the ones to decide who could fit within the Argentine nation. This "we," even if allies, was "inviting" these others to join in as a concession and not as the recognition of the right of sovereign nations cofounding the Argentine state. Expropriated Afro and Indigenous labor and Indigenous land, and the wealth that generated for white Europeans, was absent from this discourse.

I was troubled, too, by the absence of Indigenous people living in Buenos

Aires, an omission that reproduced the classification of Indigenous people as not belonging in the city, and rather as visitors from the countryside. Nor was there any recognition of the fact that Buenos Aires is a city built on land expropriated from Indigenous people in the 1500s, when Spanish conquistadores founded the city. Instead, the event reinforced the idea that the city is a white European space, that Indigenous people are rural, and that they become visible only so long as they dress and dance according to "their culture." Many scholars have noted that only if such expectations about authenticity are met will the state and non-Indigenous citizens recognize Indigenous people's rights.[8] Indigenous people, then, have to walk a fine line: They have to display their culture to be authentic but refrain from being too disruptive, lest they become seen as a threat to modernity and the nation-state.

Yet this march was also about transformation. The project of a white Argentina has attempted both to erase diversity and to align it along class lines. Here, Indigenous bodies on the street overflowed the construction of a "white" Buenos Aires and the segregation of nonwhites to the periphery. Attempts to erase the nonwhite have been challenged since the formation of the nation, and this march was another moment of that tension, one that indicates that the relationships between Indigenous people, civil society, the state, and nonwhite popular sectors need to be understood from a spatial perspective.

The march condenses core tensions that I examine in this book. The focus of my research is the people who were not invited to the march, urban Qom who invested political effort to be recognized as Indigenous and to obtain lands at the periphery of the city and beyond their traditional territories. I follow the trajectories of the Qom people to the country's capital, their making of an Indigenous barrio, their experience with urban segregation, and how they confront exclusion by shaping Indigenous subaltern assemblages. Indigenous assemblages, I argue, connect spaces, social relations, skills, knowledge, and elements from the different locations where people are situated in order to shape new activities. They do so against the forces of nonrecognition and the modalities of racial subordination of nonwhite people in the city space. While the Qom have created barrios on the outskirts of towns and cities in the Chaco, Buenos Aires has been a particularly hostile place to construct Indigenous locations, given that it is a city that Argentine elites have shaped to be seen as white European and as an example of civilization to the rest of the country. But Buenos Aires is not white, and it never has been.[9]

The convergence of the trajectories, of multiple groups including Indigenous peoples, Afro populations forcefully brought as slaves, immigrants from other Latin American countries, and migrants from Asia, among other places, shapes the city of Buenos Aires. In this book, I examine the urban experience of the Qom, one of the largest Indigenous groups, originally from the Gran Chaco region in northern Argentina. The Qom have migrated to Buenos Aires since the 1950s, like many other Indigenous groups; however, unlike other migrant groups, they have shaped Qom barrios in the city, one of which is the focus of this study. *Qom* means "people" in the Qom language, or *Qom l'aqtaqa*, but for most of the nineteenth and twentieth centuries, the Qom have also called themselves and been known as Toba, a name of Guarani origin adopted first by Spanish colonizers and later by broader Argentine society.[10] Qom barrios have been a specific form of urban occupation developed by the Qom first in the Chaco region, where their traditional territories are located, and later in Santa Fe and Buenos Aires.

While each barrio responds to specific circumstances, they all have been part of a recurrent strategy of Qom people within and beyond the Chaco region.[11] Liliana Tamagno describes the deliberate practice of creating barrios in the city of La Plata as a drive to "be together in the same place," a phrase that condenses the importance of reconstructing community for cultural survival in the city.[12] The Qom experience in Buenos Aires has been specific, given that the capital city's margins are populated by diverse nonwhite others: rural migrants, Indigenous people, Afro and mixed-race groups and their descendants—all of whom are perceived as nonwhite, populating shantytowns and peripheral spaces and involved in movements such as the *piqueteros*.

The study of Indigeneity has long departed from rigid associations between people and a bounded territory. However, its alternative has been an understanding of Indigeneity as a negotiated and shifting identity, with fluid relations to place, an approach that has left important material dimensions of Indigeneity underexamined. I argue that by making and remaking spatial assemblages, Indigenous people shape space and create a modality of political control of space or territoriality that links countryside and city. I deploy the notion of assemblage following both Deleuze and Guattari and Latour's conception of networks, to highlight how everyday life is made through heterogeneous connections across space.[13] To focus on assemblages is to focus on the material conditions of these links, which involve everything from urban infrastructure and old cell phones to dirt roads and the bush in the Chaco, so as to shape a specific territoriality. Unlike the spatiality of the state, the territoriality of Qom assemblages is not the sovereign regulation of a continuous and bounded space but is instead a form of control that needs to be regularly remade out of relationships. Unlike the notion of diaspora, assemblage does not imply isomorphism (e.g., a network that links Tobas with other Tobas), but it instead considers a constitutive multiplicity of elements, actors, and relations.

This book, in short, argues that Indigeneity needs be understood from a spatial and racial perspective, and that Indigenous territories are shaped within larger assemblages that link people, places, and relations within and beyond articulated identities. By examining the constitution of a Qom barrio in Buenos Aires and tracing its connections to the countryside, other Qom barrios, and the city center, I address three central problems in spatial, Indigenous, and racial politics.

One is the relationship between Indigeneity and urban space. For a long time, dominant discourse erased urban Indigenous people from political debate; it considered Indigenous people in cities to be "too acculturated" to hold academic interest or political grip. Activism and research conceived urban Indigeneity as a displaced condition or a moment in a process of development of popular sectors.[14] Yet Indigenous people have reconstructed identities in the city, building organizations, producing new cultural practices, and claiming the city as an Indigenous place.[15] Importantly, urban Indigenous people are not merely "displaced" and do not rely solely on their connection to "homelands." Qom youth, for example, shape their Indigeneity in the experience of the city and not elsewhere.

A second, interrelated problem is the tension around the racial organization of the city. In the 2010 march, the state, social organizations, and those organizations' supporters clearly marked Indigenous people as visitors and internal "others." In this categorization of Indigenous as alien to the modern city, well-intended allies perpetuated a project of white European nation making. They highlighted the city and citizenship as a European space where nonwhites were visitors as best. As visitors, the marchers were expected to leave when the event was over. Historically, racial control over nonwhites helped to establish a European-oriented nation-state. Yet this racial organization of space has never been fully settled. People who "look Indigenous" are restricted in their possibilities of social mobility. The exclusion of urban Indigenous people and nonwhites from the shantytowns in the bicentenary march maintained the racial organization of the city. But this has not been passively accepted either. The Qoms' experience shows that racial stratification over space is challenged in daily forms of movements through the city and in cultural practices that destabilize the city as a white European space, if only partially. This perspective traces the Qoms' openings in urban settings and their practices shaping lives within and beyond European whiteness.

A third line of inquiry follows Indigenous regulation of space or territorialities through assemblages. While the Qom barrio on which I focus is indeed a form of Indigenous diaspora that links rural villages in traditional territories with urban communities, relations extend beyond an "ethnically" marked space and unfold beyond the limits of Indigeneity.[16] Qom assemblages develop complex connections between family members, collaborators, non-Indigenous neighbors, and state officials, to name a few. The notion of assemblage highlights these heterogeneous connections that need to be made and remade and link the Chaco to the city, but that also create ways of occupying the city center when people perform "cultural work," such as facilitating workshops and doing musical performances. These assemblages are constituted in mobilities across rural and urban Qom locations and in the use of city space.[17] While the recuperation of land has been crucial, it is not enough to contain the multiplicity of Indigenous lifeways. *Assemblage* has been a term used in association with displaced and delocalized processes, connecting the experiences of migrants and refugees, and social relations deploying technologies. My perspective links assemblages with Indigenous and subaltern positions to account for relations that transcend the boundaries of one Indigenous territory and exceed the sovereign control of space by state and capital, as well as the resistances to these controls. Indigenous assemblages establish relative control over space, even if this capacity is shifting, superposed with state sovereignties, and shaped by the surrounding space of capital accumulation.[18] Indigenous assemblages reconstruct, with limitations and from fragments, Indigenous territories and lives, not within but across the space of the nation-state.

In these three lines, while integrating the question of recognition, I pivot from the emphasis on representation to focus on how these struggles unfold in the materiality of space and bodies. Examining a Qom barrio offers an entry point over multiple forms of Indigeneity generated in connection with shifting assemblages, capable of indigenizing the urban location. What is at stake, too, is a dispute over the possibilities of shaping lives that partially escape neoliberal regimes of ownership, expropriation, and desire without becoming complete outsider to dominant social structures.[19]

An Indigenous Barrio in Buenos Aires

The Qom barrio where I did my work is an anomaly. Several communities of the Kolla, Guarani, and Mapuche, among other peoples, have been recognized by the state and have been successful in obtaining plots of land through housing projects that, in the 1980s, the government offered to popular sectors at large.[20] By contrast, the Barrio Qom, where I worked, is home to about four hundred people and is one of the few places that is legally recognized Indigenous land in the Buenos Aires urban conglomerate. It was created in the 1990s by people who had migrated from the Chaco over previous decades and had been living in the city's *villas* (shantytowns) for many years.[21] In this book, when I refer to the barrio or Barrio Qom in Buenos Aires, unless specified otherwise, I mean the barrio in the northwestern district of Greater Buenos Aires where I undertook most of my work. I leave it unnamed to maintain its confidentiality. At present, there are over a dozen such Barrios Toba or Barrios Qom in Greater Buenos Aires and at the periphery of the city of La Plata.[22]

My first time in the Barrio Qom, I was visiting Miguel, a musician and language teacher in his sixties. We had met through a colleague at an event at the Ambrosetti Ethnographic Museum of the University of Buenos Aires, where I worked and where he was playing the violin. Miguel agreed to introduce me to people and show me around. The day of my first visit we went on a walk through the barrio. We followed a dirt road with small houses in a row that bordered the barrio. Our first stop was the communal dining room, where I noticed an abandoned construction site and a building that served as a community kitchen and multipurpose room. Miguel explained that the room was used for community events and weekly services of the Qom Evangelical church, the Iglesia Unida, whose abandoned construction site was alongside it. The dining room had been built by a church nonprofit that operated a soup kitchen for several years until it lost funding. Miguel did not mention the more regular users of the space, a group of teenagers who were sitting on a cement platform outside the building, hanging out and listening to reggaeton and hip-hop music. They said hi and looked curious.

The community center, located to the right of the building, operates as a secondary school and library. One room was used as storage for construction materials, as a nongovernmental organization (NGO) planned to expand the barrios' private houses. On the side of the community center was a colorful mural painted by a group of non-Indigenous students who had visited the barrio "to help." The mural was painted without consultation about the design, and it featured a man and a woman wearing vegetable-fiber skirts, a sun, and carved stone, symbols not directly connected to the Qom but generically recognizable as "Indigenous." The human figures were seminude, which had led someone to graffiti genitals on the Indigenous man. Later, some of the youth I worked with at an after-school workshop (which we organized at their request) photographed this graffiti. When we downloaded the images and were going through them, we all laughed about it. We were probably acknowledging that people who come to help have sexual imaginations about Indigenous people that they had projected on the mural. I never learned whether the youth were responsible for the graffiti.

Miguel avoided any mention of the ten precarious houses (made of wood and zinc) built by some of the barrio's young adults that were also situated in this common area. One young woman living there, who I later met, expressed her frustration: NGOs and adults had not thought about where the new generations of Qom people would live, and they were expanding existing brick houses but offering nothing to the new generations; young families like hers had nowhere to live in the barrio. That day we went to meet Lorenzo, an elder and central figure in the creation of the barrio, and then Andrea and Rogelio, all members of the neighborhood commission. After brief conversation, they suggested I organize an after-school technology workshop for children and teach them how to use the library computers that were sitting unused. They all showed a willingness to involve me in their community, despite having just met me.

Our last stop was the house of Fernando, the preacher at the Iglesia Unida, a church that had sprung up as a result of the work of North American Pentecostal missionaries in the Chaco province beginning in the 1940s. Their presence in the barrio signaled the spatial expansiveness of religious practices institutionalized in the Chaco, given that the churches are a diasporic institution, created in Buenos Aires from the model of the first one, founded in Castelli, Chaco, but also because, through church activities, people travel and expand their spaces of religious engagement.[23] Fernando was concerned with the Comisión Vecinal (neighborhood commission), the civil association that managed the barrio, which had delayed presenting its yearly reports, limiting its capacity to start new projects.

On our way back, Miguel led me past another house, from which I could hear Christian songs. This was a second church, managed by Iván, a pastor from another Evangelical denomination that was neither Qom nor part of Iglesia Unida.[24] Simón, a Qom man and Iván's father, had created this church in the *villa*, and when families moved to the barrio, Simón moved it to his own plot of land. Iván had taken over, but some people criticized him and his church for not being fully Qom: Iván is the son of a Guarani woman and a Qom man, and almost half his church members were not Indigenous. But the church was bustling with activity and visitors from both within and outside the barrio at all times of day. Both churches are relatively autonomous, despite receiving funding from other Evangelical institutions, and both design their own programs under Qom leadership. As such, both are vital political organizations mediating with other institutions and connecting Qom villages and barrios.

Miguel explained the layout of the barrio as we came to the end of our stroll. His house was situated on the barrio's eastern edge, with an open field for grazing cattle across the way. The only paved street in the barrio runs from east to west and is the western edge separating the barrio from the Catholic school beside it. Iván's church borders the northern edge of the barrio; the common areas with the young people's informal shacks are at the barrio's southern edge. Beyond them, a large plot of land was being developed with new houses for people from many backgrounds. On the ground, these divisions are difficult to discern, and people move across the borders as neighbors. In delineating the barrio, Miguel was defining this place through its spatial limits and clarifying what was and what was not part of the Barrio Qom. To do this, he had to work to erase some of the barrio's relations to its neighbors. To present the barrio as an Indigenous place, it was necessary to depict it as spatially and qualitatively distinct. More significantly, this disconnection had to be constantly re-created, because relations with neighbors blurred the borders of the barrio. In this short stroll, therefore, I got an overview of some of the defining social relations of the barrio, which is within Greater Buenos Aires (also known as AMBA, for Área Metropolitana de Buenos Aires), yet different from it. Moreover, I was quickly and effectively integrated into the barrio myself, for my offer of volunteer work was accepted and organized.

In the following chapters, I explore the spatiality shaped by the Qom living in Buenos Aires; I trace Qom mobilities in the city that challenge urban segregation. I start with the arrival of the Qom to Buenos Aires and follow the relations that shaped a Qom barrio and that connected people in the barrio to the city center, to other Qom barrios, and "back" to the Chaco.

Key Concepts: Urban Indigenous, Racialization, and Assemblages

Urban Indigenous experience needs to be analyzed spatially, given that the recognition of Indigenous rights is enacted in particular places. Urban Indigenous people in the Americas have often been considered, even by some

Indigenous organizations themselves, as "less" Indigenous than those living in rural areas.[25] In research and activism, an ongoing question is whether urban space generates an unsolvable contradiction: Latin American cities are colonial spaces hostile to Indigenous life, and thus are not a space for Indigenous life to be reproduced. For them, *Indigenous and urban* becomes an oxymoron, an impossibility.[26] Indigenous people in urban contexts have responded to this paradox by sustaining relations to rural homelands and by actively indigenizing the city space.[27] More importantly, Indigenous peoples have always been a part of urban spaces, and cities are built on Indigenous land—a tension that manifests when, for example, Mapuche people renamed Bariloche as Furiloche in activist circles and public communications, its Mapuche name.[28] The Indigenous city has also been a central space of political organizing, as seen with the rise of the Movimiento al Socialismo party in Bolivia that took its Aymara leader, Evo Morales, to the presidency.[29] Historically, Indigenous people have always traveled to cities to exchange goods and have always built and lived in cities, even when those facts are erased from the dominant history.

People with Indigenous ancestry who live in the city may not make this urbanity their central identity, either, because they have lost connection to their Indigenous communities of origin or because their ancestors hid that identity to avoid violence. Many people, while still racialized as nonwhite and recognizing their Indigenous ancestry, have no direct links to a specific Indigenous nation and are unaware of their exact genealogy. These people are part of the group categorized as *negros*, which in Argentina is a reference not only to Afro ancestry but also to a generic nonwhite identity that includes the Indigenous, mixed-race people, and the lower classes.[30] Urban location, therefore, generates a further complication in that Indigenous people become racialized as *negros*, part of generic dark-skinned popular sectors, who have known but possibly untraceable Indigenous ancestry. This nonrecognition of Indigenous lives in the city, and the disconnection between an "authentic" rural Indigeneity and *negros* in the city, means that racism is both ever-present and mostly unacknowledged. The Qom become linked with both groups, perceived as *negros* when they walk through city space but recognized as Qom when associated with cultural practices shaping their authenticity. In both positions, their Argentineanness is unstable.

Nation-building ideology defines Argentina as a white society, which leads to a denial of nonwhite existence and, indeed, of racism altogether.[31] Racism toward the Qom and (and as) *negros* is largely unrecognized as such. But at the same time, because Buenos Aires has historically been the center of a spatial project led by national elites to create a white and European society, nonwhiteness is heavily policed and dreaded in the "white" city.[32] Unlike their experience of racism in the Chaco, in Buenos Aires, the Qom experience forms of policing, regulation, and segregation that are part of larger processes of policing nonwhiteness in urban space.[33] These experiences are shared by nonwhite migrants who arrive in a white city.

Given that the Qom have been incorporated into the city in two distinct ways, as "authentic" Indigenous people and as generic nonwhites called *negros*, from the shantytowns, the barrio is a crucial location from which to understand urban racial formation. In fact, the shantytowns where Qom people used to live are a racialized space, one of *negros villeros* while the barrio is considered a piece of the Chaco in Buenos Aires.[34] The Barrio Qom is a site of specific interest to understand the difference between a *villa* or shantytown and an Indigenous barrio, the complexities of being nonwhite in the city, and what happens when the Chaco (a region associated with Indigeneity) and Buenos Aires come together in one place.

Examining how Qom people build Indigenous subaltern assemblages moves our focus beyond spheres of social action such as the economy, politics, and kinship, and includes but expands the reach of institutional practices: Indigenous struggles for land rights thus unfold as much in the interactions with state institutions as in family gatherings, in a religious service, and in the production of handicrafts. A focus on assemblage enables an inquiry as to which are the relevant dimensions and the tracing of associations rather than the "slicing" of social reality in advance. Gilles Deleuze and Félix Guattari's notion of assemblage and Latour's interest in networks become relevant in this context, as Toba mobilities bring together a heterogeneity of elements dispersed in different places, institutions, and relationships that are put into new relations and to new uses.[35] Assemblage recognizes agency not only as an action emerging from an individual but also as capacities that result from the emergent qualities of associations beyond individual action and that include specific material characteristics of nonhuman elements, infrastructure, knowledge, and skills. Assemblages produce activity through multiple connections between elements put into new functions, including between rural and urban Qom, as well as with state institutions and through the mobilization of policies that make space for Indigenous lives in the city. Mobilities are thus a series of connective practices that link spaces and structured relationalities (e.g., state institutions, family, Qom organizations) and that traverse urban spatialities, repurposing and actualizing their elements into new associations in the assemblage.

The notion of assemblage has helped to describe the extensive kinship relationships of diasporic communities, accounts for the expansion of neoliberal relations, makes sense of new techno-political forms of governance (e.g., securitization), and names forms of autonomous political organizing. I focus on heterogeneous assemblages, which are not "outside" the sphere of the state and capital and yet they are not fully subordinated either: Neoliberalism uses assemblages to expand over heterogeneity, and assemblages from below transverse spheres and constitute overlapping material arrangements that envelop and sustain Indigenous lives. In assemblages, elements are extracted from their former "function" and put to new uses, as social relations are constantly reshaped in their interactions with material dynamics.[36] Qom people from the barrio create assemblages that distribute packages to relatives in the Chaco or solve problems for people in one place by asking a relative to temporarily move elsewhere. Assemblages produce new activity that is not contained in one element alone but emerges from multiple connections between heterogeneous places (e.g., a bus terminal, a living room used as a workshop).

My intervention is to pair the assemblage with notions of Indigeneity and subalternity, in order to contribute to the understanding of assemblages composed from below (in line with the work of Verónica Gago) and to identify forms of political practice that intersect with and also exceed markets, institutions, and congealed forms of Indigeneity as bounded and fixed, immobile and territorialized.[37] In considering assemblages as Indigenous, I locate them within a historical process in which assemblages are the modality in which Indigenous lives reconstitute within and against ongoing forms of colonization.[38]

I examine assemblages from a particular perspective. Qom and Indigenous territories, I argue, can best be understood as a series of horizontal connections that control space, limited but not fully determined by the hierarchical organization of space by the state and market relations.[39] Indigenous territory is thus not so much a homogeneous, continuous, culturally bounded space (a perspective criticized for decades now) or a territory nested inside another territory.[40] Both these perspectives follow the model of the nation-state's territorial-based sovereignty.[41] Territory as assemblage includes the negotiated and nonexclusive regulation of space that Coulthard and Simpson identify as a grounded normativity and that Cañuqueo in northern Patagonia identifies with the right to use land without claiming absolute sovereign control.[42] Assemblages, unlike structures, are not fixed systems but are constantly remade, each time with a different shape and function, reconstituted through everyday routines.

Subaltern politics, from a Latin American perspective, includes peasant, Indigenous, and popular forms of organization that operate within and beyond the realm of formal politics.[43] To consider assemblages that are both Indigenous and subaltern implies recognizing the often blurry dominant categories of Indigeneity and the fact that many people targeted as Indigenous by colonial powers and later by the state may not identify as such or find affordances in formal Indigenous politics.[44] Racialization, living in shantytowns, and lacking an ID are thus experiences that align them with border immigrants; indeed, in their daily movements around the city, Qom people are usually taken for migrants because their features are associated with people of Bolivian and Paraguayan origin. They are stopped by the police for document checks and threatened with prison. Subalternity, in other words, encompasses but also transcends Indigeneity.

It is in the material and affective practices of spatial mobility that an Indigenous life is formed, creating networked territoriality beyond circumscribed localities and identities. Indigenous assemblages extend life and politics beyond either urban marginality or bounded, traditional ethnic identity to focus instead on practice and territory as processes.

Urban Racialized Indigeneities and the Qom Experience in Buenos Aires

Indigenous and Afro populations were an important part of colonial Buenos Aires in the sixteenth to nineteenth centuries.[45] But the nation-building project of constituting a white Argentina in the 1880s pushed Indigenous and Afro people, especially those already integrated in urban life, to give up their identities and become "Argentine," which was defined as white.[46] Assimilation into whiteness produced a subordinated incorporation that maintained a higher class and symbolic status for European-descended urban elites as *whiter*, and later it allowed white European immigrants the social mobility to form the bulk of the middle classes.[47] At the turn of the twentieth century, the people arriving in Buenos Aires who were unassimilable because of their darker skin or because they refused to give up their Indigenous, Afro, and peasant lives were subalternized and pushed to the city's peripheries alongside rural immigrants. The *villas* initially created by European immigrants became spaces of nonwhites. Spatial segregation, along with labor market subordination and racial discrimination within institutional life, positioned *villeros* as the most precarious sectors of the working classes. While at mid-century, white European immigrants were able to leave the *villas* to achieve social and spatial mobility (often through the positive value toward white Europeans), nonwhites remained. Adamovsky identifies this as a class and racial separation, whereby European immigrants became the middle class, supported by political elites promising a citizenship aligned with the civilized world.[48] A separation of middle class as white and subaltern *villeros* as nonwhite took place, too, in an unrecognized way. While Argentina did not have racial segregation laws; and while nonwhite people were able to move to the middle classes—and some *villeros* continue to be white European—in the majority and in the social imaginations, middle classes are European descent and working class and subaltern are nonwhite.[49]

When, in the 1940s, peasants who had Indigenous ancestry but had started to prioritize a class position arrived in Buenos Aires in search of industrial work, they expanded the existing shantytowns. Urban elites viewed internal migration as a menace to the white European city, calling newcomers *cabecitas negras* (little black heads) and denigrating them as uncivilized and uncultured. Shantytowns, became spaces exclusively of *cabecitas negras* when most white Europeans moved out of them. In the 1950s *Cabecitas negras* turned into just *negros*, a pejorative term coined by Buenos Aires elites to refer to all nonwhites in urban spaces. In spite of the blunt racial dimension of the category, dominant discourse denied for decades that this was indeed a racial classification, insisting that Argentina is a raceless society.[50] In subsequent decades and through to the present, Latin American and cross-border migrants (especially from Bolivia, Paraguay, and Peru) were also pushed to the *villas* and racialized as *negros*.[51]

Latin American immigrant communities in Buenos Aires have had to make efforts to organize as Bolivian or Paraguayan and against the generic categories of "immigrant" and "negros."[52] They have created community organizations to support settlement, obtain legal status, and claim rights, such as being allowed to perform Day of the Dead ceremonies.[53] Yet building ethnically marked spaces has not been a priority for them. While some *villas* and working-class neighborhoods are associated with one particular community—for example, the barrio Charrua is known for its predominantly Bolivian population—shantytowns are multicultural places, with transnational migrants living alongside internal immigrants of various regional identities. The cycles of migration and the specificities of Argentine racism have led to the creation of immigrant settlements with people from multiple origins, all of whom are implicitly racialized as nonwhite *negros*.[54]

The specificity of the racial organization of space beyond the Chaco and in Argentina's biggest cities creates a context for the unfolding of an urban indigeneity. The Qom have also created modalities of life in the city that are not replicated by other Indigenous nations. Studies in South America have highlighted how urban Indigenous people become "brokers" between the city and rural locations, especially in negotiations with the state.[55] In Santiago de Chile, Mapuche organizations understand the city as part of Mapuche territory and strive to reclaim it.[56] Similarly, Mapuche scholars and activists in Argentina understand the city in connection to rural areas and as a part of Mapuche territory, and urban life as one way of being Mapuche.[57] In the Ecuadorian Andes, Otavalo people seek to be part of the city as modern and middle class while maintaining their distinctiveness through cultural production—but not by creating barrios.[58] In contrast, El Alto in Bolivia is a parallel city to the capital La Paz, in which the majority of its million inhabitants identify as Aymara.[59] The Qom in Buenos Aires occupy barrios that are situated between these two extremes, neither a large demographic creating a parallel city nor disseminated through urban space. In the Chaco, the Qom were subject to forms of proletarianization that incorporated them as seasonal workers with an ethnically marked identity; for this and other dynamics, they were able to stay as communities and did not have to hide their identities. On the flip side, their economic subordination and exploitation have been extreme, and they have become among the poorer populations of the country. Thus, the Qom strive to create smaller barrios that seek to be integrated into the city.

What it means to be "Indigenous" or, in this case, "Qom," is co-constructed in relations with multiple state levels, and in regional and provincial contexts.[60] In the Chaco, most Qom people enact their Indigeneity through the struggle for legal recognition of their territories, the re-creation of communities, the use of the Toba language in activating cultural practices, and through sustaining relations with the bush, rivers, and marshlands.[61] In Buenos Aires, a sense of being Qom is reconstructed through the use of language, kinship relations, and links to other Qom communities. But new forms of experience linked with urban subalternation also emerge. While most people I worked with self-identified as Toba (then the common ethnonym for Qom), their experience in the *villas* upon arriving in Buenos Aires often brought them into close contact with a racialized and impoverished urban population and racialized them as *negros*, or the subaltern urban poor. Alongside this Indigenous identity, I examine the impact of this racialization as *negro* and subalternation in the *villas*. Qoms' perception of themselves as urban Indigenous became a force in the creation of a barrio that emerged from past experiences in the Chaco, from their life in the *villas*, and from encounters in the city.

Doreen Massey defines place as a product of intersecting trajectories and encounters, and as the result of "the non-meeting ups, the disconnections and the relations not established, the exclusions."[62] For the Qom people I worked with, the city emerged as a place of new and unexpected encounters, for instance, with border migrants in shantytowns. Encounters were thus moments of creative construction of places and a sphere of multiplicity, for in these encounters with other actors, multiple relations unfolded at the same time. The *villas* and Barrio Qom, are shaped too in the disconnections: Qom and nonwhite subaltern people are not welcomed in some areas of the city, they are silently excluded from the rental market, and they cannot move freely through the "white" city center. If places result from trajectories that meet up, they also result from relations elsewhere, and for the Qom, this is what happens in the Chaco. To account for networks created by these Qom families, I take a perspective on mobility to contribute to an understanding of how the movement of people, objects, information, or ideas enable actions that are coordinated across space.[63] By mobilities, I mean the material organization of movement and the dispositions for moving, and also the emergent lines of escape that evade forms of organization of movement and escape plans, what John Urry calls flows.[64] More than a classification of movement, I am interested in the function of movement in the composition of assemblages. In the next section, I describe how I deployed a mobile methodology to trace the assemblages that create and shape life in the barrio.

Moving Alongside Qom Assemblages

My research extended over eighteen months between early March 2009 and late August 2010. Most of my work took place in the Barrio Qom in the Sauces district, which is a pseudonym I use to protect the confidentiality of the dynamics I analyze, and in the Area Metropolitana de Buenos Aires, Greater Buenos Aires. I visited the barrio several times a week, walked with people to do groceries, and to the health center; I took the bus, train, and subway with them as they moved through the city. I commuted with people from the barrio to downtown Buenos Aires, went with them to government offices in the city, and attended workshops they delivered in middle-class schools. Additionally, I accompanied some of the non-Indigenous activists working in the barrio, observed the work of NGOs, and had long conversations with missionaries. I interviewed government employees working with people in the barrio, including workers from the municipality, the social worker in charge of the barrio, and employees at INAI, who gave me an overview of the ways Indigenous legislation was being implemented.

As I got closer to some Qom families, I accompanied them in their travels beyond Buenos Aires to the city of Rosario and the Chaco, where they visited relatives or attended events. In the Chaco, my travels took me to the central area of the province, around the city of Castelli, which has some of the area's oldest Qom urban barrios and is a former meeting place for Indigenous people hired to work on cotton farms. I also visited the towns of Espinillo and Bermejito, the latter of which has become a regional tourist attraction because of its proximity to the beaches of the Bermejito River. I visited a rural farm near Bermejito and traveled with many families from Buenos Aires on a bus that broke down and was held by the police to investigate if we were women being trafficked. These travels in rural areas involved walking through trails in the bush, biking, and crossing rivers by boat. These trajectories were not straightforward, effortless, abstract lines through which objects and people "flowed," but rather movements of bodies navigating rugged terrain and advancing against the frictions of social territories—for example, making a detour to avoid non-Indigenous properties or a police truck in the city center. Connections implied effort and force to overcome social and material frictions. I walked and traveled alongside people to record how difficult or pleasurable it was to move; what people talked about, remembered, and reflected on in the process of moving; and how they found their way en route.[65] Only by moving with people between different places, talking as we moved, was I able to reconstruct how people experienced different places, what they enjoyed and missed about them.

I also visited Fuerte Apache, a *villa* or shantytown in Buenos Aires where some families had lived. I had to be very persistent to visit this place, as people wanted to break their links with this place. The multisited nature of this project, in short, emerged from the fact that people's actions in one place were always taking me to others. This is how I traced the scope and reach of the assemblages they build and operate in. My intent has been to reassemble the social relations, shaping people's experience of space in Buenos Aires and beyond, and to map, rather than re-create, their experience linking the Chaco and the barrio.[66]

As a middle-class, settler *porteña* of European descent, and an anthropologist, my position offered limits and possibilities for collaborative research.

FIGURE 1.1. Biking to the river in the countryside around Bermejito. Photo by the author.

My relations with other Qom people in Formosa gave me an entry point in the barrio, as I had worked with Qom people in the city of Formosa for my undergraduate research work. There, I had been an ally in case of a massive police attack on the community I was working in. Being an Argentine anthropologist working with issues related to Indigenous people from the Chaco region is not an unlikely trajectory, given the discipline's engagement with the Indigenous of the Chaco.[67] Indeed, my connections with the barrio were mediated by other anthropologists working in the area—significantly, Florencia Tola, a colleague and friend, introduced me to some of the people in the barrio. As part of Qom protocols, which involve asking about family relations, I was regularly asked for updates on the well-being of other anthropologists to whom I was connected; they were treated as my kin in these interactions. I was also recognized as a (then) young, female-presenting person among the many volunteers and researchers who establish connections with the barrio, and I was often asked whether I was a missionary or a social worker, as these are the social roles that generally interact with the community. In my interactions, Canada appeared as a generic location in the Global North, and many people associated me with European missionaries or visiting Evangelical pastors. I was regularly asked whether I knew preachers and missionaries from the Global North.

It took some time for me to establish trust with nonpublic figures and to see more personal aspects of the lives of leaders, who nonetheless were very approachable and willing to speak about the public aspects of the barrio. The position of a researcher is not an easy one, as many people in the barrio have experienced extractivist practices from researchers who come, write a book, and leave. I learned that building long-term relationships, engaging in a project with the barrio's association, staying in touch through the years, was as important as the potential impact of my arguments. This collaboration or critical ethnography became the best approach for me to establish a relationship with the barrio, which does not erase the complexity of our engagement.[68] My fieldwork involved undertaking activities in the barrio. I organized a workshop with youth in the barrio and a *Qom l'aqtaq*-language class for the general public at the University of Buenos Aires. I did several of these activities with other anthropologists, linguists, and ethnohistorians, as it became more productive to work together. This was never a "lone anthropologist" project in which I detached myself from my previous setting to immerse myself in a new social world.

Book Overview

This book unpacks Qom's production of the barrio as a reaction to urban racism and spatial segregation, but also as a location from which to reestablish Indigenous subaltern assemblages, through a series of movements with and across the locations that make up their lives in Buenos Aires. I examine how this superposed territoriality challenges, if only partially, the space of a white Argentina. To do this, I follow Qom trajectories as a series of displacements and connections.

In Chapter 1, "Ending Up in Buenos Aires: Histories of Movement from the Chaco," I analyze the migration of the Toba from the Chaco to Buenos Aires as a complex and nonlinear series of travels shaped by gendered forms of mobility. I follow the trajectories that took people to Buenos Aires and propose gendered typologies of this experience, including men looking for a partner and "strong" women sent to expand their family's networks. I argue that these movements are profoundly affective and marked by experiences charged with particular intensity, such as a moment of family dissolution or the expansion of experience generated among men who completed the then-mandatory military service. I argue that rather than a planned migration, people describe their movement to the city as a set of conjunctural forces and circumstances that made them "end up" in Buenos Aires. Mobility is thus advanced as a better perspective for understanding displacement, given the life in the city was a result, too, of multiple back and forth, circular movements, and a conditional situation in the city. Importantly, mobility helps us undo any easy divisions between rural and urban Indigenous as fixed identities and locations.

In Chapter 2, "The *Villas*: The Spatiality of Race in Buenos Aires," I turn to the Qom experience in the shantytowns. As they settled in the *villas*, Qom families lived alongside and as a racialized collective, historically categorized by middle-class residents as *villeros* (shantytown dwellers) and *negros*. This chapter discusses the Qoms' experience in the shantytowns, which they described as unbearable but also energizing and enriching because of their connections with Peronism and participation in the "*villero* movement." I thus modulate the rejection by some Qom of the life in the *villas* and, more particularly, of being identified as *villeros*, as a narrative that perhaps is better understood as responding to the mandate of a single and unified identity as part of state recognition. To put this narrative ethnographically in tension, I explore the experience of young people who, by contrast, decided to stay in the *villas* and are proud of this belonging. The chapter considers the tensions created by the spatial racialization of Qom bodies in Buenos Aires.

In Chapter 3, "Making a Barrio Qom in Buenos Aires: Space and the Politics of Recognition," I delve into the reasons the neighborhood is constructed by its residents as a preferable living environment in comparison to the *villas*. I provide an account of the chronology behind the establishment of the neighborhood, which initially stemmed from the recognition of families residing in the barrio as genuinely Qom by NGOs, professionals, and organizations. This recognition played a central role in garnering the necessary support for obtaining juridical personhood granted directly by INAI, at the time more progressive than municipal or provincial institutions but harder to reach both geographically and socially. I explore the interrelation between space and identity, which emerges not from a sense of place or a clear political struggle but from generating a new place out of multiple encounters and relationships. This process involves not only a homogeneous state entity and a distinct Indigenous collective but also various levels of institutional functions shaping space.

Chapter 4, "'Encountering the Indigenous': Middle-Class Humanitarianism," examines one of the prominent aspects of the present-day neighborhood: the continuous influx of visitors from the urban middle class, driven by an interest in "exploring Indigenous culture," aiding in poverty alleviation, and demonstrating solidarity with the struggles of the community. The chapter focuses on these interventions as endeavors to improve and develop the barrio and its residents, encompassing contradictory and multifaceted projects. It turns to the urban middle class and their interventions as part of organized civil society. These visitors can be regarded as Argentine and thus as white European by default, yet they re-create their whiteness in this intense interaction with the Qom in the barrio. The chapter explores the significance of the barrio as a place of unusual activity, the cultural productivity of these encounters, and the way this place is exoticized by urban Argentines who are attracted to it in search of "real Qom Indians."

In Chapter 5, "Subaltern Assemblages: Extending Spatial Control Through Multiple Associations," I explore the networks that Qom families create through their movements connecting multiple places. I focus on dynamics that cyclically re-create these networks, such as the circulation of objects, particularly handicrafts and donations, between the city and "remote" rural communities. Additionally, I explore the spatial connections forged through encounters within the Qom Evangelical church, examining how these moments strengthen and reconfigure existing relationships and reorganize life. Last, I explore the expansions of Qom families through movement from rural to urban space and through the simultaneous use of multiple heterogeneous locations. I analyze these connections as exemplary instances of Indigenous, subaltern, and specifically Qom assemblages comprising individuals, places, and objects that engender new activities through their spatial and material interconnections.

After the Indigenous march for Argentina's bicentennial in May 2010, I asked the people in the barrio whether they had considered turning up and participating. They replied that, aside from the fact that they had not been invited, they had been too busy to go. Many of them said they had to wake up early the next day for a workshop on "Qom culture" or to send their children to school. In other words, it was not simply that they were excluded from highly visible political events such as the march; they were constrained by the everyday relations and commitments that connect the barrio to other places in the city and kept them busy. This entanglement of trajectories that produced the barrio as a distinct place is the focus of the chapters that follow.

CHAPTER 1

"Ending Up in Buenos Aires"

Histories of Movement from the Chaco

Winding and Entangled Trajectories to Buenos Aires

"I never thought I would end up living in Buenos Aires" was one of the first things Martín said about how he came to the city. He is a man in his sixties who owns a small house in Barrio Qom in Buenos Aires and a cabin in Castelli, a city in the province of Chaco, where he was born and used to live. Martín misses his relatives in Castelli, and he would like to return there one day. He remains in Buenos Aires because his only son and his family moved there, and he enjoys living with them. Martín lived in many places before moving to Buenos Aires. He was born in a small village north of Castelli, became orphaned at a young age, and was raised by his uncle, who had a small farm, where he planted cotton. He later moved to Castelli and traveled back and forth to cotton plantations, where he worked during the harvests, returning to Castelli in the offseason when he would study the Bible. After the breakup of his first marriage, he moved to live with an uncle, in the city of Rosario. There, he met his second wife and lived with her for a decade, but they could not get pregnant and eventually split up. Alone, he moved back to Castelli, and lived there for many years. If it were not for a phone call from his nephew requesting help to build his house in Barrio Qom in Buenos Aires, he would still be living in Castelli.

Many people remember how they imagined Buenos Aires from the Chaco; they thought of it as an affluent city. Then, living in this distant, vibrant city seemed very unlikely. "Ending up in Buenos Aires" meant that travel there was unplanned and that living in the Barrio Qom had become a final stop after many previous back and forth movements. Even among those who had always wanted to live in the city, Buenos Aires was, at the time, an unusual destination for this internal mobility of Qom people. Yet most people had prior experience of moving; they had been born in rural villages and had moved between several locations, often to other Qom barrios in towns or cities in the Chaco before coming to the capital. These trajectories were winding, repetitive, and complex, and each turn was quite unpredictable.

"Circumstance" and prior experience was not the only explanation people gave me about moving to Buenos Aires. Initially, people told me they moved because of economic and political reasons. In their narratives they simplified their trajectories, describing a linear move from a place in the Chaco to Buenos Aires. They explained that they wanted to "get better jobs and salaries" during a time of emergent industrialization in Buenos Aires in the late 1960s and 1970s, and to escape exploitative labor in the Chaco. They identified economic constraints in the Chaco: the "lack of work" created by technological transformations in the cotton industry that drove Indigenous people out of the labor force in the late 1970s. Some also said that "the farm they lived in was not big enough to support all of their family members," a product of the decline of the price of cotton and the ongoing agricultural expansion that expropriated untitled Indigenous lands. Moreover, people told me that they moved to Buenos Aires "to send children to school" and access basic health services. Qom moving to Buenos Aires had an experience not unlike other rural-to-urban migration processes taking peasants to big cities in Argentina since the 1950s, and it matched, too, other processes of urbanization in Latin America.[1] These answers located Qom trajectories within larger sociopolitical processes: to escape the well-documented land expropriation, labor exploitation, and political subordination in the Chaco region.[2]

While these were strong forces that pushed people in the Barrio Qom to move out of the Chaco, they are not enough to fully explain their trajectories. Soon, I found that many of the first generation to move to Buenos Aires enthusiastically narrated their travels and relocations during their youth, traveling to nearby villages for fun and joining trips organized by an Evangelical church. Telling me these stories from their present location in the barrio, some of them also explained that coming to Buenos Aires emerged from affectively intense moments that pushed them to leave a bad situation or search out new options. Feeling optimistic, breaking up with a partner, or having a desire to explore triggered many of their trips.

FIGURE 1.1. A Qom Man living in Buenos Aires during a visit back to Castelli, where he lived as a young adult. Photo by the author.

In this chapter, I analyze the forms of mobility of people who in the Barrio Qom in Buenos Aires and reconstruct the trajectories these mobilities generated. I focus on the forms of movement that conditioned and allowed people to travel and on the specific trajectories leading to the city. Mobilities result both from power relations and dispositions for movement that enable people to travel in certain moments and certain ways and that push people to forms of immobility.[3] I conceive of trajectories as specific histories of movement, of people, objects, or ideas shaped in three levels of interactions.[4] First, I consider the economic and political processes in the Chaco that worked as push factors and what pulled people to Buenos Aires. Second, I analyze the forms of intense mobility experienced by young Indigenous people in the Chaco and the gendered dispositions to move that are part of growing up. Third, I follow the trajectories of people before they "ended up" in Buenos Aires and bring together the entanglement of conditionings, dispositions, and affective intensities that triggered and shaped their movements. In tracing these trajectories, I found some unexpected commonalities among people who ended up in Buenos Aires, as, for example, many of the men connected their movement out of the Chaco to having been orphans at a young age. Having undergone a specific critical experience (a moment of affective intensity) was common to the people who arrived first in Buenos Aires. I show how Qom people who later created the barrio in Buenos Aires have extended the usual forms of mobility.

I consider economic and political dynamics of internal migration; however, I argue that these are limited. Migration push and pull approaches have worked on an ideal model of a rational individual moving alone and who migrates as a choice or a way of escape. Migration paradigms thus treat movement as an exception, presuming it to be the outcome of either a deliberate rational plan or a severe threat.[5] These assumptions then create distinct legal categories of migrants and refugees and produce policy based on this restricted understanding of human mobility. This model has never correlated to the multiple experiences of mobility, many of which are not rational, are in groups, and combine choice and the escape of real constraints and threats.[6] I incorporate a discussion about Qom mobilities to these current reexaminations of migration as mobilities. In addition, Qom people engage in travel as a coming-of-age activity, shaping independence and use travel as a response to moments of intensity that make people respond beyond the dispositions for moving.[7] Migration perspectives have also paired displacement with processes of ethnic identity reconfiguration in a new location and the assumption that diasporas will re-create their cultural specificity with variation but strong connections to the homeland.[8] These analyses are limited too in that they tend to understand culture as homogeneous and pay less attention to the capacities and positions of people who move, although age and class are many times a considered variable.

By engaging with affective mobilities, I explore which types of intensive variations trigger movement and which capacities are needed for someone to travel as far as Buenos Aires. Not all the Qom people facing displacement in the Chaco ended up in Buenos Aires, and labor exploitation became intolerable at one moment but not another. Tracing the forms of mobility and the affective variations in people's trajectories ending up in Buenos Aires is a way to unpack why people decided to move at one particular moment and circumstance.

"Ending up" is a phrase Qom people use to describe that coming to Buenos Aires was not part of a long-held plan. Importantly, considering the three dimensions—structures, cultural practices of mobility, and circumstance—situates mobilities as actions that reshape Qom assemblages. Mobilities expand assemblages over new spaces and reconfigure what assemblages can do as a result of this extension of a community over space. These three dimensions of trajectories do not neatly contain one another. Rather, they are entangled relations that simultaneously pull people in different scales (e.g., regional and national) through competing forces and intertwining forms of power that may operate simultaneously. Mobilities that expand assemblages cannot be reduced to a capacity to "escape" from relations of domination, but neither are they only forms of constraining people: subverting one form of power (e.g., escaping labor exploitation) implies getting caught in others (e.g., becoming objects of state assistance in Buenos Aires). "Ending up" condenses this affective and experimental nature of movements to Buenos Aires and identifies how assemblages were reshaped by Qom people who moved to the city and continued to be related to rural villages.

The Colonization of the Chaco: Regulating Indigenous Mobilities

The families in the Barrio Qom moved to Buenos Aires to escape the subalternity, poverty, and dispossession that result from ongoing advances of state, agribusiness, and *criollo* (people of mixed Spanish and Indigenous heritage and low socioeconomic status) and European small farmers over their lands. As in other parts of the Americas, settler colonization was a form of land dispossession that attempted the complete control of Indigenous land by erasing Indigenous life and replacing it with settler ownership and control.[9] In Argentina, the vectors of dispossession were the army in the late nineteenth century, *criollo colonos* (farmers of mixed-race origin), and large land owners of (mostly) European origin. After land redistribution in the twentieth century, provincial police, local government authorities, and missionaries set the institutional mechanisms responsible for maintaining the structure of dispossession and keeping Indigenous groups reduced to less productive lands.[10]

For any project of territorial control, the regulation of movement is central, given, as Milton Santos argues, the effective regulation of territory demands controlling space through law and its economic functions (e.g., defining areas of resource extraction and processing) but also (re)shaping uses and daily activity.[11] For the process of construction of state territorial power in the Chaco, the last region under Indigenous control, it was central to restrict Indigenous mobilities over their lands and to regulate them as a new labor force.[12] Before the state military conquest, from 1880 to the 1920s, the Indigenous groups of the Chaco controlled their territory and mobilities.[13] Land expropriation took decades and a multiplicity of repeated incursions and overlapping projects of the Argentine army—and later the provincial police, local authorities, missionaries, plantation owners, and poor *criollo* farmers, and is a process that continues in the present.

Before their incorporation into the state, warfare between different groups, and repeated attempts by Spanish and later Argentine armies to invade the territory, the seasonal availability of natural resources, horses, and the cattle trade were some of the factors that structured the mobilities of Indigenous groups.[14] During the state's expansion over their lands, mobility was an Indigenous strategy to escape the army's violence, by hiding in the bush, where they could survive for months at a time.[15] This option became limited when the army blocked access to rivers and hunting grounds, and land was distributed among big landowners, European settlers, and poor *criollo* peasants.[16] Qom people I met explained this process as the end of their autonomy: "Freedom ended when the army occupied the region and plantation owners divided the land with fences," older people explained. In the eastern Chaco, Indigenous people were forced to gather in mission stations and *reducciones* (state reservations) that lumped together different ethnic groups. Some were able to remain outside these state institutions in vacant areas between the new *estancias* (ranches).[17] Families in the Barrio Qom in Buenos Aires came from different villages and towns in the central Chaco region, each of which is inhabited by previously unrelated groups. The biggest reservation in the area was Napalpí, but many of the people I worked with grew up in titled and untitled farmlands around the cities of Castelli, Pampa del Indio, and Bermejito.

In the first half of the twentieth century, mission stations and reservations exerted a disciplining influence on Indigenous communities, shaping habits necessary for wage labor, while missionaries focused on bringing them into the fold of Christianity. Although the Catholic Church achieved some success, the Qom people were particularly drawn to the Evangelical Baptist Church. The missionary endeavors and wage labor had repercussions on patterns of mobility. Trips to the bush away from mission stations and reservations were a form of escape from church discipline.[18] People in the Barrio Qom in Buenos Aires remember the missions with some ambivalence, as were places that restricted their freedom but also protected them from military violence. Likewise, they recalled working on cotton plantations as both a means of earning money and an arduous task that involved whole families. Many groups in the central Chaco, around Castelli, remained beyond the orbit of mission stations and reservations, occupying less productive lands where they had modest farms and lived on subsistence activities, such as the small-scale commercial growing of cotton and seasonal work on farms. In the central and eastern Chaco region, Indigenous labor followed economic cycles. Forestry exploitation, the industrial production of tannin, and sugar production were the initial activities, followed in the 1930s by the rise of cotton as the region's main cash crop. Both cotton and sugar production relied heavily on the cheap labor of Indigenous people and poor *criollo* farmers to produce the "extraordinary revenues" celebrated by national and provincial governments.[19] The *ingenio* (plantation and sugar mill) Las Palmas was the first agribusiness organizing space for capitalist production in the region.[20] Owned by British investors and subsidized by the national government, Las Palmas employed thousands of Indigenous people as seasonal workers at harvest time.[21] Moreover, in the 1930s, as the national government promoted cotton production by subsidizing companies, some Indigenous groups, among them relatives of people in the Barrio Qom in Buenos Aires, were able to set up as small cotton farmers on their own lands.[22] However, they could not maintain production for long, and when in the 1960s, commercialization became harder for small producers, they had to seek employment as workers in larger farms. Production drastically declined in the 1970s, and Indigenous people were expelled as workers and many abandoned their farms and moved to the nearest towns.[23]

Castelli is the biggest town in the central area of Chaco province and was an organizing node for the cotton industry. Many people in the Barrio Qom in Buenos Aires come from that area, owned small farms, and worked in the cotton harvest. Qom families worked together in the harvest and traveled to Castelli to meet contractors, who hired them as seasonal workers on different farms. At the end of the harvest, contractors brought workers back to Castelli, and people returned to their villages. The rest of the year in the villages, Qom lived by fishing, hunting, gathering, and engaging in subsistence agriculture.[24] Many of the people whom I met in the barrio gave me detailed accounts of cotton picking as children accompanying their fathers, and later as adults, especially when I traveled with them to the Chaco and the view of cotton fields evoked for them multiple memories of the harvests.

The mobility of Indigenous families as workers was initially highly regulated by missionaries, plantation owners, and provincial authorities. The 1924 massacre on the state reservation of Napalpí, south of Castelli, exemplifies some of the tensions around the control of Indigenous mobility, given that the conflict emerged when local authorities denied Qom, Pilagá, and Moqoit (also known as Mocoví) workers permission to travel to work on the harvest in the neighboring province of Salta, where they could get better salaries. When Indigenous workers gathered on the reservation of Napalpí and their discontent took religious and messianic overtones, *criollo* and white settlers in the nearby towns feared a rebellion. One morning, municipal police and armed civilians surrounded the reservation and killed four hundred Indigenous people in the course of a few hours; a military aircraft sent days later from Buenos Aires chased down survivors.[25]

This event suggests that the regulation of Indigenous movement was of central importance. The Qom people were not free workers, able to move to where capital paid the most (a basic principle of a liberal labor market); rather, they were a source of cheap labor whose mobility was closely regulated by local, provincial, and national authorities. Landowners and the police and army acted together and massacred over four hundred people, including children. They did not hesitate to use violence to control a potential disruption of this regulation. That the national government backed them by sending troops shows that the systematic project of Indigenous dispossession by violence was a unified state approach. Everyday forms of violence continue to this day. *Criollos* and local officials often justify the killing of Indigenous people by the police as a side effect of cattle theft and "trespassing." People in the barrio have memories of this kind of violence, from which they say they escaped, using phrases such as "I left the villages because I did not want to be bothered anymore." *Bothered* often refers to violent encounters with *criollos* in the bush, tensions over land.

People in the barrio have memories of the arrival of Evangelical missionaries to the Chaco region in the 1950s. John Lagar, a North American Pentecostal preacher, created the first mass baptism movement in the region, and Mennonite missions also attracted followers to the churches they created.[26] Both denominations trained Indigenous preachers who, in turn, created their own churches and sought state registry as legal religious associations (what became an important experience to organizing as communities in the 1980s), if short-lived. Especially significant was the Qom Evangelical church, the Iglesia Unida, created exclusively by Qom preachers in the 1950s. It quickly spread to most rural villages and urban barrios in the central and eastern Chaco region and influenced all aspects of community life.[27] The subsequent conversions brought about new moralities, including gender divisions, while Evangelical churches also integrated elements of traditional shamanic beliefs regarding health and illness.[28] Currently, the Iglesia Unida, alongside other Evangelical churches, serves as an institution enabling travel and connecting villages and barrios. In addition, many people in the barrio acquired literacy skills by joining a church and learning to read the Bible, not through formal education. Learning the Bible serves, too, as a pathway to becoming part of church commissions and preachers, roles that stretches beyond religion and include community organizing and leadership.

When in the 1970s and 1980s, seasonal work in the region shrank abruptly, the *ingenio* Las Palmas went bankrupt, and families intensified survival practices by fishing, hunting, and gathering in the patches of forest they could access. In the same period, missionary groups and church-related NGOs linked to liberation theology (e.g., Endepa, or Equipo Nacional de Pastoral Aborigen; Incupo, or Instituto de Culturas Populares) began to support land claims. In the 1970s and 1980s, many groups successfully recovered lands at a time when there was no Indigenous legislation in the country. Belgian missionaries worked in an area called the "interfluvio," north of Castelli, and in the 1980s, helped obtain the titling of 140,000 hectares for local Indigenous villages, leading to what became one of the largest legally recognized Indigenous territories in the country.[29] Many of the families in the barrio grew up in this area, and some are sons and daughters of leaders who organized this land claim. However, without credit access, the options for making these lands productive were restricted. The processes of land titling did not stop an economic crisis from unfolding or displacement to towns and cities.

As mobility from rural areas to the towns of Bermejito or Castelli, or to the city of Resistencia, became more frequent in the late 1960s, Qom people created more stable settlements in the cities. Qom settlements emerged, too, outside of the Chaco region in the cities of Rosario, Santa Fe, and La Plata.[30] In this period, some Qom living in urban areas organized land claims, many of them successful. In the 1970s and 1980s, provincial governments in Formosa and Chaco handed out land titles that turned periurban settlements into formal Qom barrios.[31] This process is not without contradiction: While it was a significant recognition to Indigenous participating in urban life, it also allowed governments to settle previously mobile, rural Indigenous groups in urban areas and away from rural lands. In the 1990s, municipal and national agencies supported the creation of urban Qom barrios outside the Chaco. In these barrios, people made a living from state assistance, temporary employment, and selling handicrafts.[32] When possible, people continued to gather resources from the periurban bush.[33]

The experience of working with the Iglesia Unida and NGOs in making land claims generated an awareness of a common experience with other Indigenous groups, which shaped a new identification of Qoms as *Indigenous people*, the term later adopted in provincial and national legislation.[34] As the category consolidated as a form of interaction with the dominant society, the Qom became intertwined in development practices and state politics, a relation that would intensify in the 1990s, after the creation of Indigenous legislation. All these dynamics are part of the prehistory of the Barrio Qom in Buenos Aires.

In sum, the history of Qoms' spatial mobilities in the central Chaco is the result of combined processes of economic and political subordination and of attempts by Indigenous people in the Chaco region to counter them. The mobilities out of the communities expanded existing assemblages and created new ones as people who moved sustained relations with the rural communities. Thus, Qom groups avoided discipline and confinement by escaping to the bush and moving to vacant less productive lands. To escape labor exploitation on large farms, they sought jobs in towns. In connection with missionaries and NGOs, and together with their own demands and activism, they created new assemblages that allowed groups to recover part of their lands but also made them more dependent on state assistance. These movements reshaped assemblages and opened new possibilities in the context of multiple forms of violence of land dispossession, forced assimilation, and structural racism that positioned Qom as some of the poorest, most exploited, and oppressed sectors in Argentine society.[35] Recovering portions of their former lands allowed Indigenous groups to fish, hunt, gather, and farm on their own territories. They created their own Evangelical church, and settlements in the towns and cities became formal barrios.

While these economic and political processes were part of what pushed and enabled people to move to Buenos Aires, they were not the only ones. Some people explained that they were able to come to the city because they had traveled intensively when they were young. They were experienced and thus had the tools to start over, far from all that was known to them.

"Looking for a Place to Be": Youth Mobilities

Entangled with the experience of labor exploitation and land expropriation were the dispositions of people's movements, cultural practices that shape Qom's sociality. Some examples are growing up and looking for a partner, taking care of distant relatives, and creating activist alliances. These practices are never rigid rules but are part of available repertoires that orient mobilities. By "young," I mean the period when teens are considered old enough to travel on their own, usually around twelve years of age; it ends when their first children are born, at which time they are considered adults.[36] In various

Qom villages and barrios, I observed many young people moving intensively and frequently. The parents of youth explained that travel is part of growing up, and I observed how they help young people to make short or longer trips. Many encourage the mobility of their daughters or sons so that they get valuable experience, especially to attend high school or contribute to the family's well-being, or to take care of an ill aunt or uncle. Families and acquaintances, however, also watch over young people's movement, especially that of young women, as they are in danger of being sexually assaulted. But also, people may spread gossip about women's mobility if they consider that their movement is excessive, or they may worry if young men and women travel only to "party."

Qom people I met in different locations highlighted experiences of travel in their youth. Some were mobile by visiting nearby villages, but others moved longer distances, from rural villages to a town or city. The duration of the trips was also variable: People traveled for one day or lived elsewhere for over a year. Young people were also among the most enthusiastic participants in church-organized trips, some of which took them to cities outside of the Chaco for several days. They could also choose (and were allowed by their parents) to move in with a relative and stay there as long as they wanted if they had, say, fought with a parent or were feeling restless. These mobilities shaped by age were an important aspect of the people's life histories in the barrio where I worked. In most cases, people said these experiences gave them the conditions and skills they would later need to travel far away and settle in a new place.

Young people's movement was often described in terms of *buscando un lugar para estar* (looking for a place to be). People explained they wanted to live somewhere different from their villages, and mobility was the key to such a possibility. It was considered a normal experience for young people to move back and forth to locations, make last-minute decisions, feel compelled to move elsewhere and then change their minds and return. A young woman moved to a town with her aunt to attend high school, but later she quit and returned home because she had not felt comfortable there. A young man from a village in the Chaco attending a teachers' meeting in Buenos Aires decided at the last minute not to take the bus back home, traveling instead to the Qom barrio in the city of Resistencia with new friends, also Indigenous teachers. In none of these cases did people express concern or try to stop the young people's decisions. The trajectories of youth tend to be quite unpredictable, and that unpredictability is considered a normal part of being young.

Some men explained that in their youth they traveled to find work, in some cases to contribute to family finances, and in others to become fully independent of their parents. Martín, who was raised by his uncle, moved out of his uncle's house when he was sixteen. He said he needed to "valerme por mí mismo" (support himself). He explained that he wanted to ease his uncle's burden of feeding so many children, so he went to Castelli to become a seasonal worker picking cotton, and when the harvest was over, he never came back. He worked in the cotton harvest on different farms for several seasons, and during the offseason he stayed in the town, studying the Bible at the local branch of the Iglesia Unida. Martín's move was thus related to finding work and gaining independence, but it was not planned in advance; he explained that one day he knew he "had to go," and without speaking to his uncle about it, he left to the harvest knowing he would not return. Traveling allowed him to be economically independent, get involved in the church, and access education. It was, therefore, not difficult when three decades later, he unexpectedly moved to Buenos Aires to build a house for his nephew and "ended up" staying.

Other men remembered their youth as a time of general unrest. Julio, a man in his early fifties who arrived in Buenos Aires in the 1980s, explained of being thirteen, "There was nothing wrong with my family, but I needed to go, just anywhere." This is synthesized in the phrase "no me hallo" (I do not find myself), which describes the experience of feeling uncomfortable or not at ease in a particular place. This can be linked to boredom or to a lack of life prospects, but it may also indicate a generic sense of unease. Julio first moved to live with an uncle in a village close by but soon felt he had to move again. He traveled north to the province of Formosa, where he had no acquaintances or relatives. He arrived at a Pilagá village, where he became friends with other young people and decided to stay. The Pilagá are an ethnic group related to the Qom who speak a different language. He got day jobs on nearby farms, stayed with some of his new friends' families, and learned the Pilagá language. After three years, he suddenly decided to return and did so.

Julio's trajectory shows that it is generally accepted that young people's travel may have no other reason than a "need to move," and those who have such an intense eagerness to move find in travel the possibility of appeasing the feeling of being out of place. Julio's unease persisted even when he had moved out of his village and moved in with his uncle, and so he traveled again. Only when he was far away, in a different province with no relative nearby, did he stop moving around. The disposition to move is thus one of the transformations associated with "growing up," which, for Julio and others, implies this need to explore other places and live elsewhere for some time. This need for young people to move is not considered something negative or problematic, and while parents miss their children, they allow it and know it may lead to becoming a more experienced person. Julio's travel solved his feeling of uneasiness, and the relations he created in the new place enhanced his capacities for action: He became economically independent, learned a new language, and created a home. These skills allowed him, years later, to move to Buenos Aires, even though he knew no one in the city.

While Julio's travel was unusual in that he moved to a place where he had no connections at all, many people in the barrio had made similar adventurous trips and had emerged more experienced. I started to notice that the barrio had been created out of a group of people many of whom had the skills of being outgoing, adventurous, and experienced. People I interviewed, especially men, bragged about knowing places and having acquaintances "everywhere." Even the extreme form of unplanned mobility known as *la joda*, or party life, is socially accepted if the young person later returns to a "right path."

La joda is a term I heard in every Qom village and barrio I visited. People who "party" spend the day hanging out with friends, drinking alcohol, and smoking; they go to parties and dance clubs in nearby towns and "hook up" with different people, sometimes *criollos* or *criollas*. Some young people travel explicitly to engage in *la joda* with young people from other Qom villages or barrios. Parents worry when their children party too much but do not punish them. As Noelia told me, "You can't lock them up." Parents encourage youth to "get out of that life" and go to church, because people "en el evangelio" (in the Evangelical church) stop smoking, drinking, and partying. Evangelicals redirect themselves onto a "good path," redirect the intensity of partying to the religious services and dance, and people develop a well-behaved form of mobility: working, going to church, and traveling for religious encounters.[37] Indeed, the transition from *la joda* to becoming a Christian is not uncommon and is a recurrent topic at religious services. People who quit *la joda* are regarded as experienced individuals who "saw the world," but then had the moral strength to get back onto a respectable path. La joda is thus an area of concern of the church, and in dialogue with religious practice, in informal conversations youth in *la joda* would tell me they were *pecadores*, or sinners. In other words, *la joda* can be a source of intense mobility among the youth, and it is an experience central to the travel trajectories of some people living in the barrio.

Related to the active sexuality implicated in *la joda*, another reason to move was to find a partner. Leandro explained that in the rural villages "all families are related, and all women are your cousins. They may be your second, or third cousins." He then added that some men don't mind, and they may marry a third or fourth cousin. But others look for someone they are not related to, so they travel. They go with the church or look for a job somewhere else to meet someone.

"Finding a place to be" gained new implications with this explanation. Travel was about exploring other places and communities where one could settle, and also about the desire to find a partner outside the immediate village, another dimension of becoming an adult. Young people often have relationships elsewhere, and it is, therefore, common for them to be constantly moving back and forth between their villages and those of their lovers. Young people described falling in love as an intense, irrational need to be with another person, and moving to be closer to them was part of that intense affection.[38] Adults said that, when a young person likes a boy or girl, "you can't stop them from wanting to meet them," showing that they regard constant mobility as part of the very experience of falling in love. When young people find a place to settle with their partners, they usually say, "Ya me quedé" (I've settled now) and then find a job or form a family.[39] Significantly, mobilities that end up in the formation of new families are another aspect of the reconfiguration of assemblages that have kin relations at the center. When a family member moves, their family of origin will have a new connection and reach in the location where the youth has moved.

When young adults find their place, and especially after having children, their mobility usually slows down. Men may still travel quite frequently (and male political leaders and preachers engage in intense travel as part of their work), but it is harder for women to leave their children and domestic responsibilities behind. Thus, the possibilities to move that are more equally available and acceptable during youth become restricted for women after they settle.

Women's Mobilities

During informal conversations with women in their thirties and forties, many told me about traveling by themselves at a young age.[40] Sofía left her village home for the city of Resistencia because she wanted to get involved in church youth groups there. Andrea intensively traveled back and forth to go to the missionary-run high school in Bermejito (a place we later visited together). Their stories described a gender-specific way of organizing their travels.

Elisa is a woman I met in a periurban barrio in the city of Formosa; she lived in a rural village in Laguna Blanca and visited her cousins in a nearby village most weekends when she was young. Later, her parents encouraged her to move to Formosa city to attend high school and helped her find a non-Indigenous family through church connections to host her. She was a dedicated student, finished high school, and went to a nursing assistant program. Soon after she got a job as a nursing assistant, and with her first paychecks, she bought a motorcycle. With it she was easily able to travel again to her cousin's villages, where she had a boyfriend. Unlike Martín and Julio, Elisa traveled to a specific place: the city, her cousins' villages. Even when she was very independent and in control of her mobility, she was not involved in the adventurous and relatively spontaneous traveling that defined the experiences of young men. Women usually traveled to places where they had relatives, or with an institution (e.g., the church, an NGO, a school) organizing their trip, and they linked their travels with a particular goal: to attend high school, take care of a relative, or attend a workshop. Women's travels were thus more organized and tended to have a particular destination and sense of purpose. Mobility enables women, like men, to establish new connections, learn, and be recognized as experienced. But women's movements are an object of closer attention and scrutiny, and if they do not follow an organized travel trajectory, they are said to "travel too much."

Cecilia is an *auxiliar aborigen* Indigenous teachers' assistant in her early twenties, with two young children, living in a Qom barrio in Formosa province.[41] She traveled very frequently to attend teachers' meetings. When Cecilia went to Buenos Aires for a teachers' workshop, she emailed me to tell me when she was coming. She stayed with me, attended the workshop, and returned home four days later. Cecilia was among the most mobile women I met, traveling since before she had children, as part of her involvement in a transregional Indigenous teachers' organization. Despite how carefully she planned her travel, neighbors gossiped that she was meeting other men. When I met her in Buenos Aires, her husband had just left her, and she was angry and sad. A few months later, I visited her in the Chaco, and she told me there was also gossip about her being "a bad mother" and leaving her responsibilities behind. Then she was frustrated and told me she would not stop attending teachers' meetings simply to "get her husband back." She had not changed her mind and was determined to let her husband go if he could not understand her involvement in the teachers' organization.

Gossip, therefore, often acts as a form of regulation that may attempt to slow down or stop movement. People link women's movement with the development of what is considered an "excessive sexuality," even when this was not actually happening, a regulation likely influenced by missionary imposed gender ideologies.[42] In Cecilia's case, mobility was related to work, and she was nonetheless the object of gossip aiming to slow her travels. Cecilia was considered a strong woman, independent, one who does not alter her choices for others' gossip—but that independence, and bearing the weight of gossip, was not easy. When her husband left for no other reason than the gossip, she became a single mother, needing her mother's support to take care of her kids while she traveled.

Being respectable is a moral category influenced by the Iglesia Unida that condemns women who have sex with many men while being unmarried or who "cheat" on their husbands. "Cheating" is approached more openly—for example, many men accept raising the children of their partners from another man while being married to and living with that woman, but this is still done in a private realm and not openly discussed. It is something I found out in intimate conversations with the people I am closest to. While there is not an essential Qom sexuality, these forms of sexuality are resonant with Qom's ethics that are distant from Christian regulation of sexuality.[43] But women (and men) who are not "respectable" are not only criticized in terms of their sexuality, but also as parents. A "respectable" woman is assumed to have her household under control and a traceable mobility. Even when her travels were well organized, Cecilia's mobility generated suspicion, and her neighbors and in-laws tried to regulate her mobility by insisting that she stopped traveling.

While women have relative freedom to move when young, they are expected to slow their mobility when they become mothers. Mobility becomes intertwined with moral understandings of what is acceptable and not for married women in Qom communities, and even when Cecilia disagreed, her husband was carried away by the gossip around her. This concern echoes feminist discussions around women's mobility. Initial feminist approaches considered control over women's movement outside the household as a form of female regulation across societies.[44] In this scheme, feminists regarded mobility as an emancipatory transgression of the push to the domestic sphere and patriarchal control. In the previous examples, mobility opened new possibilities for women and was also directed by others, as when parents insist their daughters move to help a relative.

Some women are pushed to move, requested to go elsewhere by their family, and for them, travel may not be an expression of agency, but rather of obedience to a family request. And yet when parents help a daughter move to attend high school, they are also supporting her independence. This problematizes any simple understanding of private versus public space and mobile versus immobile women. Women who travel may be under scrutiny, but they are also valued as experienced. Finally, the concern over young women's mobility is also a response to Indigenous women being targets of gendered forms of violence by non-Indigenous people in public spaces, as part of what Rita Segato names "pedagogies of cruelty," which she links to colonial and extractivist perspectives of Indigenous women's bodies as available to be taken to communicate male power.[45]

For women, mobility represents an ambiguous and contradictory experience. It may allow them to study, have a job, become experienced, and gain leadership roles in their communities but also to present frictions; it may be chosen or a mandate to follow. Thus, any simplistic understanding of mobility as unequivocal form of freedom or a simple escape is reductive. Prior dispositions to move, and experiences of their movement's regulation, manifested in women's trajectories to Buenos Aires. Only women who were already mobile arrived in Buenos Aires by themselves or initiated their family's travel.

In sum, affective mobilities are seen as a natural part of growing and as shaping capacities among adults, but among women, they implied a specific form of regulation and scrutiny, especially for adult women, married and with children.[46] The trajectories of people who "ended up in Buenos Aires" and were the first to build the Barrio Qom drew on these previous experiences of travel and expanded them. The people who ended up in the barrio were not the ones most in need. Rather, most of them embodied the effects of these intense movements as young people and were able to manage themselves during their longer-than-average and exploratory travels. In the next section, I examine the trajectories of four people who live in the barrio and who sparked their families' move to Buenos Aires.

Unusual Trajectories

Moving to Buenos Aires was almost never a one-way process. People went back and forth between locations and had lived in the Chaco region or in the city of Rosario before.[47] While moving to Buenos Aires is a shared desire of many people in Chaco, a desire shaped by media depictions of the big and affluent city and by stories about powerful Qom leaders who maneuvered successful land negotiations with the national government, moving to Buenos Aires was a risky move, and the boldest one. In the capital, there were very few established Qom people, no Iglesia Unida churches, and no organized

Qom communities. Thus, there were few networks helping others establish; moving to the Qom barrios in Rosario or Santa Fe would have been easier.[48]

If these moves were not only defined by push and pull factors or by cultural practices alone, then affect identifies the circumstances that motorized displacement, and the notion of "ending up" suggests the contingency of these mobilities. This is an alternative approach to migration and mobilities at large. Analyzing the role of affect as a form of political dissidence in Latin America, Beasley-Murray identifies affective transformation as a driver of unexpected political turns, including unexpected mass mobilization such as the Caracazo in Venezuela, or the spontaneous mobilizations to support Perón's seeding of Peronism in Argentina.[49] He identifies affect, too, as a relationship that maintains unity through time in insurrectionary moments and sustains coordinated action and perseverance.[50] By focusing on affect, he establishes a field of political study that cannot be predicted from the tensions contained within one social structure, for example, racial tensions. If insurrection and political change can be traced through collective affective transformations (for example, the sudden mobilizations of people to the streets in the *Caracazo*), so can the moments of reconstituting consensus, which are effective only if shaped in new affects and habits (for example, the development of consumerism in Argentina under neoliberal transformations). Affect draws attention to what Stuart Halls calls politics "without guarantees" to ask which affinities create new forms of collective organization (whether if a sense of Qomness, a class, or an intersectional composition) that become relevant or not.[51]

Considering mobilities from the perspective of affective politics move away from assuming that Qom people will reconstruct their ethnic identities in the city without variations. It challenges too that people who move have too much or too little agency. By inquiring what types of experiences become intolerable in Chaco, and what capacities and desires trigger a move, mobility can be understood as a result of a complex combination of context and structural dynamics; one that generates new possibilities (for example being Qom in the capital city). Affect does not ignore social structures and political rationalities; it traces their transformations and inquires into political activation, mobilization, and reorganization by resituating embodied experiences and material practice as a focus. Here I am interested in how affect has triggered movement and the extension and reconfiguration of assemblages, and how it operates at the center of assemblages to maintain active connections.

During my work, I identified regularities in the mobilities of the people in the barrio, who, as mentioned, were among the first Qom to settle in

Buenos Aires and conduct a successful land negotiation. Out of these commonalities, I created a typology that describes how these unusual mobilities created space for Qom life in the city. The typology unpacks the common experiences and capacities that both triggered and created possibilities for moving farther away than other people had and creating Qom places in new areas of the country. These unusual trajectories are thus about how assemblages expanded their areas of reach. Expanding to Buenos Aires thus made it possible to be close to national government institutions and NGOs based in Buenos Aires. Affect thus enables another understanding of the process through which territories emerge out of assemblages, as they result not from a sovereign power but from connections (composition), disconnection, and dissolution at the center of Qom politics.

The first type of trajectory I analyze is that of women who were recognized as *mujeres fuertes* (strong women) and encouraged to move to help their families. These women had studied or been engaged as leaders and thus were trusted to develop new links in a new place; some moved because they had chosen to, and others were sent by their families. This is in contrast to the second type of trajectory, that of men who had been key figures in the negotiations over land in the barrio and organized their life histories around having been *huerfanitos* (orphaned children). Men who depict themselves as orphans explain that they were left "with no guidance," "no place to be," meaning that they were intensely mobile and had no fixed home in the Chaco. A third type of trajectory, highlighted by both men and women, involved breaking up with a partner, described as a moment when people needed to create distance and go elsewhere. Finally, many adult men moved out of the Chaco because of mandatory military service, which they identified as an experience that gave them new skills but was difficult yet transformative, making them better prepared to go to Buenos Aires. These four types of experiences are affective variations and involve moments that changed people's capacities to act, transforming their associations in one place and making them move elsewhere. This is a typology of affective variation that transformed the configuration of Qom assemblages and the territory over which they extend. In what follows, I analyze four trajectories that illustrate these unusual ways of moving.

MUJERES FUERTES

"Strong women" are women who have a leadership role, are experienced and independent, and are perceived as brave. In the countryside, they are called *guapas*: women who can find their way in the bush, are skillful in obtaining resources, and know how to use a machete, climb trees, gather fruits, and collect fibers. They are also brave women who confront the dangers of the bush. Some younger women, many living, by contrast, in urban areas, can also be come strong by accessing education, getting jobs as health assistants or aboriginal teachers, being community leaders, and working with NGOs. Women who have leadership roles and organize community activities, such as running a soup kitchen, are also regarded as "strong women."[52] Some women have all these capacities at the same time. In the barrio, a few of them were primarily responsible for making their whole family move to Buenos Aires, such as Andrea, who is also the daughter of an important political leader and preacher in the Chaco.

Andrea was born in the mid-1970s, in a village in the interfluvial area of the province of Chaco, an extensive area between the river Bermejo and its subsidiary the Bermejito. At the time, the area was informally occupied by Indigenous groups and a few *criollo* farmers. It was also one of the last areas of Indigenous armed resistance during the military conquest of the Chaco and a central place in the collective memory of Qom people. As a child, Andrea used to travel with her father, her mother, and her siblings to visit relatives and other leaders in the villages of the area. They also went to work in the cotton harvest with their father several times. In her travels she got to know different villages, learned about political organizing, and became "strong" as a result of these experiences.

When Andrea finished primary school, she attended a high school created by Belgian missionaries located a few kilometers from her family farm: a boarding school for rural Indigenous children. Andrea lived at the school for weeks at a time, returning home to help with farm duties. Through this education, she met other Qom people, interacted with school teachers and foreign missionaries, and earned a high school diploma. When she finished high school, Andrea was fluent in Spanish, had strong reading and writing skills, and knew how to interact with institutions. High school prepared her for life in an urban setting. Andrea had her first child after graduating, and because she did not stay with the baby's father, she lived with her parents, who helped her raise her first child. Soon, she met her husband and had two more children.

In the 1990s, Indigenous leaders, including Andrea's father, obtained the legal title to 140,000 hectares of land where they lived in the *interfluvios* (between rivers). With the assistance of Belgian missionaries, they created the Indigenous Land Association, which coordinated communities and administered the land. Andrea's father helped her apply to get a plot of land in the area, and she settled with her husband and three of her eventually nine children. Andrea lived there for a few years, raising goats and taking care of her farm. When her older children were still small, her father asked her to move to Buenos Aires to help her sister, who had moved searching for better prospects for her children and was living in a *villa* (shantytown). He stressed that she would have more possibilities to study and support political organization in Buenos Aires. Her father considered that she was more capable of moving than any of her other siblings who did not attend high school, and her experience implied that she had a responsibility to go to Buenos Aires and supporting her sister.

Andrea was in her early twenties when she moved to Buenos Aires, where she lived in the shantytown with her sister for a year. But her husband, whose Spanish is not very fluent, did not find a job and had problems adjusting, while she had no chance to study. They both spent most of their time inside the small apartment in Fuerte Apache thinking about the community, their farm and cattle, and the bush, so after a year, they moved back to their farm in Chaco. However, her sister became involved in the land negotiations for the Barrio Qom in Buenos Aires, and two years after their return to the Chaco, she offered to put Andrea on the list of families requesting a house there. Andrea and her husband did not want to move again, but her father insisted on the importance of having a house in Buenos Aires and that she should take it, as an educated person in the family. Her sister told her the barrio would be very different from the shantytown, and together, her father and sister convinced her to move. Andrea agreed with the aim of *juntar certificados*, getting as many education certificates as she could by taking courses.[53] She also expected her children to attend high school in Buenos Aires, and even possibly access tertiary education, a level she had not attained. Since moving, Andrea had been actively involved in the barrio's *comisión*, producing and selling handicrafts, and working with NGOs and the middle-class people who approach the barrio "to help."

Andrea was responsible for her family's move to Buenos Aires, unlike some other women who come as wives following their partner's initiatives.[54] Yet she was also under a lot of pressure to move. Being a "strong woman" with unusual travel experience, holding a high school diploma, and knowing how to interact with state institutions and NGOs, Andrea was made responsible for her extended family. She was expected to contribute in a different way from that of her siblings, who had no formal education and stayed on the farm. Her father and older sister were able to influence Andrea to be a "pioneer" along with her sister and help organize families in the newly created barrio. She had to put her own and her partner's desires aside and move to establish the presence of their extended family in Buenos Aires.

Andrea's settlement in the barrio transformed her extended family's capacities for mobility as a whole because the family would have two houses where they could stay while in Buenos Aires. Andrea's sister, who became another of the barrio's leaders, along with her husband, would also be stronger if Andrea moved, as together they helped one another and were a common front on neighborhood commission. After Andrea moved, she and her sister hosted relatives from the Chaco and connected people from Buenos Aires to the rural communities. However, Andrea, who was in her thirties when I met with her, did not give up her desire to live back on a farm in the Chaco, and she periodically reminded her father that she wanted to go back. When I went to Bermejito with her, I saw how persistent she was in planning a return to her farm during conversations with her father.

A few other strong women in the barrio also moved to Buenos Aires as part of the collective "good of their families," yet others moved as their own initiative, as Andrea's sister did. These movements, part own desire and part a response to family needs, expand family assemblages and their capacity to act: It is useful to have a family member who can run errands in the city, host family members from the Chaco, or be an intermediary with middle-class groups in Buenos Aires. Andrea and her sister, both strong women, supported their family by having a space in the capital. Both were actively in touch with their family in the Chaco, a large family with multiple leaders and important networks. The sisters created this expansion by texting back and forth daily to coordinate activities with their family.

Kinship relations are actualized in complex ways among Qom, yet as mentioned, Qom people have been described as matrilocal, and many married couples—even if they do not move to the woman's side of the family—hold stronger connections on the maternal side while the men move out and lose touch.[55] Women are expected to maintain a more active connection with their parents once they have their own families, while men tend to become members of the family of their partners. This form of kinship is thus connected to the forms of mobility leading to the barrio, where men are more disconnected members while women move as part of a family. Having "strong women" in an extended family, therefore, makes a huge contribution to the overall well-being of everyone. More than fifteen years after they had moved to Buenos Aires, Andrea and her sister had extended their family's network there.

ORPHANS

In contrast to the spatial expansion of kin relations created by strong women, many of the men who first arrived in the city explained that they left the Chaco because they were orphans, and their affective family relations had been severed. As orphans, they had no significant kinship relations in the Chaco, had nothing to lose if they moved far away, and thus they took the chance to explore. Being orphans had shaped these men's entire lives and made them more mobile in their youth, with no nuclear family holding them back. I was surprised by the number of men in the barrio in their late forties or older who emphasized this experience of being orphaned, which seemed to me unrelated to traveling. I will unpack this by focusing on Lorenzo's trajectory.

Sitting under a tree outside his house in the Barrio Qom in Buenos Aires, Lorenzo narrated his life to me in a series of interviews punctuated by memories with strong affective variations. When he recalled events, he seemed to be reliving them, making gestures as if the landscape he was referring to were there in front of him, and changing his mood in relation to the events he was describing. Some of the experiences were sad, and a few times, his eyes were watery. He was unashamed of sharing his sadness with me, and I felt honored by his trust. Many other times, he laughed smoothly, and many memories made him smile frequently, too, demonstrating a deep connection to how events had affected him and a wide emotional range. His sense of having been lost most of his life, with no family support, no guidance, and no love until he met his most recent wife, was a recurrent theme. Lorenzo narrated his life starting from the moment his father died, and then went back to contrast how well he was cared for when his father was still alive.

Lorenzo was born close to the *ingenio* Las Palmas in the 1920s and was the first son of a powerful religious and political leader and *ingenio mayordomo* (foreman) at the plantation. When Lorenzo's father died, the family abandoned their house and spread out into different villages. Lorenzo's mother sent him to a nearby village to live with his uncle, who also worked for the sugar plantation. In Lorenzo's memory, at that moment he became an orphan: He had no home of his own, no guidance in life, and no family support—a status that shaped the rest of his life. Living with his uncle, Lorenzo did not attend school regularly because no one cared about his education. He quit school before completing his primary education, hung out in the train station with *criollo* children, and rode the trains with them. He started traveling to nearby towns, and activated intense mobility linked to not having a family to contain him and no clear orientation.

When Lorenzo was eleven, he started working with his uncle on the Las Palmas plantation, where they plowed the land with oxen and worked the cane harvest. Overall, he was employed for half the year. However, Lorenzo made almost no money and remembers how at the end of a season, he had enough only to buy new work clothes. When he was eighteen, Lorenzo had a girlfriend, and they had a baby girl. But the baby got sick and died, and the trauma of the death led them to split up. Alone again, Lorenzo took an offer from the Iglesia Unida to go to study the Bible in Resistencia, where he stayed for a season before moving back to work for the *ingenio*. In remembering these trajectories, he said it was very hard for him to face both the death of his daughter and the fact that he had no family support. He said he missed having his father around to guide him, especially at such difficult moments. At the time of our interviews, Lorenzo was in his seventies and still lamented the death of his father, the lack of guidance, and that he had wandered so much.

During one harvest, Lorenzo met Roberto, a Qom man doing seasonal work who was living and working in Buenos Aires and told Lorenzo how much work a person could find there. He left Lorenzo his address and insisted that he go and work there himself. Lorenzo kept on working on the plantation, but after some time, he started to feel a pain in his chest. He asked the sugar company to treat him, but the company doctor told him he was healthy. When harvest time came, he asked for a job as he had done for the past ten years, but the *mayordomo* said there was no work that season. He knew they were hiring many people for the harvest, and they were explicitly denying him work. Probably, he explained, the administration did not want to acknowledge any work-related injury he might have, and so they denied rehiring him. Lorenzo felt betrayed and angry after so many years of hard work.

Lorenzo had experienced labor exploitation for years, yet it was the experience of being denied work that he found most upsetting. He felt particularly abused because his father used to be the *mayordomo* of the area, and his whole family had served in the *ingenio*. The lack of attachment combined with the mistreatment triggered Lorenzo's first trip to Buenos Aires. He looked up the address that Roberto had written down on a small piece of paper, and with help from the union, he put together a folder with his medical record, got a train ticket, and left for Buenos Aires. Lorenzo's trajectory was thus marked by intensely affective transformations: the death of his father, the breakup of his family, the death of his first child, the split from his partner, and the loss of his job. He linked all these events and his subsequent trip to Buenos Aires to the experience of being an orphan with no one supporting him and nothing to lose if he moved far away. Going to Buenos Aires in the 1950s, with nothing but the address of an acquaintance written down on a piece of paper, was a bold move. Nobody else in Lorenzo's circle of relatives or acquaintances had moved that far away; only his father in the role of community leader had once visited the city.

Other men also remembered their mobility as shaped by their experiences of being orphans. They explained that they had more freedom to move far away because they had no strong attachments in the Chaco. They were also proud of having confronted many difficulties and becoming stronger than the average person because of this. Many of these men also had moments of intense mobility when they were young, and they had managed to support themselves at a young age. When they moved to Buenos Aires, there was no Qom church or any organized groups of Qom families to help them. This sense of homelessness among some orphan men opened up the option of moving farther than usual, of making a leap that was not as safe as moving to the well-established settlements in Rosario, for example. These male orphans and the strong women were, therefore, the pioneers in expanding Qom networks into Buenos Aires. Later, they helped others to settle in the city.

BREAKUPS

Another trajectory from the Chaco to Buenos Aires involves people who ended up in Buenos Aires to escape from a breakup, that is, people who traveled to move away from intense personal confrontations with their former partners and moved as acts of affective and spatial disconnection. One of them was Sofía, who was much younger than everyone else I met with, and arrived in Buenos Aires during my work. She was born in the late 1980s in a rural Chaco village near Espinillo and used to travel with her father to sell handicrafts. They traveled to participate in craft fairs in the provincial city of Resistencia and outside the Chaco, in Santa Fe and Rosario. As a child, Sofía went with him whenever she could, and on those trips, she learned how to travel to big cities, manage the business, and interact with *criollos* and white people. When her parents split up, Sofía was a teenager, and she moved with her father to the Qom barrio in Resistencia to attend high school there. Her father was involved in the barrio's commission, and he always participated in organizing community events and mediating with the state. Sofía started to organize youth activities in the barrio and became involved as a youth coordinator on a non-Indigenous NGO project. In this role she traveled to meetings to Rosario and Santa Fe and to small towns in the Chaco.

When I met her, Sofía had just arrived from Resistencia and was staying with relatives in the Qom barrio in Buenos Aires. She had come to the city to take a job as a live-in domestic worker in a middle-class home, because her father insisted and supported her in doing so. However, what made Sofía decide to move to Buenos Aires was a recent breakup with her partner, with whom she had a child. A non-Qom friend Sofía had met at a youth encounter, who also did domestic work, had offered her the job. Sofía did not want to take it, because it meant she would have to separate from her child and quit her work as an organizer, but she finally decided to move so she could be far from her former partner and start over. She sent her child to live with her mother in a village near Espinillo and let her father help organize the trip. He contacted Leandro, a distant relative living in the Barrio Qom, and arranged for her to stay at his place for her first few days in the city. Because of her previous travel experience, Sofía did not find it hard to adjust to Buenos Aires, and although she had never been in the city, she emphasized never got lost, as many other people did.

Sofía's travel was thus related to several factors that I have been discussing so far: job opportunities, personal strength, and support and pressure from her father. However, she also had strong motivations to stay in the Chaco: her child and her position as a youth organizer. What ended up triggering her move was the breakup and her need to be far from her former partner. People say that former partners can get resentful, become aggressive (and often try to cause harm through sorcery), and get jealous if a woman (or man) meets a new partner. Accordingly, Sofía took an option she would not have considered otherwise and moved far from Resistencia.

This was another common pattern. In many life histories, people described how after a breakup, they had moved as far away as possible: from a village to a nearby town, to a bigger city, or to relatives in another province. They explained how they actively searched for any possibility to move away and create some distance, because remaining in touch with a former partner could result in strong tensions. Many people ended up in Buenos Aires because they needed to dissipate a conflict, interrupt intense relations in the Chaco, and start over. Importantly, only those people who, like Sofía or Martín, had experience in traveling were able to move to Buenos Aires after a breakup. In this case, travel was a way of actively disconnecting from intense personal relations in the Chaco.

COLIMBAS

An important experience related to travel in general and ending up in Buenos Aires was the military draft, a system that, until 1994, enlisted civilian men for a year of training and made them move across the country in different units. In Buenos Aires and across the Chaco I met men who, after their service, decided not to go back home. When I recorded men's life histories, the draft came up time and again as an experience associated with intense mobility. *Colimba* is the popularized informal name for the process of being enrolled in Argentina's military service—it can also refer to any man who was so enrolled. The term compresses the words *corre, limpia, barre* (run, clean, sweep), actions associated with the draft.[56] Military service was universal and mandatory until 1996, when it became voluntary.[57] Each year, all men in the cohort of seventeen-year-old Argentine citizens had their national ID numbers placed into a raffle for selecting the men required to do a year (or more) of service. During their service, men received training before being distributed between Argentina's three forces (army, navy, and air force) and across the country to perform the lowest-ranked tasks in each military unit.[58] I had expected that military service would be a particularly traumatic experience for Qom men, because most Qom people have intergenerational memories of the violent military conquest of the Chaco in the early twentieth century. I was surprised to find that most of the men I talked to remembered it as a mostly positive personal experience (although many too highlighted problematic aspects), which they separated from the state violence that once engulfed the Chaco. The *colimba* was a recurrent theme in the trajectories of several men ending up in Buenos Aires and was remembered as an experience that gave them valuable skills and generated in them the desire to travel and visit new places.

Julio's trajectory further expanded during the *colimba* in the early 1980s. Julio was assigned to the navy and first stationed in the city of Corrientes and then sent to a naval base in northern Patagonia, where he learned to work on ships and was trained in parachuting. While he had been highly mobile at a young age, it was only in the *colimba* that he started to want to move to Buenos Aires. One of his friends had worked in the city and told Julio that he should go, that "Buenos Aires was full of opportunities." Julio decided he would travel there after the *colimba*, and even though he had lost touch with his friend and had no connections in the city when the time came, he did not hesitate to take a bus to a shantytown and rent a room for the night. During the service, Julio and other Qom men bonded with men of all backgrounds and places of origin and learned about places they had never heard about and wanted to see. Julio remembered that nights with his new friends in the *colimba* were spent making plans to visit one another's hometowns. Thus, military service gave men the opportunity to expand their mobilities to previously unimagined places.

Julio further explained that, in the military, Qom men had a good reputation, which contributed to enhancing their skills and the ability to travel farther away than other Qom people. The physical training and the tasks assigned to them were relatively easy to perform for Qom men. After all, they were used to hunting in the bush with rifles, and they had been exploited on plantations, so they were strong and could bear physically exhausting work with little food and for long hours. They were very good at finding their way in the bush, sleeping on the ground, and shooting with a rifle. Therefore, they were praised by instructors and recognized as skilled soldiers. Their embodied skills and strength unexpectedly became a form of capital in the specific context of the military.[59] This praise contrasts with the racism Indigenous men faced in other settings, such as schools and hospitals, where they were treated as incapable, childlike, and barbaric. It also contrasts with their experience on the sugar plantations, where Indigenous people from the Chaco were regarded as the least skilled workers in an ethnic hierarchy of exploitation.[60]

This unexpected good reputation facilitated for Qom people learning new skills in military training programs without the denigrating interactions that they experienced in schools and workplaces. And it was in the *colimba* that Julio learned to read and write, and also was trained in construction work, plumbing, and as an electrician, skills that would help him in Buenos Aires. In sum, Qom men who had participated in the *colimba* were able to move farther than others. They had confidence, networks, and skills that supported them upon arriving in the city and, later, in creating the barrio. Thus, among the people who negotiated the land of the barrio, a number of the men had served in the military.

In these four types of mobilities, there is a commonality: the breaking of the usual social disposition for moving, the habits that lead people to settle in the Chaco, either in a rural community or in a barrio. There is also a break from a direct determination of political-economic forces, such as forms of subordination through economic exploitation, land expropriation, or religious conversion. The four unusual mobilities depart from and mediate between the level of individual agency, the dispositions to move, and the political-economic conditions. Affect thus breaks the determination of habits and the larger structures and opens space for variation, while mobilities then trigger new experiences and open the range of possibilities, as in the case of Sofía. More specifically, the affective relations that trigger movement reconstruct assemblages in new and expansive ways. Institutions including the church, family and marriage, and military service are neither forces that completely subordinate people nor redefined by Qom's individual agency. Rather, they become mediations, are used for other purposes, and trigger the expansion of assemblages as networks of relations across space. The typology thus captures forms of mobility where there is either an unusual expansion of a person's capacities, in the case of *mujeres fuertes* and *colimbas*, or an important rupture in intimate relationships, as for orphans and people experiencing a breakup. It is important to highlight that expansion is not the only effect of relocating to Buenos Aires. When I met Sofía months after my first encounter with her, she narrated a very difficult situation as a live-in domestic worker, where she was not allowed to leave the house sometimes for weeks and was constantly working overtime, both at her employer's home and at their business.

"Ending Up": Open-Ended Trajectories to Buenos Aires

The mobilities and trajectories examined in this chapter show that people "ended up" in Buenos Aires because of particular historical conditionings, specific dispositions for movement during their youth, and forms of affective variations strongly shaped by gender. Movement to Buenos Aires resulted from specific circumstances (e.g., becoming orphaned, being jobless) in which some Qom people used their skills (having travel experience, education, or military experience) to solve a difficult situation and expand their options and their extended families' possibilities. To understand how people ended up in Buenos Aires, it was thus necessary to examine historical-material conditions and cultural practices related to mobility, but also to trace their trajectories, the "histories of change," and the obstacles they encountered.

In all four trajectories, people explained their move as the result of a moment of affective intensity in their relations in the Chaco that transformed a request, a conflict, or a sense of disorientation and anger, into mobility, and created the "need to move." This "need" was inseparable from broader social, geographic, and historical conditions, but it also indicates an affective intensity, the sense of being compelled to move away from where they were and travel to Buenos Aires. In tracing these trajectories, I found that most people coming to Buenos Aires had previous experiences of intensive travel, and they described such experiences as necessary to survive in the city. Significantly, many of the first people to arrive in Buenos Aires were part of politically engaged families in the Chaco, daughters and sons of religious and political leaders, who led land claims in the Chaco and became leaders themselves.

Today, moving to Buenos Aires is easier because newcomers can count on finding many established Qom barrios and, therefore, a preestablished network of connections and points of reference. Yet decades ago, Buenos Aires was an uncommon destination for Qom people living in rural areas. In their recollections, people stressed the unusualness of their decisions, as they moved to shantytowns that struck them as alien places where they had no connections. This made many of the people in the barrio "pioneers" in arriving and staying in a city where they had to *arreglarse*, or figure things out by themselves; connect with unfamiliar institutions such as local schools; and find a place to live. The relative success of their efforts to settle down in the city is explained as the outcome of physical and moral grit, embodied in the strong women and in the *colimbas*, but also among orphans who had been traveling far away from their communities. Each movement opened new capacities and new potential connections, and the chain of those chance encounters made people "end up" in Buenos Aires.

Affect explains why and how people moved within the Chaco, how mobility changed people's capacities, and what types of situations triggered and oriented people toward Buenos Aires. In this chapter, I have offered an alternative approach to understanding mobility as neither the result of political-economic relations alone nor the product of cultural practices specific to the Qom—or even the consequence of purely individual choices or agency. Instead, I have traced mobilities in their bodily and affective materiality, as embodied actions executed within and against entangled relations of power and domination, operating at different scales. Assemblage brings together the simultaneity of relations that shape forms of movement. These arguments are in agreement with studies of migrant Indigenous people that identify that migrants are generally not the most impoverished, disempowered members of a group of origin.[61] This typology also adds to the understanding to translocal activities as a set of relationships that do not only re-create the community of origin and transform the destination but also create forms of connection between several places, activities, and historical circumstances. The barrio is a form of Qom diaspora, but a perspective of diaspora alone is not sufficient to unpack the role of the military service or why strong women and orphans move more than others. The barrio is thus a specific composition that is not just re-creating an essence of Qomness whose original source is rural communities. In life histories, experiences of mobility were a necessary part of the bold move to Buenos Aires and, ultimately, the creation of the barrio. People generally moved from rural to urban places, and they often explored several locations and came back home in between, in some cases going back to their home villages in the Chaco. In movements Qomness was expanded, the possibilities of being Indigenous reshaped in the mobilities and in the city.

More importantly, most of these trajectories were defined by uncertainty. Very few people had planned to move to Buenos Aires or organized their mobility with that goal in mind. Most of the encounters and displacements were unplanned, and this manifests in the phrase "ending up" in Buenos Aires. The typology of strong women, orphans, people who had undergone breakups, or *colimbas* shows these commonalities, and the specificity of each experience. Yet the fact that many of these trajectories ended up in Buenos Aires and not elsewhere also indicates the affective pull of this city as the national capital and, therefore, as the most powerful point of reference in national imaginings of progress and prosperity.

CHAPTER 2

The *Villas*

The Spatiality of Race in Buenos Aires

Arriving in Buenos Aires, Living in the Shantytowns

In 1954, Lorenzo left the village where he lived, in the area of Las Palmas, Chaco province, and headed to Buenos Aires. He was frustrated because he had not been hired for the sugarcane harvest at the Las Palmas plantation and was ready to make a claim at the company's headquarters, as the union had advised. When he left, he had a train ticket, a few belongings in a bag, and a piece of paper with an address. The address belonged to Roberto, a Qom man whom Lorenzo had met a year earlier during the harvest in Las Palmas. Roberto had encouraged Lorenzo to "come to Buenos Aires, stay at my place, and work," emphasizing that he could "find plenty of work in the city." Lorenzo had not seen Roberto again, but had decided to accept the invitation. After a bus ride to the provincial capital and a two-day train trip, Lorenzo arrived in Buenos Aires. He described his arrival in the city in great detail: "I got to the train station . . . and I took a taxi because I felt lost. All the tall buildings, everyone moving so fast! The taxi crossed downtown, then over a bridge, and we arrived at the address I had. When we got there, I saw the place and I was so afraid [he opened his eyes, reenacting the moment of surprise]. . . . It is a *villa*!"

This was not the last time I would hear people from the barrio narrate their arrival in Buenos Aires in terms of a shock defined by two stages: first, the encounter with a city felt as overwhelming and disorienting, "so full of people and cars and buses, moving so fast" (as Lorenzo described it); second, the shock of learning they would be living in the *villas*, the infamous Buenos Aires shantytowns. The families I knew who were living in the barrio arrived in Buenos Aires between the mid-1950s and early 1990s. Depending on when exactly they arrived, they confronted different socioeconomic conditions. Whereas until the 1970s there was near full employment in the city, the 1980s and 1990s were times of economic crises and rising unemployment, the product of neoliberal "structural adjustment" programs. Despite these particularities, life in a *villa* was an experience common to most Qom people arriving in Buenos Aires, including the families living in the barrio.[1]

Most Qom people I spoke with in the barrio depicted the *villas* as places where "life was unbearable": precarious, noisy, packed, and violent. For this reason, initially, it seemed there was not much to ask about this experience: Living in the *villas* was very hard, and that was the reason they worked to create the barrio. However, later on, people told me about aspects of their life in the *villas* that contradicted their earlier descriptions of somewhere that was "unbearable." In the *villas*, neighbors were always ready to help; *villas* are home to people from all over the country, as well as transnational migrants, and Qoms enjoyed learning about life elsewhere, for example, from people who came from places "with snow." Many neighbors became their friends, and they created a diverse community that could not be reproduced in the Barrio Qom in Buenos Aires. Furthermore, young people like Luciana told me that the *villas* were no more dangerous than the Barrio Qom, and that people in the *villas* had a stronger sense of community. Why, then, did people not stay in the *villas* and make an effort to improve their situation there?

To answer this question, I found I had to engage with other experiences that people were talking about only in bits and pieces. For Qoms arriving in Buenos Aires, what was even more surprising than living in the *villas* was that many *porteños* saw them as *negros villeros* (blacks from the *villas*). They found out they were labeled with this highly stigmatized identification thanks to some very tense encounters. Gerardo, a man in his fifties who arrived in Buenos Aires in 1984, remembers that when he lived in the *villa* Ciudad Oculta (Hidden City), he was frequently stopped by the police, something he still occasionally experiences. The police singled him out because of his appearance, especially his brown skin and Indigenous facial features, and his proximity to the *villas*, and they concluded that "he looked suspicious." When they stopped him, they often questioned him for a long time and he would miss appointments. He knew, too, that *porteños* who passed him while he was undergoing such street interrogations looked at him as if he had committed a crime. He looked suspicious because he "looked poor" and was dark-skinned. The racialization of the urban poor as *negros* and *negros villeros* was something that the Qom, in common with other internal and foreign migrants, experienced upon arrival in Buenos Aires. These terms suggested their rural origins and implied that they were inevitably uneducated, potentially violent, prone to breaking the law, and thus in need of control. *Negros* did not have access to the "city proper" and were instead "thrown together" in the shantytowns, along with thousands of other rural migrants who had come to the city in search of work. As *negros*, Qoms became the objects of stereotypes, and these stereotypes prevented them from living in a regular barrio and walking unimpeded around the city.

In this chapter, I argue that what made Qom families move from the *villas* to found the Barrio Qom was less the way of life in the shantytowns than the experience of being racialized as *negros villeros* and all that implied. Given the stories that people in the barrio told me about how the *villas* were places full of a rich diversity of people, where they enjoyed forms of solidarity, the discomfort they felt in the *villas* has more to do with this racialization than with life in the shantytowns themselves. In short, that Qom families moved from the *villas* to escape racialization as *negros*, as subordinates in the racial formations of Buenos Aires. In what follows, I discuss two intertwined processes: the experiences of being racialized in the city and the productive encounters emerging in their racialization as *negros*.

Spatial segregation, however, is not all-encompassing. To unpack this dimension, I focus on the descriptions of the *villas* as places of productive encounters, drawing again on Doreen Massey's notion of "throwntogetherness."[2] If space is a sphere of unplanned encounters characterized by the emergence of multiple forms of socialization, then the movement of people and objects can never be fully controlled or anticipated. Chance encounters of people, infrastructures, and natural features, and the unexpected associations that emerge, are what she calls being "thrown together in space." The Qom who arrived in the city from the Chaco were thrown together in the *villas* with multiple other subaltern groups, with very diverse trajectories, and they created new forms of association in the city as they met people from all over and created collective mobilization in the *villas*.[3]

Regulations and associations in the *villas* changed over time. The next two sections of this chapter give an overview of urban racial formation and how the Qom were racialized in Buenos Aires. I then expand on the effects of racialization and the positive encounters in the *villas* of Qom women and men who now live in the Barrio Qom. This encompasses two periods: First, between the 1960s and the 1970s, Qom people who arrived in the *villas* were connected to the Peronist political movement; second, from the 1980s until the 1990s, there was a return to democratic government while the country experienced a series of economic crises. The experience of the Qom sheds light on larger racial logics of the organization of space in Buenos Aires, and the making of the *villas* as places where people converged to create new political subjects.

I draw on the trajectory of four families that lived in a *villa* currently known as Fuerte Apache that I visited thanks to one of the families I had closer relations to.[4] I reconstruct Qoms' experience in the *villas* mostly from conversations with them and from this visit to Fuerte Apache.

Racialized Space in Latin America

The image of the *villeros* and *negros* can best be understood alongside the marking of dark-skinned people as "other" in Argentina and Latin America. The racialization of the *villas* reflects power dynamics stemming from Indigenous dispossession and the construction of racial differences to justify and reproduce this structure. Marx's analysis of colonial economic relations, the expropriation of Indigenous land, laid the foundation for capitalist exploitation.[5] Fanon emphasized the significance of urban spatial division between white European and Indigenous and Afro space in the colonial organization of the world.[6]

In Latin America, spatial division according to race was a characteristic of colonial cities, including Buenos Aires. The distribution of bodies in the city dates back to the colonial encounter in the sixteenth century, when physical characteristics were to distinguish between Spanish colonizers and the Indigenous colonized: The Spanish colonial regime created the legal category of "Indio" as an "other" to the "civilized," modern European.[7] As colonialism unfolded, this dichotomy gave way to an array of racial categories derived from the intermingling of Spanish, Indigenous, and African populations. As in other colonial formations, the organization of race in space maintained a degree of separation between these groups and their relative oppression and privilege.

With independence throughout Latin America, the association of urban space with white Europeanness was reinforced. While mestizo national identities recognized some Indigenous and Afro ancestry, whiteness maintained a privileged association with modernity. Throughout the region, Afro and

Indigenous were pushed to abandon their identities and see themselves as mestizos in order to be recognized as citizens.[8]

With migrations from the countryside to the city encouraged by booming industry and the expansion of citizen rights, the spatial divisions maintained racial divisions that produced shantytowns.[9] In northern cities in the United States after emancipation, slums gradually became places for the nonwhite only, allowing state authorities, landlords, and the police to separate out nonwhites while enabling the social mobility of white Europeans, a form of regulating space that was not as overtly racist as Jim Crow Laws, yet still effectively organized urban space along rigid racial lines.[10] In Latin America, the city center was reserved for mestizos and white Europeans, with the exception of domestic servants.[11] In the region, the making of national identities had the city as its center, and urban Indigenous and Afro people were considered in the process of becoming modern and thus no longer Indigenous. In Peru, for instance, this created new forms of identity, as urban Indigenous became Indigenous mestizos.[12] Groups and people who had been seen as less white or who had refused to give up their identity were banished to the lower classes and the urban margins.[13]

These urban margins, far from being places of passive subordination, have been at the center of contestations of social and racial hierarchies, as well as the site of the emergence of new socialities. In El Alto, Bolivia, a twin city to the capital La Paz, people generated new forms of identification, sometimes setting aside Indigenous identities in favor of political and class affiliations, but they have also used Indigenous relations (e.g., *ayllu* structure) as a motor for new forms of political organizing. In the past two decades, insurrectionary movements organized from El Alto supported the first Indigenous president and reshaped political representation and citizenship.[14] These movements have demonstrated that assimilation and the re-creation of identity are not the only dynamics of Indigeneity in urban spaces. Life and politics are shaped in baroque compositions of heterogeneous logics and forms of socializing.[15]

In this context, the making of Argentine racial formations has two specificities. The first is that instead of promoting mestizo identity, the nation was shaped according to a white assimilationist logic.[16] The second specificity of Argentina's spatial-racial formation is the aforementioned category of *negros*, literally "blacks," associated with the shantytowns and urban subaltern groups, which signals a distant Indigenous and sometimes Afro ancestry, even as it negates such identifications. *Negros* is a form that conflates subalternity, class, and a racialized identity that is seen as having traces of

Afro and Indigenous. As Segato argues, "The non-white is not necessarily the Indian and the African but rather an other that has the *traces* of the Indian and the African, a trace of the historical subordination."[17] The notion of the trace is very important in that it simultaneously erases and recognizes. It erases the possibility of Indigenous people being contemporaneous and part of the formal city, yet it also recognizes that the expectation among the founding figures of a white Argentina that nonwhiteness would dissolve was never fulfilled.

Negros, alongside Indigenous people and Afro groups, confront Argentine whiteness and manifest its precarity. *Negros* are a constant reminder that Argentina is not white, than nonwhites are a large sector of the population (and not only a minority) and that whiteness itself has incorporated Indigenous and Afro and mixed race within it. The next section focuses on the history of the category in association to the space of the villas and how the Qom experienced being perceived as nonwhite and located in this category.

Negros Villeros: Spatialization of Race in Buenos Aires

By being identified as *negros*, Qom men and women were redirected to the city's outskirts, restricted access to certain places, and their movements through the city were regulated. By being placed in the *villas*, the Qom became neighbors of other people labeled as *negros*, and these encounters opened new possibilities in the city. Before the creation of an Indigenous neighborhood, the experience of being racialized for urban Toba people was intertwined with the experience of being segregated to the *villa* space. Segura argues that, to understand processes of urban segregation, it is not enough to focus solely on economic and social dimensions; it is necessary to comprehend mechanisms of racialization as mechanisms of spatial segregation and regulation of mobilities in the city proper.[18] Combining spatial segregation categories with racial formation allows, too, an understanding of the practices generated to counteract these experiences and perceive them as disputes over physical, economic, and political spaces.[19] The Qoms' experiences contribute to understanding how race organizes space in Buenos Aires and how these regulations are challenged and deflected. *Villeros* and *negros* were identities assigned to the Qom upon arriving in Buenos Aires, and these were new and alien to them.[20] Qom families often used *villero* in a pejorative way, for example, to refer to former neighbors, implying that they were uneducated.[21]

In labeling the Qom as *negros*, phenotype matters, for this category refers not only to a class distinction but also to racialized bodies seen as non-European and nonwhite. As *negros*, the Qom are no longer seen as Indigenous, but as people with traces of an Indigenous background. Paradoxically, the Qom and other Indigenous groups in the Chaco are generically recognized by the dominant society as "authentically Indigenous." But in the context of the city and for authenticity to be legible to others, the Indigeneity needs to be displayed, and when Qom people were taking a bus, or going to work or the hospital, they found that Indigeneity was not evident for average *porteños*. In Chaco, racial otherness associates Indigenous people with being lazy, irrational, resisting modernity, and having too many children, but not as dangerous, threatening, or as a political force.

In colonial Argentina, the category *negro* meant specifically the Afro-descendant enslaved population, as distinguished from the *indios*, whom Spanish colonizers recognized in some cases as other nations. In the twentieth century, the category expanded to name all nonwhites, including Indigenous people, probably because of the association with exploitative labor in Buenos Aires.[22]

The bases for the category's expansion can be traced to the distinction between barbarism and civilization established by Domingo F. Sarmiento, an elite writer and president, and a participant in Argentina's nation-building process. Sarmiento argued that the country's lack of modernity resulted from the tension between civilization and barbarism, and the fact that the provinces, but also Buenos Aires, were led by people representing barbarism. Civilization was linked to the culture, science, and progress of white Europeans; barbarism was linked to Indigenous and *criollo* (mixed-race) irrationality, chaos, and the violence of the provincial *caudillos*.[23] From this analysis, Sarmiento was one of the proponents of the whitening projects that has characterized Argentina, distinct from other Latin American countries. This project encouraged the mass immigration and assimilation of between four million and six million Europeans.[24] Indigenous and Afro people were expected to abandon their prior identifications and become Argentines, and Argentines were defined as white and European.[25] The category of "mestizo" went unrecognized, and people of mixed race were expected to become socially white.[26] European immigration to the country was taken as an empirical triumph of the whiteness project, even though racial diversity did not disappear. Ethnic categories started to be explicitly removed from census and institutional records, in order to sediment the ideas that all Argentines are indeed white. Thus, for example, while military conscripts used to be registered as part of racial groups, from 1900 onward, registering race was explicitly banned.[27] However, racial divisions did not cease to exist, nor did the hierarchical organization of race.

Mass immigration and politics of erasure locate Argentina as settler colonial society that shares the genocidal project of erasing Indigenous people and invisibilizing Afro-descendant populations and their enslaved labor.[28] As in other settler colonial societies, Indigenous and Afro populations are targeted under logics of elimination, in order to enable European state sovereignty and the territorial expansion of capitalism as part of narratives of "progress."[29] But unlike in North American settler societies, some Afro and Indigenous people in Argentina were able to become white.

Adamovsky further identifies the formation of the middle class as a way for elites to co-opt the middle sector of shop owners and professionals against popular insurgencies and create class and racial separation by identifying this middle sector as white and by promising their inclusion in the civilized world.[30] While this racial distinction has since been challenged by Indigenous, Afro, and *marrón* anti-racist collectives, it continues to be a central force in Argentine social stratification.

Negro as a category naming "racialized urban subaltern" emerged in the late 1930s when Buenos Aire's elites identified rural populations migrating in large numbers to urban centers as *cabecitas negras*, literally, "little black heads."[31] *Cabecitas negras* became the urban working class and soon associated with the emergent Peronist movement.[32] The elite and the middle classes saw their power being challenged and reacted by identifying (with variations) *cabecitas negras* with the tropes of barbarism that Sarmiento had developed, such as their being an *aluvión zoológico*, or a zoological flood invading the city from the rural areas.[33] These categories were developed in the cities and expanded to the rest of the country, also referring to a regional difference: "White Europeans" were urban and from the big cities in the center of the country, while rural areas were defined as nonwhite.

Negro thus resulted from the proximity in the city between groups, a project to divide white Europeans and nonwhite subaltern groups and the efforts of elites and some middle classes to restrict access of dark-skinned people to white Buenos Aires. Iconically, the birth of Peronism that took place with a mass mobilization of subaltern groups to the city center was read at the time along racial and spatial lines as *negros peronistas* taking over the city while also becoming political protagonists. While military governments in the 1960s and 1970s attempted to stop the centrality of the (*negros*) *peronistas* located in *villas* in the political sphere, *negro* was not explicitly articulated in these dictatorships' discourse. *Peronistas* (Peronists) and *subversivos* (insurgents, left-wing, guerrilla fighters) became the abnormality to be suppressed with state violence.

Qom people arriving in Buenos Aires before the creation of the Barrio Qom found themselves living in the *villas* regardless of whether they had family or acquaintances to host them. The hostels and *pensiones* (live-in hotels) for the working class in the city were too expensive for someone arriving unemployed from the Chaco. Renting a room or an apartment was also impossible for them, given that in Buenos Aires, one needed to provide a property title, as a warranty to sign a rental lease and pay a few months in advance. The result of that policy was that most working-class people and migrants had no way of entering a rental agreement, even in a working-class neighborhood. This also became a form of racial separation given often poor white Europeans were accepted in *pensiones* and low-level hotels.

The *villas* first emerged in Buenos Aires the 1940s and were originally informal and illegal settlements located on vacant lands, composed of precarious, haphazard shacks made from cheap materials. The *villas* share a similar history with other informal cities in Latin America (and slums elsewhere): rural-to-urban migrations, industrialization, and segregation of internal migrants. They also share the basic tension of being "denied" urban recognition as part of the "city proper," even though they are connected to and part of it at multiple levels.[34] The *villas* are tied to specific national processes such as the formation of Peronism, successive dictatorships, and different economic crisis.[35] They were built by the mass of migrants who were arriving, like Lorenzo, from rural areas to work in the emerging industrial sector. People settled in the *villas* with the hope of being there only temporarily, until they could find a job and move out.[36] With time, European immigrants were able to move out, but mixed-race internal migrants were not. As new immigrants from neighboring Latin American countries, also perceived as nonwhite, continued to arrive in Buenos Aires, the *villas* expanded. In the 1960s, a generation born into the *villas* started to invest in improving their homes, building brick houses and concrete floors.[37] This produced conflict with the military government, which did not want to see the *villas* as permanent settlements. Dictatorial military governments from 1966 to 1973, and especially 1976 to 1983, developed policies to "eradicate" *villas*: evicting families, destroying shacks and other structures, and putting the land to new uses.[38]

With the return to democratic government in the 1980s, evictions stopped and the *villas* were repopulated and expanded. This growth was also promoted by city and national governments that sought to generate social inclusion by "urbanizing the *villas*," developing housing projects, connecting *villas* to sewage systems, and imposing taxes.[39] Importantly, under democratic regimes, the *villas* were still regarded as backward places that needed to be reformed.

During the 1980s, with the return to democracy and in the context of economic crises, discourses linking *villas* and *negros* to criminality spread. With the arrival of new immigrants from Latin American countries, hegemonic perceptions generated a new chain of meanings connecting *villas*, *negros*, and supposedly "illegal" and "out of control" immigration with crime and violence that threatened the white elites and middle class.[40]

The cycles of the Argentine economic crisis paired with the growing numbers of impoverished people to create a sense of Argentina's darkening, and this strengthened the impoverishment of the working class.[41] The associations of nonwhiteness with crime and the consequent segregation were not unlike global processes of the criminalization of nonwhites across postcolonial cities.[42] In the 1990s, the *villas* gradually became the object of unprecedented forms of violent policing, a process that has since only deepened.

Today, the places that media and daily language name as *villas* encompass a range of very different kinds of spaces. Some are illegal settlements built on public lands beside the railroad, with no roads (only corridors), no sewage, and no running water. Others are working-class neighborhoods with paved streets and brick houses. And others are housing projects for the poor. Many *villas* have a combination of all these structures—shacks, houses, apartment buildings—oftentimes reflecting the histories of older *villas* as they changed from shantytowns to developing neighborhoods with structures several stories tall, such as in the paradigmatic Villa 31.[43] The fact that many villas are now legal and urbanized barrios, and that settlements and new state-sponsored housing developments carry the classification of *villa*, complicates the distinction.

Fuerte Apache, where many of the Qom families first lived, is a housing project for the poor built on legally owned land, with running water and electricity. It therefore fits the definition of a barrio, which has legal land tenure and benefits from basic infrastructure: solid construction, sewage, and electricity.[44] The only structural difference between Fuerte Apache and Barrio Qom is the presence of ten-story apartment buildings in the former in place of the latter's small houses with yards. Nonetheless, Fuerte Apache is seen as a *villa* by most *porteños*, the media, and authorities, who recognize it as a marginal and dangerous place. The fact that Fuerte Apache continues to be stigmatized as a *villa*, even if it is not an illegal tenement shantytown, shows that in Buenos Aires a key characteristic of a *villa* is the presence of the nonwhite poor, and likewise, the space of the villas racializes their inhabitants as *villeros*.[45]

While neither national nor municipal legislation institutionalized a racial distinction, the racial division of city space and villa space materialized in nondiscursive ways. One is the continuation of strict regulations on rent in Buenos Aires that prevented anyone from outside the city from renting an apartment in a middle-class or even working-class barrio. Another is the overpolicing of nonwhite people in the city space, young men in particular, who are targeted as suspected criminals by default. The idea of *decencia*, or decency, which Adamovsky identifies as a central trope in the making of middle-class identity, can be regarded as an attempt to regulate interracial sociality; in it, *negros* were not "decent" enough to create links of solidarity with the white middle class.[46]

As Gordillo proposes, Buenos Aires is at the center of white Argentina, "a geographical project and an affective disposition defined by the not-always-conscious desire to create, define, and *feel* through the bodily navigation of space that the national geography is largely European."[47] The presence of *negros* in Buenos Aires prevents the white elites and middle classes from fulfilling their project of feeling that they live in a European city. Schematically, as a result of this division, *negros* are forced to live outside the white city, the "city proper" and are highly regulated in their movements.

Negros villeros

One morning, during his first days in the city in the early 1990s, and after running some errands downtown, Víctor decided to explore the surroundings of the train station. After walking for a few minutes, he decided to stop and take a break. As he used to do in the Chaco when he went to town, he sat on a doorstep to rest. He looked around, observing the city, the people walking on the street, the big houses. All of a sudden, a policeman approached him and asked, "Are you about to get into trouble?" Víctor replied that he was just resting. The policeman insisted: "Do you come from the *villas*?" When he replied that he did, the officer asked for his identity document and threatened to take him to the police station for a background check. When Víctor showed his ID and explained that he had recently arrived from the Chaco, the policeman relaxed and changed his attitude. He explained to Víctor why he should not sit on doorsteps: "You look suspicious like you are planning to rob a house." He later told him: "You need to keep on walking." From that moment on, Víctor learned that in the city, unlike in the Chaco, he looked dangerous. To stay safe, he had to walk in a specific way, never stopping, having a destination, without looking at people or houses. He also learned he had to keep his ID on him at all times.

As we commuted on a bus together, Julio told me about one of the first times he and two other men were invited to play at a music festival in downtown Buenos Aires. It was easy to find their way to the venue, taking first a train and then a bus. After they played, they decided to watch the rest of the performances and stayed until the very end. When they arrived at the bus stop, someone told them the bus would not come until the morning. They had no way to get back home, as everyone at the festival had left, so they decided to ask for a *remise* (private taxi) in an agency nearby. When they got to the office, a man told them through the window that no car could take them. He explained frankly: "We don't know you, and you could rob the driver." With no other option, they went back to the bus stop and slept on the floor for four hours until the bus came. From then on, they never stayed in the city past midnight.

Andrea has been selling handicrafts since she came to Buenos Aires. When she first arrived, she sold handicrafts by going door-to-door in middle-class residential neighborhoods. She introduced herself as an Indigenous woman and never had any problems doing so. She compared her experience to that of other women in the barrio, who sometimes have problems when they beg for food in those same neighborhoods. Police and other people stop them and tell them to go back home; and some shopkeepers prevent them from entering their stores. Andrea explained that, as much as she would like to return home with food and secondhand clothes, she never liked to beg because of the possibility that the police could stop her.

It is from fragmented anecdotes like these that I realized that the experience of Qoms arriving in the city was shaped not just by living in the *villas* but also by the embodied experience of being perceived as potentially dangerous *negros* (black) in the city. While only Julio explicitly told me he knew that when the police stopped him it was because they were seeing him as a *negro villero*, the tensions people refer to point to the experience of visual recognition of an otherness that coincides with racialization in the city space.

While Qom people were used to being racialized as Indigenous in the Chaco, they did not expect to be racialized in this way. These Qom men and women were marked as being out of place in the city, their physical appearance marking them as nonwhite, potentially dangerous "others." Police, business owners, their employers, and private residents shared this perception, showing how these ideas are disseminated across social groups, even among those who are nonwhite themselves and hold racist stereotypes against nonwhites from the *villas*.[48] Following the rearticulation in the 1990s of *negros* as dangerous and *villas* as spaces of criminality, in the city center, Qoms' bodies were read as a threat to the law and to the security of whiteness. I was stopped twice by the police when walking through downtown Buenos Aires while accompanying two Toba men who were running errands, the police being concerned I was being robbed.[49] In addition, these narratives highlight how as *negros* the Qom's indigeneity was diffused. If the notion of *negros* has a "trace of indigeneity," then Qom as *negros* are seen as having Indigenous ancestry but not "authentic" indigeneity.[50] If in other parts of Latin America, Indigenous people in the city are seen as mestizos, then in Buenos Aires the Qom are regarded as *negros*.

Spatial and embodied divisions in the city are not just an effect of political marginality; as Goldberg argues, they are a form of governmentality in itself.[51] Racial segregation regulates access and movement in the city, marking whose bodies belong there and whose are out of place. The Qom bodies resting in the city, walking in the street at night, and knocking on doors in residential neighborhoods were seen as spatial transgressions and as threats to the well-being of the "normal" population. Qoms as *negros* were met with close regulation of what they did, and any action outside employment was interrupted and controlled. Ramiro Segura makes a similar observation in regard to racialized migrant people in their mobilities through the city of La Plata.[52] This form of power thus not only "fixes" nonwhite bodies in the *villas* but importantly polices the movements of nonwhites in a modality of racial profiling.

The policing of the white urban space regulates the presence of *negros* in the city by directing people to choose to move and associate according to set arrangements. Víctor learned it was easy to arouse the suspicions of the police, so he never stopped to rest and always kept his ID in his pocket. Julio learned that it was difficult for someone who lives in the *villas* to return home after midnight, so he stopped staying late in the city. Andrea did not like taking the risk of being harassed, so she regulated her actions while in residential neighborhoods, choosing acceptable activities such as selling handicrafts. If in the Chaco the Qom were also racialized as an Indigenous "other," that alterity there did not usually generate fear.[53] Being seen as dangerous was a new experience for them, and it became central to their experience of navigating urban space.

Territorialization and regulation of movement are not enough to stop or erase the *negros* and the *villas* from the space of a white Buenos Aires. *Villas* spread close to the highest-end neighborhoods, growing "beyond control," and *negros* use the city and share spaces with the white middle class. The *villas* not only provide cheap labor but also "feed" popular culture—for example, *cumbia villera*, a genre of *cumbia* music specifically played by people in the *villas*, has become a popular style that animates the parties of all social classes. The *villas* are an inevitable part of the city and were a location from which the Qoms' experienced life in the city for many years. This productivity acquired specific dimensions during Peronism.

Living in Villas Under Peronism: Affective Engagements

During the first period of Qom people arriving in Buenos Aires, *negro* as a category was associated with manual work, unionism, and Peronism. Peronism was a populist political movement, named after President Juan Domingo Perón (1946–1955), who extended worker's rights, promoted lower-class access to services, and emerged as an anti-elitist, anti-European and anti-American-imperialism social and cultural force.[54] While it spread to other social sectors later on, the urban and industrial manual workers, organized into unions, were the central force in support of Peronism. Therefore, when the first Qom people arrived in the city, internal migration, the *villas*, the expansion of an industrial working class, and Peronism were tightly interconnected.[55] While Peronism did not address its supporters as *negros*, the Buenos Aires elites and sectors of the middle class did.[56] The term *negro peronista* became, too, a marker of self-identification among Perón's followers. Interestingly, Peronist militants occasionally called one another *negros* regardless of their phenotype or class, in order to strengthen their sense of belonging to "the people," but tensions between white middle-class and nonwhite lower-class Peronists were sources of tension.

Negros peronistas were seen by anti-Peronists as people of rural origin, as mixed race, and as blindly following a political leader who manipulated them with his charisma in an authoritarian political project. For elites and sectors of the middle class, the *negros peronistas* presented a direct threat. After the 1955 military coup overthrew Perón and Peronism was banned as a political party, *peronistas* became associated with *subversivos* (armed dissidents). However, not all *peronistas* were part of guerrilla movements attempting to retake power by force. Likewise, segments of the white middle class were central actors in the Peronism movement when military government prescribed the Peronist party, and Peronist militancy became a clandestine movement.

Nonetheless, during the military governments of the late 1950s and 1960s, the political organizations of *villeros* were targeted and *villas* became stigmatized as places where supposed *subversivos* were hiding.[57] This was another reason they put so much effort into evicting the *villeros*.[58] While the Qom in the barrio today do not identify as *peronistas* (only some people may), in the *villas* and during this period, they became inevitably entangled with the movement. If in the city they were seen as *negros*, their neighbors in the *villas* regarded them as fellow *villeros* and workers, and thus potential *peronistas*.

Lorenzo, who in the Barrio Qom was the first person to have arrived in Buenos Aires, had spent several months in the city between 1954 and 1955 before returning and settling. Lorenzo's narrative about his first years in Buenos Aires was organized around several spatial displacements and having lived in several *villas*. He first lived in a *villa* located very close to the port, named Isla Maciel. He was relocated to the Hotel de los Inmigrantes because of a fire, and a few months later, he moved out of the hotel and rented a shack in Dock Sud, beside Isla Maciel.[59]

When Lorenzo returned to Buenos Aires five years later, he went directly to Dock Sud and rented a place there. After a year, Lorenzo was able to buy a small wooden shack there. In the late 1960s, when the military provincial government threatened to evict the *villas*, he, along with many other people, resisted eviction. The military government agreed to give them provisional housing in Ezpeleta, in southern Greater Buenos Aires, farther from the capital. He moved there in 1968, and five years later, in 1973, authorities contacted him to tell him that "modern apartment buildings" were ready for them to move in. These were the housing projects that later became known as Fuerte Apache.

In spite of these displacements and the negative consequences of being seen as a *negro*, he always found a place to live in the *villas*, and he always had employment in the port of Buenos Aires. In his memories, Lorenzo highlights three main aspects of his experience that show that living in the villa and being part of the subaltern *negros* was a constraining experience for its negative stigma. But he also remembers *villas* as places of diversity where most people were employed as urban workers, and he remembers them as locations empowered by the emergence of Peronism, where he participated in the political experience of organizing against evictions. In his description, he highlighted that the constitution of these collective subjects, including the *movimiento villero*, which organized against evictions in the villas, allowed him to connect and make space in the city. Establishing these strong links was possible only because of the intense conviviality developed with others in the *villas*.

Lorenzo described Dock Sud as a place where he met people "from all over." He told me how when he was single, several friends got together every Friday night at his place. He cooked food, his friends brought wine, and they ate and played cards. One of his friends, El Correntino, played the guitar really well, and they all sang and stayed up late. Some of his close friends were men who worked with him in the port. He also remembered that "Italians were good with money. They were able to move out of the *villas*, to [a proper] barrio really fast, some after only a year of saving." He therefore experienced the *villas* as dynamic places with people coming and going, mingling, and having a good time. Lorenzo also described in detail his work in the port, his coworkers, how fiscally responsive he was, and how much stronger he became by loading and unloading ships and racing his friends while carrying heavy loads on their shoulders just for fun.

These experiences point to the *villas* as places where diverse people established intense daily interactions. This is what Paul Gilroy identifies as a postcolonial conviviality, which is the spontaneous and everyday interactions between people being differently racialized (of different races) that produce anti-racist cohabitation.[60] For Gilroy, this is an actual (rather than enunciated) form of cosmopolitanism that emerges from below and contrasts with the multiculturalism of media, political, and policy discourses. The intimacy in the villas brought together people with very different trajectories into a new life in common. Because of this shared conviviality in some moments, people affected by urban racism in similar forms came together and responded.

One of the most intense experiences Lorenzo lived was during his first arrival to the city in 1955.[61] One afternoon Lorenzo was drinking mate with a friend when a group of people came to look for them to join a rally to see Perón.[62] These Peronist militants were animated, had a banner, and insisted Lorenzo and his friend carry it, which led Lorenzo and his friend to soon joined them in the march. They walked through the port and into the city, with more groups joining along the way: "Oh, how many people, I could not believe it!" When they reached the Plaza de Mayo (next to the presidential house), it was harder to advance further. They pushed against other people and made a space for themselves at one side of the plaza. Then Perón came out to the balcony: "Everyone cheered, we could see him, we were so happy."[63] Notably, Lorenzo denied being Peronist, but his account indicates that a

Peronist rally was too intense and important for him to pass up. He and his friend walked to the plaza, pushed aside other people to get a good spot to see Perón, and shared in their joy when they finally saw him come out to the balcony. Marching to the plaza was so exciting that they felt like they needed to join in and walk to downtown Buenos Aires.

This was a joyful experience of joining a collective body of other subaltern people taking over the city center. One of the transformations of Peronism was the centrality that the working class assumed during this period, a class that until then had been ushered to the social and spatial margins.[64] During the rally, the collective body of what the white elites saw as *negros peronistas* occupied the main streets and parks of downtown Buenos Aires. The rally of *negros peronistas* challenged the spatial segregation of the *negros* to the *villas*. Ten years earlier, on a date now commemorated as Día de la Lealtad, when a huge mass of people marched to the Plaza de Mayo (the park facing the presidential palace) to ask for Perón's freedom from jail, a photographer shot what has since become a famous image of Perón followers sitting on a European-style water fountain in the park, with their shoes off and their feet in the water.[65] The image shows that the photographer saw the presence of the Peronist rally as a disruption in the city; he likely recorded the men's use of the fountain to rest their sweaty feet as an indication of *peronistas*' uncivilized use of a Europeanized public space. Lorenzo remembers how, given the density of the crowd, the police were unable to make any arrests until people started to go home. To avoid being caught, he made his way to the barrio La Boca and to the Riachuelo; there, he asked a boat driver to let him onto the last trips he was making to help people get away from downtown and avoid the police.

From then on, the rallies of *negros peronistas* generated similar reactions. The demonstrations interrupted the "white" European city and further challenged whites' control over the city space. Lorenzo's excitement can therefore be understood as part of the collective joy felt by subaltern groups in occupying the central spaces of white Argentina and making it their own.

In a similar way, Lorenzo remembers being part of a big port strike in 1966 to protest the transformation of work conditions that had been implemented by the military government. He explained how the government changed the pay system from one in which workers were paid per ship unloaded to one in which they were paid per day, no matter how many ships they unloaded. Even though he showed he had a clear understanding of the reasons to strike, he distinguished himself from the union. The following segment of an interview illustrates this:

ANA: Were you part of the union?
LORENZO: Me? Part of the Union? No, no.
A: But did you participate in the strikes?
L: No, no I did not. The only thing I did when there was a strike is that I did not work, I joined the others. How can I work when there is a strike?

Lorenzo followed this exchange with a critique of both the military interventionists and the supposedly fifty thousand new workers who were hired as strikebreakers.[66] In his participation in the rally and the strike, Lorenzo shows that the "throwntogetherness" of *negros* in the *villas* were productive in generating experiences of conviviality that had political traction. For example, the Friday dinners at Lorenzo's shack literally created the space for the emergence of a powerful collective subject. The new subject consolidated in union organizing and the Peronist movement but also transcended it. This narrative is also indicative of an affective and political involvement rather than one based on identification. During the strike, he was part of the mass of workers who walked out of their workplaces. He was not a strikebreaker; he was part of a collective action that almost completely interrupted port activities for a week.[67] However, he did not identify as part of the union or as a Peronist.

Becoming part of this collective body is different from articulating a Peronist political identity.[68] Lorenzo was not striking with the others because of union discourse that resonated with him and made him set aside differences to instead emphasize his commonalities with other workers. Rather, he linked himself with other Peronists in an affective, embodied way, triggered by his life in the villas, his shared enthusiasm for the release of Perón in one case, and the shared anger at new forms of exploitation. In both cases, the experience was made possible by his friendship with coworkers and fellow *villeros*. How could he not be furious about this change in pay that would reduce their salaries? How could he betray his friends who worked with him in the port, with whom he spent his days working?

These situations are thus better understood as an affective engagement in politics.[69] Thinking of politics as affective implies tracing the motor for action and association not just in the struggles of identity and cultural articulation that become significant in a specific historical context.[70] Affect draws attention on the embodied associations of people that unfold in specific places and happen beyond forms of representation. Lorenzo joined the march or the strike because of the shared excitement and shared anger, not so much because he set off his Qom identity to instead put forward an identity as a *peronista* and worker. When Qoms were "throwntogether" with other people perceived as *negros* in the *villas*, a collective body of *villeros* and *negros* came together, and that body was able to act in powerful and new ways—ways that they had not anticipated.

Lefebvre has shown that spatial practice is a sphere of both the reproduction of power relations and the emergence of new forms of interaction.[71] Parallel to an affective conception of politics, Lefebvre finds the sensing body as a place where new forms of the political can emerge.[72] Doreen Massey adds that the intersecting trajectories of people, objects, and ideas in space are a productive force, as it is in space where different relationalities and histories unfold simultaneously.[73] This multiplicity is never totally controllable, which makes it a sphere of creativity where relations escape regulation and reproduction, and new relations and new collective subjects emerge, such as the emergence of *peronistas* out of exploited workers and racialized *villeros*. These collective subjectivities have unknown capacities, and to paraphrase Spinoza, nobody knows what many bodies can do when they come together. Because power relations can never anticipate the result of encounters in space, they can never fully control what unfolds from chance encounters in space. The tension between the regulation of movement and unexpected encounters and conviviality unfolded in the *villas*. In the *villas*, the Qom as *negros* became subjects to be controlled, but also, by coming together with "people from all over," Lorenzo developed capacities he had never imagined. Further, as part of a collective subject of *negros*, *peronistas*, and people from the *villas*, he could stop the port's activity or momentarily take over the city center.[74]

The *villas*, in short, were places where new collective subjects were constituted out of a multiplicity of trajectories. People arriving from different points of the country with no previous connection started to share their everyday experiences and, significantly, urban racism, and they started to come together against to confront those forms of exclusion. Through these experiences and actions, they started to have a history in common. This commonality was not just the effect of being denied recognition as citizens (of being only a subaltern "rest"). Their life in common in the *villas* generated its own creative forms of relating that went beyond the denial of them as "normal" citizens. Joining these collective bodies is thus affective and unfolds spatially, connecting *villa* and port, *villa* and downtown Buenos Aires. It is a coming together from which new forms of action emerged.

During the 1960s, Lorenzo was also part of the *villero* movement that resisted evictions and fought for better infrastructure.[75] In 1967, during the military dictatorship of Onganía, Dock Sud, the *villas* where Lorenzo lived, received several eviction threats. This was part of the military government's policies to "eradicate" shantytowns and keep Buenos Aires a middle-class (and white) space.[76] Lorenzo joined other families and a group of university students who together demanded new housing from the local government. He was unaware of how dangerous such political associations and claims were at the time, when any Peronist militant could be killed by the dictatorship. They succeeded, and the government promised that they would be relocated to temporary houses until they could build a proper barrio. The temporary location was in the district of Ezpeleta, in southern Greater Buenos Aires, farther away from the capital than Dock Sud—part of a trend to push subaltern and nonwhite people farther and farther away, and something that Afro populations experienced, too.[77] In 1968, Lorenzo moved to the new barrio that would become his and his second wife's home until 1973, when authorities confirmed they could move to the new permanent homes. These were modern apartments in Ciudadela, closer to the city center and on the border between the capital and the AMBA, in a new barrio called Ejército de los Andes.[78] They moved a few months later to the modern apartment in a ten-story tower that had everything they needed: gas, running water, and electricity.

Fuerte Apache: A Place of "Apache Indians"

The Qom families arriving in Buenos Aires and the *villas* from the Chaco in the 1980s and 1990s entered a very different environment from the one earlier migrants like Lorenzo had. Argentina at the time was struck by a series of economic crises. Neoliberal "structural adjustment policies" mandated the privatization of state services and the shrinking of government services, while the pairing of the currency to the US dollar (which made importing goods inexpensive) dismantled national industry. Unemployment grew, reaching unprecedented levels and impoverishing the working class, who had achieved levels of relative well-being during Peronism.[79] People living in the *villas* who were formerly employed as manual workers could find only temporary employment; they were hired illegally, with poor compensation and no rights. *Villas* had become a permanent location for the urban poor, and as rural-to-urban migration increased, the *villas*' population escalated.[80]

Fuerte Apache was expanded in the 1980s with the construction of new towers, and it grew with the informal construction of shacks around the apartment buildings.[81] During this period, Fuerte Apache, together with the other *villas* in Buenos Aires, came to be associated with criminality.[82] While unemployment generated the emergence of youth gangs in the *villas* and poor neighborhoods, they were held as responsible for the city's higher crime rates when violence and criminality was widespread across social classes.[83] Significantly, Fuerte Apache was identified as the most violent place in Argentina. Furthermore, a place originally known as Ejército de los Andes came to be named Apache Fort, and was therefore imagined and racialized as a fortified Indigenous stronghold.

Silvia, a woman in her late forties when I met her, grew up in Fuerte Apache, and, along with several people from the Barrio Qom, told me about the event that led to the name change. Newspaper articles and journalistic narratives about the event confirmed Silvia's memories, yet she and other Qom people interpreted the event in a particular way. In the late 1980s, José de Zer, a TV journalist who was well known for sensationalist coverage of crime and supernatural events, reported on a shooting between a gang and the police in the *villa* of Ejército de los Andes.[84] The gang had been involved in a robbery, and the police were trying to capture them. The gang members regrouped to their apartments in the projects and shot at the police from the windows of an apartment on a high floor.[85] According to Silvia, José de Zer reported: "The criminals are shooting from one of the towers making the barrio inaccessible to the police. No matter how hard they try and how many officers they involve: the criminals are shooting from a high floor, making the barrio inaccessible. It is as inaccessible as a fort! As an Apache fort!"

From that moment on, the media renamed the place Fuerte Apache, and most people in Buenos Aires learned about "Fuerte Apache's dangerous criminals." Interestingly, this *villa* was attributed an Indigenous identity but one that evokes the warlike "Apache Indians" as represented in Hollywood films. Fuerte Apache has a cinematic referent in the 1970 movie *Apache Fort, the Bronx*, referring to the borough of New York City and its African American neighborhoods, and José de Zer probably had the movie in mind when he chose that name.[86] If the *villas* were a place of *negros* that had "traces of indigeneity," an Apache fort was a place where Indians were powerful delinquents and thus were equated to "Apache Indians." And "Indians" were fighting back against the "white" city. This name therefore captures white middle-class fear and desires about the *villas* as violent places of nonwhiteness. The name resonated in such a strong way that almost nobody today knows or uses the official name of the barrio.

In synthesizing the visceral fear and anxiety that the presence of the *negros* generates among the white middle classes, the name Fuerte Apache associates *negros* with Indians, assumed to be a real threat to the city.[87] This takes us back to Foucault's idea of racial formations as emerging from a war situation, one in which the enemy has become internal and threatens the implicitly "white" society as a whole.[88] Fuerte Apache indirectly evokes the armed Indigenous people who threatened Buenos Aires from the Pampas in the colonial era and in the early days post-independence. These are the *negro Indians* who have continuously prevented Buenos Aires from becoming a fully white city, as desired by white Argentineans. Fuerte Apache thus frames indigeneity in Buenos Aires through reference to North American "Indians," perhaps to distance the direct links that the *negros* have with the Indigenous nations whose traditional territories were occupied to build the city, which constantly haunts white Buenos Aires.

Silvia further stressed that the journalist who named the place Fuerte Apache knew about the Qom families, who coincidentally lived in the same building where the shooting occurred. According to her, the journalist believed that the Qom were protecting the gang with supernatural powers, and so effectively that the police could not reach them.[89] "Everyone was afraid of us and they thought we protected the gangs with a special power, that we made them invincible," she said. For her, in short, the press renamed the whole barrio Fuerte Apache because the Qom families living there had made it inaccessible to the police. Even though this is probably a personal interpretation, this story is nonetheless very significant. It brings the *negros* and the Qom together back in a circular move. The Qom became *negros* in the *villas* of Buenos Aires because of their nonwhite phenotypes, but in a process that diluted their indigeneity. When the *villas* were perceived as a threat, the notion of indigeneity still present in the category *negros* returned to the forefront, and the press gave one villa the moniker Fort Apache. In Silvia's account, the presence of the Qom in the housing project turned the *villas* into an indigenized space also imbued with a supernatural power to resist the police.

Negro again becomes a category that names nonwhites who are implicitly recognized as being connected to indigeneity. While public discourse insisted that Indigenous people live only in remote rural areas, their presence continued to haunt Buenos Aires from a villa called Fuerte Apache. The naming of the allegedly most violent *villa* in Buenos Aires as Fuerte Apache only strengthens this idea that the Indigenous people never completely vanished from the city, making their elusive, phantasmatic presence even more powerful.[90] For a very different context, Michael Taussig has argued that because colonizers in the Amazon feared the terrifying savages, they were always ready to unleash violence on them.[91] Likewise, after the incident that led to naming this *villa* Fuerte Apache, and linking it indirectly to the never vanished Indigenous People the place started to be depicted as one of the "most dangerous places in all Argentina." This was part of the criminalization of the *villas* part of global criminalization of slums under neoliberalism, one criminalization never detached from colonial anxieties about a return of the Indigenous People that the colony and later the state aimed to erase.[92] Under this logic Fuerte Apache became the object of unprecedented policing methods in the late 1990s.

In the 1980s, a group of Qom families from the Chaco arrived in Fuerte Apache, where Lorenzo was living. They first stayed with acquaintances and soon found out how difficult it was to get an apartment there. They considered occupying the premises of abandoned shops, and so they contacted Lorenzo to ask him for advice. Lorenzo remembered telling them that "they had to act quickly and all together, given a single family would get evicted. They had to occupy the premises at night and never leave, until the police would accept their presence." The group did as Lorenzo said and were successful. The premises had poor infrastructure: no bathroom, no running water, and no electricity. But they made the best of it, they connected their new home to electric lines, organizing a kitchen and washroom. They lived there for two years until they were able to move to apartments like the one Lorenzo lived in.

Different Qom people who lived in the *villas* told me how they gradually became integrated in the *villas*. Children started school and made friends; women did chores alongside female neighbors and watched over their young boys playing soccer from their balconies, sometimes with the now internationally renowned soccer player Carlos Tévez, whom many people remember.[93] Antonia was pleased to send her children to a school that also had a high school. The men got jobs in construction and many times found employment through their neighbors. Raúl remembers how convenient the location of Fuerte Apache was: He was only forty minutes away from the city center. It was easier for him to get to work when he lived there than when he moved to the Barrio Qom, which is roughly three hours away from downtown Buenos Aires. These families remember how they became part of the *villas* and enjoyed many aspects of living there.

According to Raúl, during this period their neighbors learned that they were Qom and started calling the apartments the place of "los Indios" (the Indians). He once surprised a taxi driver when the driver asked if it was true that Indians lived there, as rumors said. Raúl replied it was true and then pointed to his daughters, who were just joining him in the cab, "They are Indians, and I am an Indian too." The driver was very surprised and remained silent for the rest of the trip. This interaction indicates that the Qom had a reputation as "Indians" both inside and outside the *villas*, and that the identification generated curiosity but also fear. At the same time, the Qom were not readily perceived as having racialized features different from other *villeros*, and the taxi driver had no clue he was talking to "an Indian." Inside and outside the *villas*, they had to clarify they were Qoms. Otherwise, people saw them as "regular" *negros*. This is one more example of how Qoms fit into the category of *negros*, especially when associated with the *villas*, and how Indigenous bodies in Buenos Aires are perceived as *negros* rather than Indigenous. Interestingly, Afro people in the villas and Buenos Aires are many times called *negros negros*, with the modifier of the category *negro* to emphasize that one is an Afro *negro*, and they are perceived as such only when they have stereotypical Black characteristics, for example, dark skin or curly hair.[94] *Negros* as an all-encompassing category thus names Indigenous appearance and non-white bodies irrespective of the differences that exist among people and the Qom fit that form of racialized identification.

Growing Up in Fuerte Apache

When I hung out with younger people who grew up in Fuerte Apache, I was surprised they insisted that they did not know much about Toba culture and would encourage me to talk to their parents instead. Most refused to have recorded interviews but were happy to hang out, taking me into their daily lives and including me in their conversations. I reminded them that I was interested in their lives too, and so I joined in as they did chores, went to town, and visited. For them, growing up in Fuerte Apache was a different experience from that of the people who arrived in Buenos Aires as adults. Showing similar forms of attachment that many people in Buenos Aires have toward the barrio where they live, for these youths, Fuerte Apache was *their* barrio, and many of them did not feel a need to move out or to create an Indigenous place. One of them was Silvia, who, with hesitation, agreed to do a life history with me. She spent her youth in Fuerte Apache and to my surprise structured her narrative around her addiction to drugs as a teenager. As soon as we sat down, she started narrating that experience. Silvia is currently an active member of the Qom church, and her narrative is sometimes organized as a *testimonio* a moment in the religious service when people are invited to share experiences with the congregation. *Testimonios* about being lost and then finding the way back are part of the recurrent themes, and for some of the second generation (of Qom people growing up in Buenos Aires), being lost is associated with the villa. While she described her adolescence with regret, she also narrated her experiences as rich ones that allowed her to explore the city and learn to be streetwise, skills she still uses as a single mother and in the convenience store she runs out of her home. Being streetwise, she says, allows her to deal with suppliers, clients, and moneylenders.

Silvia's narrative brushed over her childhood in rural Chaco, where she played with friends in the bush all day long, and then briefly described arriving in Buenos Aires and the villas and the harshness of that time. Very soon in my first encounter, she starting talking about her use of illegal drugs, mostly *paco*, a variation of crack. She first tried with a boyfriend in high school and soon she was hooked. She remembers how good the experience was, given that when she was on drugs, she forgot about all the problems she had, missing the Chaco, fighting with her parents especially her mom, a very strict, Evangelical woman, but especially her sense of hopelessness, of no prospects. School became unbearable after the experience, and so she dropped out and began to spend most of her time with her boyfriend doing drugs and immersed herself in *la joda*, a term she used. When she began using drugs every day, things got more complicated. She lost a sense of time and place and started to depend on drugs to function. She could not always pay for the drugs, and thus became indebted to dealers who would harass her and her family. She distanced herself from her family to keep them away from dealers and lender trouble and moved in with her boyfriend, who stole car stereos and later joined a gang and engaged in bigger thefts. At one point they were living in a very nice house in a gated community with other young couples. One day she realized she had no idea where that place was or how to get out of it.

This sense of being literally lost is what she describes as triggering her desire to "get out of that life." During the time of negotiating for the barrio, she got in touch with her family. Her mother was disappointed with her but requested a house for her in the barrio nonetheless. She decided to move back with her family and into the new barrio. Moving out of the *villas* and into the barrio was the turning point in her life: She stopped taking drugs and cut all relations with her previous boyfriend and friends. She depicted the villas as "hell for me" and the barrio as a "calm place where I could hear the birds sing again." She stressed how both worlds were opposites and how she made an explicit effort to never go back to the villas again. However, she did not express a need to create an Indigenous place, as the older generation did.

Outside the formal interview, Silvia talked about one of her sisters, Alex. Alex is the only person from the group of Qom families in the barrio who is *travesti*, a Latin American trans identity of men who transition to women; may get breast implants but often keep male genitalia.[95] Alex started to behave as a woman when she was a teenager in the villas. There she began hanging out with gays and *travas* (short for *travesties*) and had a boyfriend for the first time. She was living with her boyfriend in the suburbs, not too far from the barrio, and she visited the barrio regularly, helping her sisters by regularly dropping off and picking up her nephews from school. When I met Alex, she was very warm and open and funny, but she was always in a hurry. She chatted for a bit but was visibly very aware of her surroundings and never stayed long. Additionally, if a neighbor came to visit or to ask for help, she went inside the house, staying out of sight, avoiding any interaction with people she did not trust.

Silvia explained that she and Alex were the focus of a lot of gossip in the barrio and were regarded as "lost children." She interprets her addiction and Alex's transition as something that happened only because of their urban experience, which erases the fact that there are drugs and *travesties* in the Chaco, too. However, Alex's experience is significant in that the barrio had not been able to create a safe space for her yet, and she was visibly very aware and tense during her visits. While all young people had a hard time finding a plot and establishing it, she had to move farther away to be able to live outside the gossip around her, and while she had a loving and caring relationship with her sisters and other people in her generation, it was hard for her to relax in the Barrio Qom.

These accounts show that children and teenagers were having experiences in the city that were very different from those of people who had arrived as adults. While Silvia regrets having gotten into drugs, it was also a moment when she was very close to her friends, so she could forget about the problems in the *villa* and live in another place, in a middle-class gated community. For Alex, too, the *villa* was the place where she transitioned, and it is now her home with her partner.[96] For both sisters, life in the *villas* enabled other possibilities.

For Elisa, a third sister in the family who still lives there, Fuerte Apache was, in contrast, the best place to develop a "normal" life and start a family. Elisa is one of the Qom youths who remained in the *villa* when the rest of her family moved to the barrio, which challenges both the stereotypes around the criminality of Fuerte Apache and the dominant narrative about the Barrio Qom. Visiting her in Fuerte Apache provided me with this alternative view.

Getting to Fuerte Apache with Raúl, Elisa's father, was quite easy. I met Raúl at a train station only twenty minutes from downtown Buenos Aires. After a ten-minute bus ride, we were in a regular working-class barrio with modest, two-floor houses and quiet streets. I recognized Fuerte Apache only because of the high-rise towers, supposedly the "most dangerous location in Argentina," and yet I could not feel the "disturbing presence of the monoblocs" described in the media. Rather, I saw the carts of a Sunday market and a playground. The ten-story buildings were similar to other housing projects in the city. The only reminders of the tensions around this place were the three officers from the Gendarmería (Gendarmerie) who were standing beside a pickup truck and holding their rifles at the access to the villa. Raúl made me walk as far from them as possible, and we crossed the street quickly, without making eye contact. We relaxed and slowed down only when we were inside Fuerte Apache.

We walked past the market and arrived at a soccer field with synthetic grass and a tidy fence. "The field was a recent donation of Carlitos Tévez. My son played here, sometimes with him, when this was a dust field," Raúl explained. When we arrived at Elisa's complex, we walked up the stairs, knocked on the door, and a smiling young woman let us in. Elisa is a housewife, and her husband, Mario, works as a staff member of a maintenance company.[97] They have two children who go to school in the *villas* and a baby. When the children came to greet us, Elisa mentioned that Mariana, their oldest daughter, was "first in her class," and she showed me a school photo in which Mariana was carrying the Argentinean flag, an honor given only to the best students.

While Elisa stirred a sauce and we chatted in the kitchen, she told me how when her parents moved to the Barrio Qom from Fuerte Apache, she wanted to stay. But she was fourteen and was too young to stay by herself, so she moved with them to the Barrio Qom. Only a few months later she went to Fuerte Apache to visit her older sister who was still living there with her boyfriend's family. She first stayed for a few days and in an enormous act of hospitality the family invited her to stay permanently with them, too. When she met her current husband, she moved in with him and his family.

Elisa explained to me that she does not like the Barrio Qom because it is too far away from the city, too isolated, and people are not as friendly. She did not know anyone in the barrio. Furthermore, she argued that Fuerte Apache is actually safer than the Barrio Qom. The only time she got robbed of a new bike, it was in the Barrio Qom. She had never been robbed in Fuerte Apache. That is why she gets angry when people portray her barrio as a dangerous place. In Fuerte Apache, she was hosted by and found neighbors who helped her find job and supported her during her pregnancies. When her husband got a job and they had enough money to move out of their in-laws' place, they did not hesitate to rent an apartment in Fuerte Apache. After lunch, Elisa showed me her wedding photographs and stressed how much different friends had helped her to prepare the party. Past four in the afternoon, Raúl suggested we head back, and we walked to the bus stop uneventfully.

In our conversation, Elisa constantly stressed that Fuerte Apache is an average barrio and that the Barrio Qom is not so different in regard to safety: They are both more or less dangerous. Elisa stressed that she was unable to adapt to the barrio and chose to keep sharing her everyday life with her community there. Indeed, her boyfriend's family was generous enough to host her and her sister indefinitely, taking care of two extra teenagers with limited resources and in a small apartment. Elisa's account reveals that for some families that moved to the barrio, not everything was automatically better. Moving away from the *villas* implied detaching themselves from the relations established there, and that was not necessarily an easy change. This was a very different version of the barrio's creation from the ones I was initially told by people living there.

Elisa mentioned that there was only one period in which she felt truly afraid in Fuerte Apache and that was when the control of the villas became militarized, which happened right after her family had moved to the Barrio Qom. She remembers that "for some time you could see many military uniforms in here; they were green and blue and some of those combat uniforms you see only in the movies." Elisa explained that these security forces took over the barrio: "They were carrying all types of weapons, not just the normal guns police have. They were carrying machine guns, rifles, all long guns, and they were loaded! They always had their hand on the trigger, ready to shoot—a real danger! I got very scared when I took the children to school and had to pass through several controls. What if they pulled the trigger by accident? What if they shot a kid?" Interestingly, she saw the presence of the military forces (rather than gangs) as the main source of violence in Fuerte Apache. She was describing the fact that in 2004, in response to discourses identifying the growth of violence and criminal activities in shantytowns, the province of Buenos Aires (under the control of Felipe Sola) ordered the provincial police to withdraw from patrolling the complex and called for military intervention. Fuerte Apache became the first villa to be policed by the Gendarmería Nacional, a federal force that normally controls only the borders or makes interventions in the event of unmanageable social unrest, as riot. From then on, the Gendarmería constantly policed the barrio.[98] El Fuerte was the laboratory for this type of militarization of shantytowns that later extended to other *villas*.[99] The Gendarmería became a stable presence, regulating the movement of bodies of *negros* in and beyond the *villas*, and on my visit to Fuerte Apache, the Gendarmería was the only indicator that this was not just another working-class barrio. In the decades that followed, the national government promoted the growth of the Gendarmerie and generalized its presence in the repression of social protests, roadblocks, and land conflicts.[100]

These new articulations of race, with assumed uncontrollable violence and criminality, are not processes taking place in Buenos Aires alone. Most cities in Latin America and the rest of the world have developed forms of policing of internal others.[101] Goldberg found that in the 1980s, racial segregation in North American cities became the locus of new anxieties around "barbaric" forms of violence from the slums toward white spaces.[102] This anxiety justifies new forms of control and policing that is used to legitimize the killing of dark-skinned—especially young and male—bodies. In Latin America, the criminalization of impoverished areas is linked to both economic marginalization and intertwined processes of racialization.[103] In Buenos Aires, as reported by the Coordinadora Contra la Represión Policial e Institucional every year, this implies the regular killing of male youth by police and gendarmes, especially in the *villas*.[104]

The militarization of stigmatized formal and informal neighborhoods is a way that the founding relationship between the civilian population, the state, and the use of force changes its orientation. Following Weber's classic definition of the state and Gramsci's distinction between coercion and consent, the presence of the state in the *villas* is not through civil institutions but through repressive functions.[105] The militarization of slums creates them as places of exception, spaces of interruption of the civil law, where a population is defined as not deserving of rights and state care.[106] The *negros villeros* do not hold full civil rights, and if they are killed, their death does not count, *gatillo fácil* (police abuse killings) go often unreported in media and unreported as worth of investigation. The constant presence of military forces who, as Elisa remarked, display war weapons and are always ready to shoot makes life in the policed villas a concession more than a right. Negros in the villas are not just "left to die" through the deterioration of state services but are also actively killed by the police. Police see young male *villero* bodies as an imminent threat and do not hesitate to pull the trigger and kill them, as they regard them as always already a threat and to "normal" citizens. However, this is a resisted process. The long tradition of political organization in the *villas* has stopped evictions and guaranteed the maintenance of basic state services, and people have also mobilized and legally challenged the police abuses and violence.[107] Silvia was more concerned with this aspect of her life than with her Qom identity, which she held as important, too, but not as the main focus of her political activation.

The images about *villas* and *negros* as sources of danger (strengthened by the militarized control of the villas in 2004) had profound effects on the spatial arrangement of the city and the regulation of the *villeros*' movement. Qom people who were living in the *villas* in the 1980s experienced the beginning of this process and a limitation on their movements across the city space. It was during this period that men were stopped and interrogated by the police simply because they were in the city. It was after the naming of Fuerte Apache as such that the families who had formed the handicraft cooperative started to think about moving out. The desire to move out of the *villas* is something they share with other *villeros*, as many people who currently live there express a desire to live in a "regular" barrio, where they do not have to advocate for basic infrastructure or confront stigma, where they can avoid heavy policing; but the Qom families had specific opportunities to escape this.

A Different Shade of Nonwhite

Raúl arrived in Fuerte Apache in the early 1980s and became a construction worker. When employers asked him where he lived, Raúl would avoid saying it was a *villa*. Raúl equally avoided telling his coworkers he was Qom, afraid of how they would react and of putting his job at risk because of stereotypes of Indigenous people as not trustworthy. Eventually, Raúl opened up and told his coworkers that he was Qom. People were initially skeptical and would say, "No way you are Indigenous!" However, once they believed him, he received increased attention: His coworkers asked about his life in the Chaco, about his hunting skills, about what he ate. His friends respected him for his experience in the Chaco and his knowledge about the bush. Raúl soon learned that in Buenos Aires, being an "Indian" was not as bad as it was in the Chaco, and it was also more respected than being a *negro*. His indigeneity—paradoxically also a subaltern identity—could undo some negative aspects of being *negro*. Furthermore, for the people arriving in the barrio in the 1980s, one of the economic options that they developed was producing and selling "Indigenous handicrafts" at fairs or door-to-door in middle-class neighborhoods. Through this commercial activity, they became even more aware of the interest in an "authentic" indigeneity generated among people in Buenos Aires, and of how fear of *negros* was erased in those relations. Displaying an authentic indigeneity became a way to escape the extraordinary forms of policing in the *villas* and the regulation of their movement in the city.

The possibility of being recognized as Indigenous and specifically as Qom from the Chaco changed the attitude of the people they interacted with in the city. The ability to clarify that they were not *negros* but *Indigenous* by displaying Qom culture allowed them to escape the suspicious gaze that *villeros* are confronted with and helped them establish relations with schoolteachers, Indigenist activists, and anthropologists. When they remained in the *villas*, as Elisa, their indigeneity remained ambiguous. Even for people who might have wanted to be seen as Indigenous, such as Silvia, who expressed that she wanted people to recognize her as Qom too, but people from outside the barrio saw her as a *villera* instead. Creating the barrio as a distinct place marked as a Qom space thereby allowed these families to carve out an urban indigeneity that constituted a different shade of nonwhiteness, one associated not with criminality and danger but with an ideal around Indigenous culture.

Of course, for many Qom people who have been re-creating forms of knowledge, cultural practices, and life in general, opening up space for Qom life was of key importance. And yet there were many moments when people in the barrio had a melancholic tone in their memories about the *villas* and transmitted a sense of having lost something by moving away. This was expressed to me indirectly. In one of my last visits to the barrio, as I was saying goodbye, one man broke the dominant local narrative about *villas*. We were alone in his home and drinking mate in the living room when Mariano, a construction worker in his sixties, remembered that when they left Fuerte Apache to move to the barrio, he considered becoming a drug dealer. Once his family had moved out of the *villas*, he could sell drugs for a while, keeping his wife and children safe somewhere else. Maybe he could finally make some good money. He had a friend who was already in business, and he could help him expand it. However, he decided to give his apartment to relatives and abandoned that project, afraid of getting involved in criminal activities. Yet he emphasized how tired he was of never making it out of poverty no matter how hard he had worked, and all his life, in the Chaco and in Buenos Aires. He had always remained poor, and his adult children were likewise living in poverty, too. This story is complex in that Mariano was considering engaging in illegal activities, and he was also sharing his intense hopelessness in regard to getting out of the cycles of intergenerational impoverishment that the creation of the barrio was not able to undo. Importantly, Mariano told the story with a tone of disappointment, that he had missed an opportunity. His story, in short, highlighted another unexpected connection emerging from the *villas*, which was not an easy path but perhaps an opportunity to leave poverty. Mariano could perhaps experience the extraordinary, fast forms of enrichment typical of the neoliberal decades, when some sectors of society engaged in speculation, corruption, state privatizations and also illegal economies, got rich quickly.[108]

Buenos Aires is a city generally understood to be "white," both in public discourse and, until recently, in mainstream academic research. The experiences of Qom people who began arriving in Buenos Aires in the 1950s simultaneously undermine this conception while illustrating how such conceptions are created and maintained through the forms of racialization, spatial segregation, and regulation of movement that are central organizing forces in Buenos Aires. Attention to these forces opened up an understanding of the *villas* in connection to race and indigeneity, which spatializes nonwhiteness beyond process of recognition and ethnic formation. Qoms' experience in the *villa* is multifaceted, and people who eventually created the Barrio Qom had negative experiences in the *villas*, but not so much because of other *villeros* or the place itself (as initial narratives suggested). Rather, it was their economic subalternization and ongoing forms of being pushed to unemployment or the lower sectors of the labor market, as well as the exceptional forms of spatial regulation and policing that defined the *villas* as places of illegality, that affected their lives the most. While the people who created the barrio made a lot of efforts to disconnect from *villas*, they also remembered positive forms of socialization there. Building on those positive experiences, some younger Qom people created an opposite narrative, and people like Elisa remained in the *villas*. She did not see the barrio as a safer, cleaner, greener, or generally more desirable place.

The chapter has highlighted two unexpected effects of the expansion of Qom assemblages to the city. The first effect is related to a transformation in their racialized position: Instead of being recognized as Indigenous, they were incorporated into a broader, nonwhite urban category and labeled *villeros* and *negros* rather than "Indigenous." This shift meant both a loss of Indigenous recognition and a new racialization that was spatially and socially imposed. Living in the city's marginalized areas, however, also opened up encounters with other racialized groups and diverse ways of life. The second tension emerges from how urban space restricts and defines nonwhite mobility and indigeneity. "Toba" or "Indigenous" identities are acknowledged only in specific urban settings where "authentic" cultural practices can be displayed, often for middle-class recognition. Possibilities of mobility through the city also shifted in regard to recognition. When wearing sports clothes and walking through downtown Buenos Aires, Qom men were often seen as *negros* and potential criminals. When using markers of indigeneity, that suspicion and anxiety was suspended, replaced by an often open curiosity among *porteños* to learn about Qom culture.

Encounters in the *villas* created different collective subjects that had an impact in Qom's urban indigeneity. As part of a *villero* collective, the Qom were able to do new things: meet friends, appropriate spaces in the city, participate in strikes, take drugs in an attempt to forget about their problems, scandalize the media by being seen as "Apache Indians," or become respectable families in "the most dangerous place of the country." They also had an impact on the shape of the *villa* and perceptions of it, even if only modestly. From the *villas* and later from the barrio, the Qom as urban Indigenous demanded that the Barrio Qom and the *villa* be recognized and included in the city "proper." Yet paradoxically, some of the capacities created in the *villas* were lost with the creation of the barrio, which is the subject of the next chapter.

CHAPTER 3

Making a Barrio Qom in Buenos Aires

Space and the Politics of Recognition

A Barrio Qom in the City

When Mariano, a man in his thirties who lived in the Qom barrio in Cortaderas, visited schools downtown to teach "culture workshops," he started his presentation by telling the story of his arrival in the city. Like many others, he had first lived in Fuerte Apache, one of the city's most infamous *villas*, a shantytown, and his strongest memory of the place was how it saturated the senses: Electric lights shone all night, loud *cumbia* music was ever-present, people were arguing, and even gunshots were frequent. When the barrio was created, by contrast, people there had access to a "peaceful place," where they built detached houses with gardens that were surrounded by rural lots and grazing cattle. With a few variations, this was a narrative that most adults repeated throughout my work. The creation of the barrio was considered a "return to the Chaco," and the barrio stood in constant tension and relation to the Chaco, to Buenos Aires's *villas*, to other Qom barrios, and to Buenos Aires's city center.

Residents of the barrio discussed its history in reference to how the barrio contrasted with and connected to other locations, echoing Doreen Massey's insight that spaces are shaped by the physical movement of people, along with layers of sedimented "stories so far."[1] Each of these stories and movements connected the barrio from within different Qom assemblages. The stories they told extended Qom territory in the past and present and provided geographical coordinates of the organization of space. Stories also presented the process of change and people's experiences within them. From the perspective of the barrio, the Chaco was remembered as rural and peaceful. In everyone's memories, including those of children who were born in the city and had been to the Chaco only on holidays, the Chaco was a place of abundant food, of beautiful bush and forest, and they recalled their traditional lands with a glow on their faces and in enormous detail. In this tension with the *villas*, the Barrio Qom was a "return" to some positive spatial features of the Chaco: a place with green open spaces, with children playing outside, and yards where people could cook over an open fire. The barrio, in its semirural location in Greater Buenos Aires, was regarded as a better place for Qom in the city.

The barrio was a result of complex negotiations with the national state to create a Qom place in Buenos Aires. These efforts were built off past organizing experiences to create Qom barrios in other cities within and beyond the Chaco, and those efforts had to be extended and transformed in this new context. Not coincidentally, and as explained in Chapter 1, the barrio's founders included members of families with long political experience who had made successful land claims to recuperate parts of their territory in the Chaco and who had been organizers in the Iglesia Unida and had worked with NGOs. Yet these experienced people were confronted with new and unexpected challenges.

Land negotiation in Buenos Aires had to confront the fact that there was no Indigenous community in the city at the time and the capital was central to the project of a white Argentina, a project that marginalized nonwhite people. The Qom families were a numerically small group among subaltern groups in Buenos Aires. They engaged in negotiations with the National Institute of Indigenous Affairs, which had little experience in dealing with urban indigeneity, as its focus was primarily on rural Indigenous territories. The claim was traversed, too, by the racism of Buenos Aires residents toward shantytown dwellers, as highlighted in the previous chapter, and their efforts to assert their Indigenous identity. This success in creating the barrio was intertwined with relationships with the middle class and state institutions in which the recognition of authenticity was relevant as an extended relationship in time and space.

In this chapter, I address the history of the creation of the barrio as an effort made against many odds, one in which recognition was not easily granted. Even when it was given, it did not imply obtaining lands in the city's capital. The negotiation separated Qom people from other Indigenous people and migrants in Buenos Aires who created other forms of appropriating and indigenizing urban space. The Qom barrio was created simultaneous to the consolidation of Bolivian and Andean Indigenous people's organizing and before those groups turned a *villa* into the barrio Charrua, identified starting in the early 2000s as a Bolivian (and Indigenous) space.[2] Creating the barrio was also a very different strategy from that of making migrant associations of Bolivian, Paraguayan, and Peruvian migrants, which connected people spread out across the city.[3]

The barrio contrasts with other dynamics of internal migrant Indigenous and Qom settlement. The migration of Indigenous people to Buenos Aires began in the late 1950s and 1960s, primarily involving the Qom, Guarani, Kolla, and Mapuche communities, which are still the largest Indigenous groups in the city. Many Qom people initially settled in Isla Maciel, a neighborhood that comprises both Indigenous and non-Indigenous working-class, rural-to-urban migrants. After a fire, the Qom community relocated to Dock Sud, situated not far from Isla Maciel and at the periphery of Buenos Aires city. Engelman's analysis reveals that as demographic pressures and evictions led to the displacement of people from the *villas*, an informal settlement established by the Qom people in the Almirante Brown district emerged as part of a second wave and second ring of peripheral settlements.[4] Unlike the Barrio Qom, these settlements gradually underwent regulation as part of general urbanization policies that sought to regularize working-class settlements and incorporate them into the city. In the early 1970s, financial plans enabled families to purchase plots of land from the state, and Qom families replicated this approach in other neighborhoods, gradually acquiring ownership of their land plots.[5] Finally, the barrio also contrasts with later strategies of Indigenous groups that, from the 2000s, created multiethnic communities in Greater Buenos Aires but did not make land claims.[6]

In short, this chapter shows how the barrio was created as a different place in the city, a site of urban and Qom indigeneity, resulting from spatial trajectories, perceptions of place, and active claims over space. If, as Massey suggests, places are made through movement, they are always already connected to other places, not only through classifications but also through the material travels of people and objects. In the shaping of Qom barrio, there was not only a deliberate political strategy for connection but also an active disconnection, a partial attempt to deflect the powerful historical forms of segregation of the nonwhite in the city. Thus, in the creation of the barrio there was also a reconfiguration of Qom assemblages, emphasizing associations with people who saw them as Qom and providing an alternative entry point to the city. To make and present the barrio as an Indigenous place, it was necessary to create it as a distinct place: different from the shantytowns where they used to live and different from the barrios around them that hosted subaltern and racialized migrants, many similarly Indigenous or of Indigenous ancestry but who could not trace an ancestral link to a specific people (an identity recently articulated as *marrón*).[7] While creating the Barrio Qom countered part of the racial stigma of Qom as *negros villeros*, moving out from them generated negative effects, as relocating hindered the rich daily relationships that the Qom had established in the *villas* over several decades that had helped them adjust to the city.

The creation of the barrio located the families under a different government jurisdiction, the National Institute of Indigenous Affairs (INAI), and with the policies of Indigenous organizations, which overlapped with a multiplicity of forms of power that regulate the city's margins, including progressive municipal policies to regulate the rampant inequalities between gated communities and highly impoverished areas, and provincial politics with complex party relations, which they sought to avoid. Becoming a legally recognized Indigenous community defined in terms of identity politics offered new possibilities, but it did not imply autonomy. An important constraint was the constant demand to prove their indigeneity, despite having been legally recognized by INAI. The barrio is thus a success story of an Indigenous group being recognized at the periphery of Argentina's capital. This experience became a model to other processes of state recognition of urban Indigenous communities, part of the institutional memory of the INAI, influencing what the possibilities of being Indigenous in the city can be.

I begin by reconstructing the history of the formation of the Qom barrio in Buenos Aires, to explore how these interactions have shaped the layout of the barrio. My focus then shifts to the legal aspects of recognition as an Indigenous community and to land donations. Finally, I unpack "Qom cultural work" activities undertaken by many families, teaching and promoting Qom history and traditional way of life to non-Indigenous *porteños*, the urban white middle classes. These activities can be viewed as the commodification of Indigeneity, but they also represent active efforts to create a life as Indigenous and urban within the context of economic hardship. They foster connections that indigenize the city by shaping assemblages that establish links between the capital, the periurban barrio, and the Chaco.

FIGURE 3.1. Two teens pose by a Jesus Christ statue known by locals as "The Virgin." The statue is a reminder of the Catholic Church's donation of lands. Photo Technology workshop reproduced with permission.

Land Negotiation in the City

Lorenzo, one of the first Qom people to arrive, and a person with prior political experience, was one of the organizing figures. He explained that when he was laid off from his work in the port at the end of the last military dictatorship in the early 1980s, he started to produce handicrafts for a living, just like people in barrios in the Chaco do. In the early 1990s, Lorenzo was invited to give a talk at a middle-class school in the city center. He enjoyed how engaged the children and teachers were with his stories about the Chaco, and after the talk, he sold many handicrafts. Soon he received other invitations. The demand was so strong that he contacted Qom families living in Fuerte Apache to join him. These workshops were an important starting point, moments in which Qom families were recognized as Indigenous by school communities in the city of Buenos Aires. This type of work mobilizing their Indigenous identity is something Qom engage with in the urban Chaco and brought to Buenos Aires. Julio, who lived in a *villa* known as Ciudad Oculta, also engaged in cultural work even before he met other Qom families. In Buenos Aires, people like Julio and Lorenzo intensified handicraft production, first to supplement their income from contract work and later as their main source of income when economic crisis pushed them into unemployment.

Carlos, who lived with Lorenzo in Fuerte Apache, further explained how they met other Qom families in the *villas* and began collaborating on workshops focused on "Qom culture." Carlos's wife, Antonia, was also very engaged, and she and her sister Andrea coordinated the work and brought Raúl and his family into the group. Carlos and Antonia expanded their connections with other urban Qom when they attended a parent-teacher meeting at their daughters' school in Fuerte Apache. During this meeting, he introduced himself as Qom, which provoked surprise among the other parents because, in his words, "nobody in the *villas* expected Indians to be living there." Their narrative used the pejorative "Indios" to stress the perceptions of non-Indigenous people about Indigenous people even in a marginal location as the *villa*, given that *villeros* sought to be seen as "modern" working-class citizens and not as "backward Indians." After the meeting, a few people approached them, introducing themselves as Qom, too. It is worth noting that when Antonia and Carlos met the other parents, they perceived them as other shantytown residents. It was only when they said, "We are Qom," that a few other parents responded by identifying themselves as Qom as well. No physical markers made these Qom people stand out from other people living in the *villas*, not even to the other Qom people in the room. While in some contexts, Qom people do identify and discuss individuals who either "look" or "do not look" Qom, here they were indistinguishable to one another from other shantytown residents. This suggests that Indigenous appearance and features are present in the broader community of shantytown dwellers who have known or unknown Indigenous ancestry. This is another dimension of how people in the shantytown are racialized, of how people perceived as nonwhite get pushed to the *villas* by, for example, being unable to access rent in other neighborhoods.[8] After this initial encounter, Lorenzo met Julio, and he and his wife joined from Ciudad Oculta; together with Antonia and Carlos, these families started working together, giving workshops at schools and producing and selling handicrafts.

These encounters, unplanned and not an organized political strategy, created relations that were a motor for spatial transformations, reshaped the composition of groups in the *villas*, and initiated the creation of a specifically Qom place. According to Massey, space comprises a multiplicity of encounters in an ever-changing flow of spatiotemporal events: "If space is a simultaneity of stories-so-far, then places are collections of those stories, articulations within the wider power-geometries of space."[9] "Stories" are not tied to place but result from unfolding movements and the coming together of different experiences in space. Places, then, are collections of encounters and cannot be detached from the trajectories or stories that connect them to other locations. The barrio, as I show, is the result of the encounter of the trajectories of people who met in the Buenos Aires shantytowns and in schools and fairs and started working together. Their story highlights that the larger social context affected the temporality of the families who were organizing. It was in the context of severe economic crisis, marked by widespread unemployment and a resulting availability, that this meeting of Qom families led to the formation of political organization.

For these families, being Qom became a center around which they set to work together, organizing workshops and producing handicrafts. As work intensified, they decided to create a cooperative for handicraft production. With the assistance of middle-class people, they applied to become a legal cooperative for craft production, and they rented a store in Fuerte and set up shop. But after a year, the expenses were too high, and the co-op failed as a commercial enterprise. They struggled to maintain consistent sales, and the profits generated were insufficient to support full-time dedication to the venture. Antonia further explained that potential customers were afraid of visiting the shantytown to buy crafts. The cooperative was created in the *villa* and could have been a foundation for organizing as Qom without leaving the shantytown. But its failure may have driven the search for a different political strategy, toward the establishment of a Qom neighborhood, mirroring the strategy adopted by Qom communities since the 1950s, when they formed neighborhoods in cities in Chaco, Formosa, and Santa Fe. While the project in the *villa* dissolved, the cooperative gave them the experience of working together and connections with middle-class people—teachers, students, researchers, and activists—who wanted to support them. This experience was thus an initial articulation of a shared Qom identity in the city, which would allow them to negotiate for the barrio on these terms.

The possibility of re-creating knowledge and cultural practices marked as Qom is related to the fact that the Qom, along with other Indigenous groups of the Chaco, tend to be regarded as "the most Indigenous" of all Indigenous groups in Argentina. When Carlos stood in front of a school classroom and told stories about his life in the Chaco, about how he hunted in the forest, worked in the cotton fields, and witnessed his father's shamanic power, nobody questioned whether he was an authentic Indigenous person. Delivering workshops, Lorenzo, Andrea, Carlos, and Antonia were undeniably Indigenous, and this became the core of their collaborative relation with NGOs and the middle class. Perceptions about their authenticity were produced and supported in these encounters with middle-class people; in telling stories about their life in the Chaco, they became understood as a paramount Indigenous life. This authenticity created an affective traction that kept Qom people and middle-class people working together over the long term.

In the early 1990s, teachers participating in a workshop at a Catholic school were particularly moved by Carlos and Antonia's account of the difficulties of living in the *villas*. They contacted the local bishop and asked if the church had lands in Buenos Aires that could be donated to these Qom families. The bishop got involved and identified the lands suitable for donation. When the negotiations started, a Catholic NGO, which I call Christians for Indigenous People, joined in helping Carlos and Lorenzo make the legal arrangements. Julio provided the connection with another NGO, which I call Raíces, that offered support to build homes. Both NGOs identified as indigenist; they were formed by non-Indigenous activists and professionals who advocate for furthering rights and reparations for Indigenous people. Raíces provided technical and professional assistance. With the families, they wrote a funding proposal to the national government for a social housing project, and they hired an architect who designed house plans and later obtained the legal permits for the project. In this history, several lines and actors came together to create the Barrio Qom: a Catholic school and the Catholic Church, NGOs with their technical support, middle-class allies, Indigenous activists, and artists.

The leading roles of Julio and Carlos in the land negotiation sparked disputes over authority between them and their families, with Lorenzo, as an elder, acting as mediator to facilitate decision-making. For most of the history of the commission, Julio and Carlos alternated in the presidency. Their tensions led to factions supporting one leader or the other, although these disputes were never strong enough to create feuds, and families often collaborated with one another. The division was not the only factor demarcating families in the barrio. People organized along other lines, too: where in the Chaco region they were from, whether they were religious or nonreligious, and which of the two Evangelical churches they attended were also significant organizing forces in facilitating workshops in schools.

The land-titling process progressed rapidly. A Catholic NGO with experience supporting land claims in the Chaco assisted the families in applying as an Indigenous community to INAI. The provincial legal recognition of urban Qom communities had supported the creation of Qom barrios in the Chaco, but the province of Buenos Aires did not have a registry of Indigenous communities at the time, and it implemented one only in 2014, so the only option was to apply directly at the national level. Indigenous legislation had been established with the reform of the National Constitution and implemented through Law 23.302, in 1994, a year before the families applied. This law had not yet been implemented for an urban community in Buenos Aires.[10] When I requested to see the application form at the INAI, I was told it was confidential, but one Indigenous official at the institution offered to give me some oral details. He explained that this was the first time that recognition was accompanied by community land title in the city.[11] The uniqueness of the barrio, unlike other settlements of the Qom, Guarani, and Kolla, is that there was an early community recognition accompanied by land for that community and outside traditional territories. It thus served as a precedent for other urban communities, including various Qom barrios and communities of the Guarani, Kolla, and multiethnic backgrounds that would go on to apply to the national registry from the 2000s.

In 1995, the bishop's office identified a Catholic school built on a large plot of land in the far periphery of the Buenos Aires Metropolitan Area (which, as all church property, the state had donated to the church). The school had around two hectares of land that had been a farm. The land was legally divided and donated to an Indigenous association that is now the barrio's comisión. The day the land title was granted, the press, renowned indigenist activists, artists, and allies turned up, filming and taking photographs of the signing of documents. The construction work, directed by Raíces and using families' labor, advanced very quickly, and in 1996, the first families moved to the barrio. Each family also mobilized the help of relatives from the Chaco who came to work on the construction. Some of these people, such as Miguel, ended up staying in the barrio and building their own houses there. All the families who moved in either had been part of the handicraft cooperative in the *villa* or were relatives of those cooperative members.[12]

The organization of urban space is a product of power dynamics and hierarchies. For instance, at the turn of the twentieth century, Argentinean elites constructed *petite hotels* in the Recoleta neighborhood, close to the city's administrative center and surrounded by parks and museums, while the racialized working class were relegated to informal settlements and exposed to environmental hazards, such as pollution from the Riachuelo River near Dock Sud, where Lorenzo initially resided. However, space also represents a dimension in which hierarchies are unstable and subject to challenge, a concept described by Massey as the "horizontality of space." This does not erase a hierarchical understanding of space, but rather emphasizes that the two coexist and interact in tension. Massey argues that "the horizontality of space is a product of a multitude of histories whose resonances are still there."[13]

In the Barrio Qom, traces of life in the *villas* persist as connections linking the barrio to the *villas* despite the separation between them. Several men still work in occupations they initially developed in the *villas* with former neighbors, and some have married people from the *villas*, maintaining ties with relatives living there. The horizontality is shaped, too, in the connections linking the barrio and its residents to the Chaco. The practice of creating handicrafts serves to maintain these relations with the communities around the city of Castelli in the Chaco and in the area of Bermejito in central Chaco, where many families have their origin and still maintain ties. As discussed in the last chapter, handicrafts foster close, daily relationships between the barrio and rural Chaco communities due to the urban Qom's reliance on natural fibers and materials from the Chaco's bush for handicraft production. Similarly, the Iglesia Unida, with headquarters in Castelli, organizes events that bring together urban and rural Qom people, providing logistic and material support for travel and reconnection several times a year. This is another way the barrio is shaped in historical horizontal connections that become re-created in Qom translocal assemblages and in spatial contradictions that shape power inequalities, such as the urban segregation pushing Qom, rural migrants, and urban poor to the peripheries. The barrio's location in Buenos Aires materializes these tensions between connection and physical separation; it shapes the organization of space in the barrio, while the horizontality of space—for example, unexpected encounters with neighbors—can put contradictions into tension.

Geography: Arriving in the Barrio Qom

To get to the barrio from the center of the city of Buenos Aires requires combining forms of transit, in order to move to the margins of the city and the last ring of AMBA. This is, therefore, also a trip across the relations that make these places different: an affluent and middle-class city center and a periphery, surrounded by exclusive gated communities, that grows poorer the farther it is from the center. I describe this trip because it locates the barrio as an Indigenous location within the city and within AMBA. Together, Buenos Aires city, formally the Ciudad Autónoma de Buenos Aires, or informally simply Capital, along with its periphery, the Area Metropolitana de Buenos Aires, usually called AMBA or Conurbano, make up an extended, uninterrupted urban space with a population of almost thirteen million people and one-third of the country's total population.[14] This makes the urban mass of Buenos Aires the second biggest city in South America, after São Paulo.

To get to the area where the barrio is located, the fastest way is to take a train from the Retiro central station. The train crosses the General Paz highway, which divides Buenos Aires from the ring of districts in the province of Buenos Aires that surround the city.[15] As the train advances, the landscape transitions from apartment buildings to barrios of single houses with good infrastructure, including paved streets and sidewalks. Later, the houses become smaller, and the streets are sometimes unpaved; between stations, open fields have self-made brick houses with no cladding and zinc roofs. There are no visible services, and open-air informal garbage dumps emerge in empty plots. The landscape becomes more rural, some plots are empty, others have cattle, and others are sports clubs. All these are features of what in urban studies are identified as effects of informality, of poor integration to the city, signs of urban segregation.[16]

As with other Latin American cities, Buenos Aires periurban areas are often marginal neighborhoods. While AMBA is a vast area that extends in a ring around the city of Buenos Aires, and also has middle- and upper-class neighborhoods, it is imagined in many media and popular representations (especially when named as the *Conurbano*, meaning a conurbation, and the informal name of the area) as a place of poverty, shantytowns, and illegal activities and delinquency.[17] It is, though, a place of great diversity, which grew out of several waves of internal and international migration starting in the 1940s, including self-identified Indigenous people from at least twelve different Indigenous nations. According to the 2004–5 Encuesta Complementaria de Pueblos Indígenas, or Complementary Survey of Indigenous Peoples, the most recent study by the National Institute of Statistics, 14,500 Qom people live in Buenos Aires City and AMBA together. Shaping sharp inequalities standing spatially side by side, the AMBA has areas of working-class formal barrios, clusters of middle-class neighborhoods, and secluded affluent gated communities, all in often tense proximity.[18] Together AMBA and Buenos Aires city host 248,500 self-identified Indigenous people who account for roughly 2 percent of the total population.[19]

In sharp contrast with the impoverished areas, as the train advances, affluent gated communities become frequent, too. The district that I call Sauces, about thirty kilometers from downtown Buenos Aires, grew during the 1990s, when tax exemption policies supported the creation of an extensive industrial complex. The complex soon created its own migratory wave of people from around the country (and neighboring countries) who arrived seeking employment in its booming industries. But because the industries employed only highly specialized workers, most migrants did not find the jobs they expected, and in fact, the district saw high unemployment rates by the mid-1990s. One municipal social worker explained to me that many unskilled migrants end up working, instead, informally and casually as cheap service employees in the gated communities, as cleaners, gardeners, and maintenance personnel, not as formal factory workers as they had expected. In the 1990s, the gated communities that had started to emerge in the 1980s multiplied and grew ever more rapidly. As elsewhere in Latin America, they attracted elite and upper-middle classes from downtown Buenos Aires into *barrios privados* (gated communities) and *countries* (referring to gated communities, which also have amenities and sports infrastructure), both of which are enclosed spaces, with private security.[20] In addition to security, the gated communities promised a "country lifestyle," life in a safe, peaceful community closer to nature that was separated from a "class promiscuous" city.[21] Implicit was the idea that the walls of these gated communities would create this separation.[22]

The train terminates in a small center of the Sauces district, renovated with small shops targeting the middle and upper classes, but most of its passengers at this point are working class. The middle and upper classes prefer to travel by car on the highway or to take a private, door-to-door shuttle. They consider the train dangerous and slow.[23] Travel to and from Sauces therefore also re-creates class and racial separations, as different social classes and racialized groups have unequal access to speed and comfort when they travel. These unequal spatial relations, which also encompass spatial mobility, are what Massey calls power geometries: the power of one place over other and of social groups to organize the space of city, district, and country and to organize market and circulation flows. The different access and use of transport is another dimension of the spatial divisions within the district, which is organized around the coexistence of areas of poverty with others of affluence in sharp separation and tense proximity.

From the train station, there is a bus to get to the Barrio Qom. Passing fields with grazing cows and empty grasslands with precarious fences, one arrives in an area of new but impoverished neighborhoods, some with legal ownership of plots, others built informally in open lots. The newness is evident in the half-finished constructions, red-brick houses that look self-made, and the presence of construction materials that signals that the whole area is under expansion. Other houses are made with leftover materials; they are precarious houses made of wood and pressed cardboard roofs. These places host working-class migrants who are new to the city (from rural areas and neighboring countries) as well as younger Qom who had no space in the barrio and were negotiating with the municipality for land titles.

The barrio hardly stands out from the other settlements. Its only difference is that brick houses follow a single design, and the community center is the biggest building in the area. A mural on one side of it contrasts with the otherwise white walls of the few houses with exterior paint. The now-covered mural used to show a dark-skinned Indigenous woman with bare breasts who was modeling clay, and a dark-skinned Indigenous man, with bare chest, throwing an arrow. Above the image, the name "Los Qom" clarified any doubt as to the identity of the neighborhood. In the context of the vast diversity that shapes the Conurbano, Barrio Qom is a small place with only around three hundred people. The barrio's relevance is not in numbers but in its significance as an Indigenous place created in Buenos Aires far from the Qoms' traditional territories.

The location of the barrio in the city indicates tensions between the hierarchical organization of space and its horizontality. The organization of differentiated places in the city, the city center and periphery, and the association of places with different social classes, with the possibilities each has of producing and reproducing their lives there, is what Lefebvre calls "representations of space," projected by the state and market.[24] Lefebvre stresses that spatial practice and people's perceptions of place challenge and escape dominant forms of spatiality. Hierarchical and horizontal production of space, in short, are in constant tension, a tension in which assemblages intervene when reorganizing activity. When the Qom in the barrio visit relatives in the *villa*, they reconnect both places and complicate the Qoms' distance from the shantytowns. These links resituate Qom politics in Buenos Aires with struggles and issues in the *villas*, for example, their role in the naming of Fuerte Apache as an Indigenous location, the shared concern with overpolicing of nonwhite young men, and the desire for consumption and adventure experienced in the *villas*.

Foucault describes governmental power as classifying groups in (among others) racial terms, "fixing" them in place and creating the conditions for people to act according to their political interests.[25] The spatial layout of Buenos Aires, in its multilayered complexity, enacts a form of governmental regulation by separating spaces of whiteness and pushing the nonwhite to areas in the Conurbano where barrios are impoverished, services lacking, and infrastructure deficient, as was the experience of Qom families arriving in Buenos Aires who found no place to live but the *villas*. Grossberg adds that governmental power shapes territorialities, regulating how people circulate and access spaces. In this case, racial regulation of space means that the Qom and *villeros*, as nonwhite, can access gated communities only as cleaners and maintenance personnel. While the Qom managed to move away from the *villas* to a barrio with larger plots, and away from spatial and racial stigma, they continued to experience the daily forms of racism that other *villeros* did as well when, for example, they were navigating urban space and were constantly stopped and harassed by police. The barrio, moreover, is still segregated and even farther from downtown and white middle-class spaces. The responses of Qom to the novel impositions of regulation, justified by the perception of insecurity, that reinforce spatial hierarchies are complicated in that Qom people participated, even if indirectly, in the stigmatizing the *villas* when they claimed that *villas* are dangerous and unlivable.[26]

The location of the barrio in the "last ring" of neighborhoods in the Conurbano of Metropolitan Buenos Aires is paradoxical. This placement aligns with the prevalent perception that Qoms are nonwhite and nonurban, and the Conurbano is often associated with being nonwhite, an area of *negros*. This location situates them in close proximity to impoverished neighborhoods with difficult access to services. However, this semirural ring does not have the same stigma as the well-established *villas* or shantytowns, which creates symbolic separation from the broader Conurbano. Furthermore, getting to and from the barrio by train takes a long time, making commuting to work in the city more difficult and expensive. Shantytowns are much closer to the city center and thus more convenient for anyone looking for a job there. Because of the distance, few people from the barrio work daily in the capital. Yet the barrio is also relatively accessible from the capital. By car, the trip is even more convenient: The same highways that connect the gated communities with the city center can be used to get to the barrio in less than an hour. When people in the barrio work in collaboration with these groups, the capital becomes very close because they get rides to schools and fairs.

The barrio is close to the capital when relations with people from the middle class are fluid. For the middle class who visit the barrio, its location is "far enough" to be Indigenous, yet "accessible enough" to be visited. For the people in the barrio, it is far from government offices, jobs, and any possibility of making the capital into a familiar place. This matches Doreen Massey's take on places as the result of embodied movements and of planned and unplanned encounters unfolding in space. Places are collections of encounters and cannot be detached from the trajectories that connect them to and disconnect them from other locations. But these encounters are not completely free associations. Instead, different bodies have unequal possibilities for being placed, for projecting, for shaping places, and for directing the movement of people and resources toward or through them.

The shaping of a specific Qom space resonates with dynamics of partial escape from state regulation and commodification of space that Simone calls the "surrounds." Surrounds are spatiotemporal arrangements that develop in the gaps opened up by the encroachment of neoliberal relations (including making places into private property, arranging space to maximize consumption, and evicting informal settlements and economies) over urban and rural space.[27] The barrio emerged from opportunities created by multiculturalist policies during the neoliberal era that opened a small space for Indigenous recognition and for people to partially escape racial stigma and overpolicing. As a surround, albeit with limitations, the barrio influences and accompanies the progress of neoliberal spatial regulation in the Conurbano, given that it pushed the state to recognize (however unstably) nonwhite existence beyond notions of criminality and backwardness. These assertions of nonwhite dignity in the surrounds of a white Buenos Aires emerge in different modalities, including the Bolivian Indigenous existence in the barrio Charrua and fairs, and newly *marrón* identities as recognizing Indigenous ancestry, which also drove the emergence of Qom barrios. Thinking of surrounds as components of assemblages links the hierarchical organization of space of neoliberal governmental forces, with the gaps left and the instability of the horizontality shaped in assemblages, which never completely undo stratification and create new boundary-making practices in the multiple forms reappropriating space. For example, the Barrio Qom had no way to receive endlessly more Qom families, but it did support the creation of other barrios, one of which was under negotiation by some of Andrea's cousins during my fieldwork. Against the association of "state" and "market" as unequivocally hierarchical, and subaltern and Indigenous as horizontal and insurgent, assemblages redistribute resources and activity by connecting with places of hierarchical organization. Negotiations with the bishop were a form of tension for the recuperation and reappropriation of land. Then again, horizontality is an unstable set of relationships shaped in assemblages that need to be constantly re-created; they encompass new forms of hierarchies (e.g., the generational differences between Qom) and are set against the violence of expropriation over space, bodies, and lives, or what Da Silva identifies as racial capitalism's extreme forms of dispossession.[28] For the Qom, the ongoing dispossession of land in the Chaco and then their segregation in the shantytowns, and later the limitations of making a living in a situation of extreme impoverishment are the most visible forms of this racial dispossession.

Important parts of the Conurbano are indeed a result of spatial planning's pushing the working class and migrants away from the city of Buenos Aires. Many policies and regulations, such as restricting access to renting in downtown, have redirected lower classes, the unemployed, and migrants arriving in Buenos Aires in the twentieth century to the borders of the city and into informal settlements.[29] But the area is also the location of middle-class neighborhoods of houses and gardens, connected to the train and close to affluent gated communities. When, during the turn to neoliberal policies, the media started identifying the area as allegedly responsible for the rise of crime, the response, as in other big cities, was to extend policing and surveillance there.[30] The media further imagined AMBA as the location of nonwhite others, a place of *negros*.[31] Media pushed the argument that the Conurbano is where lower classes have the upper hand in determining national and provincial electoral victories. Statistically, the Conurbano is an important electoral district, yet these arguments come with racist references about the future of the country being decided by an uneducated, impoverished, dark-skinned population who are supposedly easy prey to demagogic populism.[32]

The barrio is the result both of past trajectories and of these daily connections. As such, it is in distant proximity to the capital and in close separation to the rest of the Conurbano. Its location is the result of everyday forms of movement and the encounter of past trajectories that shaped the barrio as an unusual place within Buenos Aires's power geometries.[33]

Uncontested Urban Indigeneity

In the barrio, the traces of the *villas* were erased and connections to the Chaco are emphasized. The Chaco, as the source of the barrio residents' indigeneity, became a condition for the existence of the barrio. Families legally "needed" to have lived in the Chaco to obtain land in Buenos Aires and create the barrio. In this section, I describe the legal recognition of the families as Indigenous that allowed for their registry as "Indigenous" and based in the city, which also allowed for the donation of lands. The state grants this legal status only to groups that INAI recognizes as Indigenous community. In this process, the spatial experience of having lived in the Chaco was constitutive of the legal recognition of the families as urban Indigenous.

The creation of the barrio as an Indigenous community managing land collectively in the city challenged, if only partially, long-held notions of Buenos Aires as a "white city." It forced the recognition of the existence of Indigenous people in Buenos Aires by granting an Indigenous community the right to have a place in the city and to legally own land in that place. This recognition is in contrast to the *villas*, many of which continue to be informal settlements—even if some have achieved land titles. Such recognition is also unusual in the field of Indigenous politics. Even when legislation allows for granting groups lands that are not their traditional territories, and legislation clarifies that historical reparation means granting land within their former territories or "in lands that can warranty survival," the tendency has been for such groups to have to prove previous and continuous occupation for a successful land claim.[34] Granting land in Buenos Aires to a group of Qom Indigenous people originally from the Chaco region therefore reshaped the organization of difference within the city space, if only partially.

It is not surprising, then, that the Barrio Qom's land negotiation attracted numerous Indigenous activists from other Indigenous groups living in the city and that the titling generated high expectations among Indigenous organizations. It was recognized as a moment in which possibilities for Indigeneity in the city were changing, as Manuel, a Mapuche activist in Buenos Aires, told me. He explained that with the creation of the barrio, other Indigenous groups living in the city also had started hoping for land. However, the creation of the barrio did not generate a wave of Indigenous recognition in Buenos Aires until the 2000s, when more Qom barrios and multiethnic communities started to emerge. Yet these new barrios were less successful in claiming such large plots. Indeed, many communities have gained recognition but without obtaining lands, while the large barrio Charrua, with sections of *villa*, is articulated first as for Bolivian migrants and secondarily as Indigenous because of its transborder origin.[35] Indeed, Bolivian indigeneity is oftentimes secondary to a class and political affiliation, undetachable from it.[36] The Barrio Qom did not end up setting a baseline for more rights and larger plots; it continues to be an anomaly. The slow pace of recognition may be related, as Manuel himself suggested, to the difficulties other Indigenous people in the city have in being recognized as such. Only with the Kirchner governments in the 2010s and the expansion of rights did a new wave of recognitions take place. But by that time, global pressures on land, the rise in the urban property prices, and the pressures of international tourism were working against land donations. This was a time when Bolivian communities confronted violent conflicts in response to their urban land claims.[37]

With the formation of the barrio in the early 1990s, the groups that converged to help the families leave the *villas* for a new barrio recognized them as Qom, as descendants of the populations that before Spanish colonization inhabited what is today the Argentine territory, maintaining precolonial habits and knowledge alive and unchanged. In Argentina, the Qom and other major Indigenous groups from the Chaco (the Pilagá and the Wichí) are usually seen as indisputably Indigenous. From the period of state formation to the present, they have been considered the paramount "other": hunter-gatherers who have re-created shamanic conceptions of the body and nature, who were the last to be colonized by the Argentine state, and who speak their native languages as a first language, even in urban areas. In the media and in the Buenos Aires common imaginary, Indigenous people who come from the Chaco are true and unquestioned, with romanticized images of them in the bush and as victims of party politics.

This unquestioned recognition had two unplanned but complicated outcomes. It reinforced the specific criteria of recognition with national Indigenous policies that was part of larger multiculturalist recognition while also demanding that the Qom continue to fulfill these characteristics. Because the Qom families could meet social expectations and the state criteria, in the 1990s, their recognition also defined the conditions of potential exclusion of other groups, which in contrast to the Qom could be considered "not authentic enough," such as the Guarani people. During my work, I also visited a multiethnic community making a land claim against a gated community, and they were having a hard time gaining recognition as a community of people of multiple origins. These criteria also distinguished the Qom from other Indigenous groups who have lost their language, having become part of city life since Spanish colonial times. The Qom have been distinguished as even more authentic than Indigenous groups in Patagonia, who were colonized in the same period as the groups from the Chaco but underwent an even more radical process of state-sponsored social dismemberment, with genocidal intent. Many peasants and urban families hid their identities to survive and have had to confront a history of being considered "not really Argentine" by government authorities and some anthropologists.[38]

In Buenos Aires, many shantytown dwellers also self-identify as Indigenous or as having Indigenous ancestry. Significantly, in the past few years, a new identity, *marrón*, has emerged to signal Indigenous ancestry among urban subaltern (and often villa dwellers) whose specific ethnic genealogy may or may not be known.[39] However, even when they may be recognized as Indigenous and Indigenous descendants by others, or counted as such in surveys of the National Institute of Statistics and Censuses (INDEC), no *villas* have been able to obtain a land title of the shantytown as a form of "historical reparation" (the legal figure under which Indigenous nations obtain land).

Despite commonly held assumptions, Qom "traditional life" in the Chaco has not been a mechanical continuation of habits and knowledge from precolonial times. Rather, it has emerged from complex colonial processes and centuries of the Qom people's effective, active resistance.[40] In the nineteenth century, national military forces advanced through the lands of Chaco Indigenous groups and reduced them to mission stations and state reservations. In these institutions, Qom were disciplined to agricultural labor and subjected to policies directly attempting to erase their cultural specificity and identity. Subordination also included extreme forms of violence, such as mass killings, which continued until the middle of the twentieth century.[41] The perceived authenticity of the Qom, therefore, is not a form of difference that "survived" modernization, but rather one shaped in violent forms of subordination and ongoing dispossession of Indigenous lands.

Qom were indeed able to regroup in reservations and mission stations and to occupy unused public lands in small sections of their former territories. Because there was economic interest in employing the Qom as cheap and seasonal labor in the emergent cotton and sugar agro-industries, and given that many of the lands to which they moved were of no economic interest, they were able to maintain communities where they reproduced their life during the offseason.[42] They were also able to re-create shamanic forms of knowledge and healing within the Pentecostal religious service and the Iglesia Unida. The Qom cultural re-creation, which was seen as problematic before the 1990s and considered an obstacle to their integration as "modern citizens," became a positive trait for a politics of recognition that redefined national legislation in the 1990s.

Because of Argentina's growing debt and dependency on financing and renegotiation of international loans in the 1990s, it became a national state priority to define which Indigenous groups would be recognized and consulted and which would not. The criteria of authenticity were shaped by international criteria and the double-edged sword of recognition: If for decades Western nation-states pushed Indigenous groups to "integrate" and modernize to be part of dominant societies, the new criteria required them to have remained unaffected and their cultures unchanged. In Argentina, these criteria allowed for the recognition of the Qom and the Mapuche, but they also erased their histories of struggle given these were the nations that maintained territorial control until the state violently crushed them.[43]

Furthermore, the criteria divided "good" forms of Indigeneity, or for Rivera Cusicanqui the "indio permitido," based on culture and nonconfrontation, from "bad" ones.[44]

Charles Hale calls the 1990s politics of recognizing ethnic and racialized minorities as agents of their own development "neoliberal multiculturalism."[45] Multiculturalism was initially celebrated as a democratizing move that would allow Indigenous and Afro communities to represent their interests in the face of government and corporative abuses, for example, by limiting resource extraction on Indigenous land. However, Hale shows how this form of government operated in Latin America by turning Indigenous people into subjects responsible for their structurally derived limitations. Among other contradictions, Indigenous communities are blamed if, for example, they become involved in resource extraction. Indigenous groups became accountable for the self-management of "their" problems while protecting corporate interests. This has not prevented contested politics but has created mechanisms for containing and redirecting claims through channels of consultation, participation, and "accountability."

In Argentina, neoliberalism encountered the friction of Indigenous organizations actively shaping national and provincial policy since the 1980s and significantly the 1994 constitutional recognition. Organizations also intersected with working-class political experience and Peronist organizing in the city and rural areas.[46] Briones calls attention to the specific construction of aboriginality shaped at the different scales and jurisdictions of state action and within transnational politics. When the Qom moved to Buenos Aires, they not only changed provincial jurisdictions but also became more directly linked with national institutions and the international pressures on the institutions to follow international policy trends.

It is not a coincidence that both the barrio's creation and the neoliberal transformation occurred in the 1990s. The creation of INAI, Argentina's National Institute for Indigenous Affairs, which granted recognition to the barrio, resulted from the activism of Indigenous people and external neoliberal pressures to adopt Indigenous politics as a way of mitigating potential conflicts in agribusiness and resources extraction.[47] When INAI recognized the barrio, it therefore re-created local and transnational criteria of authenticity that privileged the experience of authentic Indigenous people over other groups whose recognition was more contested.[48]

Povinelli, in the Australian context, identifies this as the double edge of recognition, meaning that while state recognition opens up significant rights, it also demands very specific qualities from those groups it recognizes. Recognition limits novel forms of cultural production and sociality and often labels them as "made up" expressions. By categorizing groups in such terms, it restricts the possibilities of the recognized and the unrecognized alike.[49] The families creating the barrio had to continue to display their indigeneity, making constant references to the Chaco and erasing their experience in the *villas*.

Meanwhile, Qom youth who were born in the city and participated in forms of suburban youth socialization have not been able to acquire plots of land and have become a less clear object of NGOs' attention, because they are considered "too urban." Once Qom families achieved recognition, they found themselves inhabiting the tension described by Povinelli as the central principle of multiculturalism, where subaltern groups are forced to identify with "the impossible object of an authentic self-identity."[50]

In summary, in Buenos Aires, the criteria of authenticity and the definition of a field of particular Indigenous politics turned the historical specificity of the Qom experience into an expression of "real" Indigeneity. The making of the Barrio Qom was the product of the Qoms' indigeneity in the eyes of non-Indigenous actors; national Indigenous politics; the effects of transnational neoliberal multiculturalism; and Qom efforts to come together as a group and actively re-create cultural practices—practices that are neither essences nor pure political strategies but habits re-created within families and in church and union organizing. Thus, Qom families in the barrio weaved the project of a new place, which resulted not only in new articulations of Qom identity but also in the creation of a life out of histories of encounters and the shaping of space.

When middle-class groups from Buenos Aires started to invite Lorenzo and other Qom families to deliver workshops at schools, they created a turning point; at the time, families were unemployed and with few economic alternatives. When the families created the handicraft cooperative to centralize and share in the production of handicrafts and the organization of workshops, "cultural work" became more than a way to make extra money. While the co-op failed, the families gained the experience of organizing such activities, and they gained connections and recognition in schools and with NGOs.

When they applied to INAI and obtained legal recognition as a community, the Qom became an Indigenous group that could formally receive a land donation, manage it, and administer resources. As in the workshops, in this legal domain, Qom authenticity was unquestioned. As part of the application, the families had to provide a historical "proof" of their origin, and they were able to prove that, despite having different communities of origin, they all belonged to the Qom people of the central Chaco area, and those communities had historical relations with one another. When families received recognition as a community, the land donation became effective. Lorenzo and Julio further explained that they considered organizing around other legal constructions. They weighed the possibility of recovering the structure of a cooperative or registering as a *sociedad de fomento*, the legal construction for neighborhood associations. In the end, Lorenzo explained, it was best to obtain the legal figure as an Indigenous community, given that the land would be immune to legal confiscation and they could apply for projects as Indigenous people. It is not that the other figures would imply for them abandoning a Qom identity, but at that point, they were open to different legal structures that would enable them to create the space for families to live together as Qom. This complicates, and even inverts, the idea of strategic identification, as the Qom were willing to use the legal structures available to them strategically, to build a Qom place in the city, whether or not they were legally recognized as Indigenous.

When the Qom made their application to INAI, the provincial registry had not yet been created. The 1994 legislation of the province of Buenos Aires recognized the "existence" of Indigenous people in its territory but not recognize the "preexistence" of Indigenous groups there. It therefore did not recognize the territory as Indigenous land that had been colonized. For a long time, this legislation discouraged the emergence of land claims in the province of Buenos Aires, as Indigenous groups had to prove their origin in another province in order to be recognized. The limits of recognition in the provincial legislation are another symptom of the fact that the province and city of Buenos Aires are European settler places and that Indigenous people are seen as migrants, newcomers to the area. This situation started to change in 2014, with the creation of the provincial registry for Indigenous people. The early 2000s was indeed a period of organization and recognition in AMBA and the province at large.

When the Qom became a registered community, a new period started for the families: They became responsible for the land donations and for managing a housing project. As a recognized association, they had a number of new legal obligations as a community with *personería jurídica* (legal status). The legal registry imposes a structure similar to NGOs, so the barrio had to elect commission representatives to manage land distribution and the housing project. As a commission, members were responsible for calling and holding meetings and keeping written meeting records and accounts, which were due every year to fiscal authorities. These requirements are challenging for all organizations: Bureaucracy is confusing, ever-changing and time-consuming. Later, the commission partnered with INAI and university researchers for a "cultural revitalization project." While the commission was very skilled and received support from other NGOs, it experienced difficulties and fell behind in paperwork. To solve this, it partnered with other NGOs, which became a way of engaging institutional structures with hired professionals that made projects easier to manage. However, this also restricted their independence and manifested the baseline of the issue that is the structural exclusion of the Qom from higher education. Administrative tasks drastically restricted the exercise of the rights they achieved.

Historically, Carlos and Julio alternated in the position of president of the commission. Since its formation, the neighborhood has been divided into roughly two groups of families, each group related through kinship or affinity to one or another the leaders, and each related to one or other of the Iglesia Unida churches. This division is not exact and does not create feuds among opposing families: There are multiple overlaps with families associated with both sides and friendships that traverse the division. People also agree to work together when there is a community event, such as a Children's Day celebration or when women come together to cook for everyone. The creation of the barrio and its commission has, therefore, generated a field of politics as in other Qom barrios, where leaders compete to represent the community while kinship and church alliances overlap, extend, and enter into tension with forms of political organization. The big difference from other Qom barrios is that party political brokers are almost nonexistent here, as the barrio's population is lower than the thousands of people in the shantytowns, and thus it is not a significant electoral constituency or voter bloc. The commission and its members are not constantly involved with provincial party politics, as are neighborhoods in the Chaco or the *villas*.[51]

The Qom families' request for legal status as Indigenous people was, then, partly a strategy but also a series of contingent decisions emerging from the context and the encounters in the city. Yet once the path of becoming a community was followed, recognition turned the barrio into an entity, and families into a new group in the city's racial and spatial formation. The barrio was a new type of space that created an opening in the city's socioracial categories and put them into a new relationship with the state. Yet the legal status obtained to administer land was an opening that paradoxically also created a closure, as it singled out particular Qom families as authentic and thus worth being "saved" from the *villas* because they met certain criteria. Attaining legal status was thus also a social and spatial separation whereby a group of Qom families were singled out from other nonwhite urban poor to create a unique place. For the families moving to the barrio, recognition implied a change in their everyday habits, as many of them became both the hosts and the administrators of the multiple visits of middle-class people to get to know the Qom. And yet this cannot be reduced to only strategic essentialism.

While I share in the deconstructivist project of problematizing any idea of immutable cultural essence, especially as presented by the work of Spivak, in this process, indigeneity is not reducible to a cultural construction that is purely a strategic political action enacted as a last resort.[52] First, the Qom closely examined options for shaping a barrio, and they even considered using a legal figure that would not focus on their Indigenous identity. Thus, they were open to become a cooperative, strategically use that legal recognition to create a new place. Moreover, to ask about the indisputability of the Qom's indigeneity in Buenos Aires is to consider how they were able to connect with other actors in ways that other people living in shantytowns could not to problematize the conditions of those relations rather than deconstruct their content. In the city, Qom families re-create cultural practices, such as the value in reciprocity shaping ongoing forms of collaboration and forms of knowledge about the world that emphasize the mutual relationships with plants, animals, and waterways. Furthermore, the closure of the category of indigeneity was not unexamined. The generations of people growing up in the barrio have engaged in cultural production challenging the imposition of a closed definition of Indigenous, subaltern, and Qom, such as is seen in the musical productions and lyrics of the hip-hop group Eskina Qom.

At the time of my fieldwork and still, the production of handicrafts was a central activity of adults in the barrio. Only a few men had full-time jobs, either hired by the municipality or in the private sector, as gardeners or maintenance employees. Most of the employed men worked in construction under short contracts across AMBA and downtown Buenos Aires. Others had sporadic jobs as maintenance or cleaning staff in the district's industrial complex. Women, for the most part, had no formal employment, although a few had sporadic domestic work. Among domestic workers, a few, including Sofía, whom I mentioned in Chapter 1, were live-in domestic workers and visited the barrio on weekends. One woman ran a convenience store from her home, and a few had been employed as cooks in the barrio's community center. A few women also begged for secondhand clothes in the city and resold them to neighbors. In contrast to the Chaco, where most families receive state subsidies, only a few families in the barrio received state assistance. Few people had pensions or benefits from the federal government, such as the *asignación universal por hijo*, a universal child benefit that pays a fixed amount of money per child to unemployed families. Because most people were registered as still living in the Chaco, they were not eligible for Buenos Aires's provincial programs. A few people received subsidies from the government of the Chaco through relatives or political patrons living there. This lack of employment and disconnection from state assistance put most families in a position of economic precarity. For example, while families were not experiencing a nutritional emergency, they were not eating as much or with as much variety as they would have liked. Most families had only one meal a day—a big stew with rice or pasta and vegetables—and whenever they had some cash, they spent it on meat first.

This context thus made teaching workshops and selling handicrafts an important economic alternative. More than half of the adult men and women produced handicrafts and did "cultural work," delivering workshops, giving talks, or, less frequently, playing Qom music in schools and festivals in downtown Buenos Aires. Many families worked in the production of large quantities of handicrafts and sell them to shops, at markets, and at fairs. The handicrafts made in Barrio Qom are animal figurines and necklaces made of store-bought clay, then painted. Some families with contacts at shops and schools involved all their members in the production of clay handicrafts. More importantly, the production of handicrafts always peaked around Multiculturalism Day on October 12, celebrating the arrival of Columbus to the Americas. Around that time, people in the Barrio Qom often receive multiple invitations to participate in events at schools, markets, and fairs to promote "Qom culture." While they do not always get paid for the workshops and talks, they often get donations of clothes and food or are allowed to sell handicrafts at the event. Here, the Qom both live up to expectations (as when they describe traditional fishing techniques) and provide novel elements to present themselves (as when they narrate their work at cotton plantations) to broader non-Indigenous society, creating a specific indigeneity in the past urban experience in the *villas* and in the encounter with the urban middle class, for whom they need to become legible as Indigenous but also with whom new articulations unfold.[53]

If the perceptions of their authenticity as Indigenous people allow families to generate much-needed income, this recognition transcends income generation and a politics of strategic essentialism. The engagement of Qom people in Buenos Aires follows a more complex dynamic than the simple performance of expectations for monetary benefit (as the Comaroffs argue), or to obtain the legal status of community, as strategic essentialism would suggest, although these goals are also part of this relationship.[54] If mirroring expectations is a form of becoming intelligible and even visible, I would add that it is a process of translation in which the identification of stereotypes is an entry point to create a relationship, but where there is room for ironic citation of the stereotypes used to establish the contact, to be unpacked later so as to expand the understanding of the experience of being Indigenous in the city. Irony was indeed part of the relationship they had among themselves, as when young women teased one another about being "Indians" or *villeras*, or when a non-Indigenous woman was about to marry the brother of one of her Qom friends and everyone joked about her becoming "Indian." In these interactions, joking implies understanding, intimacy, and the possibility of introducing tension to and mocking the negative dominant ideas about indigeneity.

The expansion from stereotype to a challenge of that stereotype takes place when Qom people narrate to schoolchildren the history of their arrival in Buenos Aires, using a feather headdress that does not follow Qom traditional dress, consciously identifying that this is what is available to them now, and that this is what makes them visible to urban children as real and alive *indios* (literally, Indians). This co-construction of indigeneity becomes the way to intervene in the "white" space of the city of Buenos Aires and claim a form of Indigenous existence there. Becoming visibly and legibly Indigenous in the urban space, they assert a presence that would otherwise be dismissed, denied, and policed, but once presented, that indigeneity is also moved in other directions. Thus, for example, in the performances, there are mentions of the Napalpí massacre of the 1920s, a historical event most people in Buenos Aires know nothing about. If the Qom did not make their indigeneity clear, it would have been almost impossible to establish the relationships that give them access to schools and fairs, that open spaces for their workshops and invitations to festivals. The workshops, craft production, and performances emerge out of a co-construction of indigeneity between the state, the middle class, and the Qom. The Qom participate in the limited space that multiculturalism opens, one in which difference can become visible if it is reinscribed as nonthreatening, folkloric, and traditional.[55] This limited opening of multiculturalism allows the Qom and the Indigenous movement at large to push for legal recognition. Yet the terms of recognition relocate the Qom and other recognized nations in a position of subordination as they need to prove authenticity and struggle for the implementation of the rights they have achieved.[56] The Qom in the barrio as the "vanguard" of urban Indigenous, and urban Qom and the younger generations more generally, navigate as they expand indigeneity as a process that does not end at the moment of recognition. Ending their analysis at the moment of recognition is perhaps a limitation to Povinelli and Coulthard's arguments against state recognition, as they consider it to be irrevocably the subordination and capture of indigeneity.[57]

Most people in the barrio agree that they have not worked as a community for the past few years. As Miguel explained in our tour of the barrio, "all families are working individually" because selling handicrafts and doing workshops is an activity that pushes families to "work by themselves." Individual work and competition contradict idealized images of what an "Indigenous community" is expected to be as a group in which everything obtained is shared equally. This expectation was reflected in the fact that people I worked with felt they had to explain to me why they did not work together. However, this expectation of sharing and cooperation does not consider the basic dynamics of the market economy in which families are involved. The expectations of the middle class are important, because when they are not met, groups get disappointed, momentum is lost, and helpers and allies distance themselves from the barrio. The constant distancing and the constant arrival of new groups both shape a cyclical temporality of these relations in which the Qom, too, become tired and disillusioned. The fact that the Qom do not meet the expectations of many long-term, middle-class supporters defines the intensity of relations and also the temporality of their disillusion, which is the subject of the next chapter. The power of that disillusion is another dimension of the pressures of conveying social expectations to build relationships with non-Indigenous groups and state institutions.

The cultural work of promoting "Qom culture" also implies differences in access to the city and forms of mobility. Those who are more active as cultural workers are usually older men and women who grew up in the Chaco but have more experience and orientation in the city than others. They know and can evaluate different ways to reach a place, have connections in the city, and may stop at an ally's home to have a meal and recharge before or after an activity. The others rely heavily on the train and do not have places to rest in the city. The possibilities for families to navigate the city center as Indigenous people are thus not equally open to all.

Because youth in the barrio were not born in the Chaco and do not have histories of an "Indigenous life" there, being a cultural worker is not an option for them. They accompanied their parents but were not able to take over their activities. In the early 2010s, the limit to the reproduction of authenticity meant that young urban Qom were not given space for cultural work. While young people can learn some stories from their parents, they cannot narrate in the first person of having hunted, fished, and gathered fruit in the Chaco, experiences that constitute their parents' authenticity. If youth talk about cultural practices in the barrio in Buenos Aires—for example, speaking their language—they are not perceived as truly Indigenous because those practices did not develop in the Chaco. The ambivalent belonging to the barrio is spatially materialized, too, as youth have had to make their homes in shacks on the barrio's edge and outside it. The barrio offered no formal plots or housing access to young adults who grew up in the city and were starting their families. Their new constructions can be seen as marginal but also as part of the spatial dynamism whereby many young people choose to stay around the barrio—by building new homes, they also expand the barrio's reach. Young Qom who grew up in the city have revealed new uses for space and expanded the barrio to points beyond it.

An Indigenous Barrio in the Conurbano: (Dis)connecting Locations

This chapter has traced the multiple relations that assemble the barrio as a space in its (dis)connection with other places. I have explored the way the barrio's residents separated from the *villas*, as well as their position in the city's formations of race and space, to constitute another space: a recognized Indigenous community with land title in the city's capital. The barrio fit general categories of authenticity and won recognition in the urban space, and yet, alongside other communities claiming recognition, it also challenged and rearranged, if only partially, those same ethnic and racial categories. I have also traced the co-construction of recognition in the interactions between the middle class, families, and state agencies, and I have highlighted the fixing of categories but also the generational variations in Indigenous and nonwhite identifications. If the creation of the Barrio Qom was an act of the first-generation migrants from the Chaco that allowed them to get out of the *villas*, the actions leading up to it were not planned. Other Qom barrios emerged out of the relocation of shantytowns and the creation of popular multiethnic barrios in the second and third rings of the metropolitan urban area. Yet many inhabitants experience the barrio as a place that has reconnected them to the Chaco. As Esteban explained, "Getting the land for the barrio was like going back to the Chaco."

In conversations about what he remembered of the creation of the barrio, Manuel, a Mapuche activist who lives in Buenos Aires and accompanied the Qom in land negotiations, connected this to the fact that the Qom are seen as the most "Indigenous" of all groups: "You know, there is one thing about the barrio. The Qom are the most Indian of all of us in the eyes of the rest of the society: They all speak the language, know how to hunt, and have lived in rural villages. That is what society wants to see." This contrasted with his own experience of growing up without being able to self-identify as Mapuche for fear of being discriminated as school, and seeing his parents forcing themselves to speak only Spanish to avoid unemployment and violence in urban spaces. As the "most Indigenous" (under the eyes of white *porteños* and the state) of the urban Indigenous people, the Qom in the barrio attracted more interest and more assistance than other groups. Indeed, Carlos, remembering the time he slept at the bus stop because he missed the last bus, told me that as an Indigenous musician performing late, he spent several nights sleeping in the park. I asked whether he had trouble with the police, as they generally evict people from the parks at night: "I had my guitar with me, and an Andean vest. [Unlike when I lived in the *villa*] when I work as a musician, I had no problem with the police anymore."

In this Indigenous place, youth are in an ambiguous situation, for many of them spent their childhood in Buenos Aires's *villas*. They are therefore not recognized as fully "Indigenous," as they lack rural experience and habits. They listen to *cumbia*, reggaeton, and hip-hop, and most drop out of high school, as they perceive themselves as having no prospect of further education. They are part of suburban youth cultural circles of manual labor, soccer, and *cumbia* clubs (when they can afford them). While these young people were recognized as Indigenous children when the barrio was created, they were not part of the initial plans for the barrio and cannot access the status of the adults who own a plot of land.

The connections that produce the barrio as part of larger assemblages need to be traced back to their multiple points of origin: the trajectories bringing people from the Chaco to the *villas* and allowing people to move out of the *villas*. There are also trajectories moving forward that link the barrio to people who "come to the barrio to help" and that connect families to other Qom barrios and rural areas in the Chaco. But trajectories can both connect and actively disconnect. The barrio was connected to the Chaco and actively disconnected from its surroundings and from the *villas*. The barrio as a place is not an enclosed location, but a site that attracts, connects, slows down, and redirects the trajectories of people, objects, and ideas. Movement not only transverses and destabilizes places but also assembles and disassembles places with others.

CHAPTER 4

"Encountering the Indigenous"

Middle-Class Humanitarianism

Weekends in the barrio were regularly full of activity. Cars would park by the community center in the morning, bringing people who "helped" with the barrio: University students organized a literacy project in the mornings, a group held a drumming class in the afternoon, and people from the neighboring wealthy gated communities frequently brought clothing donations and prepared hot chocolate for the kids. The Qom referred to these groups (including researchers) as "people who help" (*gente que ayuda*), and soon, I started to notice their significance. As I tried to arrange my first interviews in the barrio, I had to deal with the residents' busy schedules, competing with these people who help. On most occasions, when I visited someone, at the same time they were also fielding several phone calls and hosting other visitors. Being busy receiving visits was a central aspect of many of the families' everyday lives.

These people who help were mostly progressive, college-educated, middle-class, young or middle-aged people of white European background who lived in the city center or in the Conurbano's neighboring gated communities. Many were involved in education and research, including university outreach groups, while others were religious groups from Catholic parishes or Evangelical churches, and some were engaged in leftist activism supporting Indigenous causes.

People who help came with diverse conceptions about the Qoms' needs and had different approaches to how to assist them: cooking and providing food, leading meditation sessions, teaching music, aiding children's literacy, and sharing Bible readings, among others. Most families in the barrio were involved with these groups and usually accepted their plans (including my own offers to support the barrio). Antonia explained that sometimes they were not interested in some projects, but they still participated because "it is good to work with people who are enthusiastic," as Carlos from the barrio's association put it.

Martín narrated one of his first encounters with a person collaborating in the barrio: "When I started to work on an education project, it was my first time collaborating with a white woman. She was so white that, initially, I was too shy to talk with her; I didn't dare speak." While that shyness had mostly dissipated by the time I arrived in the barrio, and people who help had been incorporated into the barrio's routines, many Qom people continued to perceive these visitors as powerful, wealthy, and "very white" (meaning not *criollo* but a European-descended whiteness). They saw people in Buenos Aires as being "whiter" than the middle classes in the Chaco.

In this chapter, I explore the Qom's encounters in the barrio with "people who help." These encounters are based on a productive divergence of interests, where people from the city see themselves as agents of improvement in the face of their perceived needs of the Qom, and the Qom see people who help as a bridge to creating a life in the city, to opening a space, albeit precarious, as Indigenous people living in the capital. The presence of helpers in the barrio speaks, too, of the fascination with Indigenous difference in "white" Buenos Aires, where the people who come to the barrio see the Qom's indigeneity as a special type of subalternity, worthy of assistance. The productivity of these close relations is thus shaped by and re-creates racially distinct groups.

When the Qom families were officially recognized as Indigenous in the early 1990s, the state recognition affected their subsequent relationships with people who help. While none of the visitors asked for legal "proof" of authentic Indigeneity, groups came because they wanted to visit an "Indigenous barrio" in Buenos Aires, and most did not work in any other barrio. Many people who help imagined the barrio as populated by Indigenous people from rural areas who had grown up hunting and gathering, who were "unspoiled" by modernity or politics. In the romanticized perceptions of the people who help, the Qom were real Indigenous people.[1] I observed this in conversations when people who help asked many questions about life in the Chaco, inquired about spiritual experiences in the forest, and enjoyed long narratives about how, for instance, the Qom smoked fish over a fire to preserve it. The people who help romanticize the Qom as naive and apolitical, unlike people in the shantytowns, whom they see as politicized popular classes.

Associated with Peronism, shantytown dwellers are represented in the media as deceptively manipulating state assistance and as associated with criminality. Those who knew that barrio inhabitants had previously lived in the shantytowns often mentioned how difficult it must have been to be surrounded by criminals and violent activity in the *villas*. The Qom were singled out as a "special" type of subaltern, unlike the shantytown dwellers who were seen as politicized, lazy, and criminal.[2] The notion that the barrio deserved help is thus another way in which it becomes a different space from the *villas*. Help constructs populations and spaces (Qom and people who help) in an asymmetrical relationship, by which people who visit reinforce their whiteness by "doing good" while the Qom reinforce the recognition of authentic indigeneity in the city. Through help, white *porteños* can achieve a connection with the Chaco, and the Qom can gain some access to an otherwise hostile and racist city space and its institutions.

In this chapter, I explore how Indigenous subaltern assemblages are produced in everyday encounters that re-create racialized Indigenous and white middle-class subjectivities and places. I trace this constitution of both groups spatially, as they shape the barrio and the city center as distinct but contested spaces, given that the Qom engage help not just as a source of material resources but also as a way of accessing and connecting to the city center. I start by describing the groups of people who help.

"Plenty of Visitors": Help and the Fascination of the White Middle Class

Initially, I felt uneasy about the proliferation of such groups in the barrio; I thought that with so many groups requiring the barrio families' attention, I would get a distorted view of their urban experience. Later, however, I came to see these interactions as a central aspect of the production of the assemblages shaped for and through the barrio, and I expanded my field of study to include these relations. To get to know the groups of people who help, I participated in their activities and meetings, and I reflected on my own experience as part of one of these groups; working with other researchers, we organized a computer workshop with youth in the barrio and a Qom-language class at the university to respond to a request to support children's education and Qom-language promotion. While the motivations of these groups who help are complex, their various approaches define different types of interaction. I generated rough typologies in my field notes to keep a record of them. Some groups see the Qom as starving Indigenous people, victims of poverty and government abandonment, and want to help them by giving them food. Others see them as having knowledge that needs to be preserved, while others see them as potentially revolutionary subjects who will engage in radical forms of activism.

The first group consists of people whose work is close to charity, who would visit a few times and not return for some time. Charity groups were generally composed of middle-aged men and women who arrived in new cars in groups of six to ten people, wearing sporty but expensive clothing and bringing material donations. This self-presentation and the fact that many were groups organized within gated communities positions them in the upper-middle classes. I interacted with some of these groups and found that many were influenced by media representations of the Qom as suffering extreme poverty and malnutrition. This perception was an instance of the Qom being portrayed as passive and deserving victims. The idea of political victims was indeed articulated during one festival people who help organized, when a woman explained to me that she was hoping the Qom would "not become politicized by Peronist militants," a sign of the anti-Peronism that permeates sectors of the middle classes and often (but not only) upper classes. She was referring to the grassroots form of organizing of Peronist *unidades básicas*, found in most popular and working-class neighborhoods, which organize soup kitchens and *merenderos*, sites for snacks and after-school care. While there was an *unidad básica* in the area, it was quite far from the barrio, and Qom people did not participate in it at the time. Thus, the direct personal intervention, expanding Qom assemblages to links with these helpers, did replace this other form of organizing.

Other groups that had a regular presence and experience in grassroots organizing were Catholic and Evangelical churches, although there were important differences between them. One Catholic group, for example, had an ongoing project with a liberation theology orientation, as I observed in one of their planning meetings. Here, a soft-spoken middle-aged woman led a conversation with members of the association, suggesting the creation of a bakery but frequently pausing to ask questions and reshape plans. Groups such as this one, from Catholic parishes, were sometimes of three to four people—and more for special events. They were "average" middle class (in comparison to the people from gated communities who were in the upper sectors of the middle class). Their cars were older, and they lived in middle-class neighborhoods. The woman leading the planning meeting was a catechist in her thirties who wore a tidy but worn pair of jeans and a hand-knitted sweater. In informal conversations, she disclosed that her parish had decades of experience doing grassroots work and that they followed Paulo Freire's liberation theology methods.

Evangelical churches considered the Qom "brothers and sisters" worthy of help but not necessarily requiring urgent salvation. Evangelical churches would organize events in collaboration with the two local churches. For instance, they organized a musicians' encounter and the visit of a renowned preacher from Korea. They would also help the barrio, for example, by donating food for community meals. Evangelicals of different ages, from twenty- to fiftysomething, dressed modestly but formally. They approached the Qom as their equals, also in that they were not "dressing down," as were other middle-class groups, who appeared to be dressed as though on a field trip to an impoverished place. Evangelicals wore slacks and polished leather shoes, shirts, and cardigans; the women wore long skirts and carefully tied-back hair.

During my fieldwork, there were two groups of university undergraduate students, one working on literacy and another from an art college doing music workshops. I was part of a third university group, composed of anthropologists and linguists, who had held a language workshop for three years, and I joined later. While the main team was no longer attending regularly, many members came and conducted research in the barrio. I both joined this team and worked alone during my fieldwork.

The barrio also attracts a few NGOs. However, the organizations (part of the indigenist movement) that helped with the negotiation of the barrio's legal personhood application and its acquisition of lands, are no longer active there. I met people who had participated in the creation of the barrio, and they acknowledged that they had become disconnected from it. They were busy helping with land conflicts and disputes elsewhere in the country, which had taken on greater political urgency, given the violence and imminence of land displacement.[3] Another NGO, Aid the Qom, formed by an affluent family, has been active in the barrio the longest and pays the tuition of some Qom children to attend the Catholic school near the barrio. This NGO is represented by a family member who works with the barrio's president and who pays regular visits and follows up on the students' progress. On occasion, this NGO donates food; thus, in its actions and class composition it represents the "charity" groups described earlier. A final group of people who help are those directly involved in politics. Many groups from the progressive middle class attempted to involve the Qom in political activities that they thought would be good for them. Such groups were composed of young people, mostly university students, including students from art school and film studies. These groups tended to have no links with one another, and many approached the barrio as though it were a place they had "discovered." A young filmmaker and his crew, for example, were producing a film he considered the first on urban indigeneity. I will come back to this, in order to focus in detail on both the NGO and the groups of activists.

Help in the barrio is not without friction. Groups tend to follow an affective arc from excitement and intensity to disillusion and dispersal. The sense of disillusionment tends to be part of the experience of all groups, even those who sustain relationships over time. The initial moment of intensity is often followed by disenchantment and disconnection. In this cycle, some groups discontinue their visits and are replaced by new ones. The groups that fade get frustrated, their high expectations unfulfilled, and they interpret the interaction as a failure. For example, one member of an NGO explained to me how the group had been unsuccessful in improving school retention among Qom youth, while others lamented their failure to turn them into urban farmers. Many groups leave the barrio at that point. But while the projects may be perceived as failing, the encounters are productive in other ways: They produce a social position for people who help and reinforce Qom people's indigeneity. The encounter is productive in racial and spatial terms, and it enables the Qom to produce a living as Indigenous people in the city.

In all these movements, from downtown Buenos Aires to the Barrio Qom, all visitors shape themselves as white and moral subjects. The trip to the barrio is a small adventure and a moral project whereby "good" white people leave their ordinary environment to visit a radically different place and people. This making of whiteness through movement beyond their everyday space and into the space of victimized "others" resonates with a colonial history, where travel is a constitutive part of (white) colonial subjectivities and spaces.[4] When travel is narrativized, it tells a tale of civilized, adventurous, mobile men who leave their homes in the metropolis to explore the wilderness of the colonies and meet Indigenous others. As part of a white middle class, they can become "generous aid workers," "recognized members of their community," and prestigious "advocates for the dispossessed." As such, in the encounters that take place in the barrio, middle-class people cultivate the progressive nature of their whiteness and reinforce their class belonging, racial distinction, and privilege. This is not a metropolitan whiteness based in the Global North but an unstable whiteness, one that has been othered in association with Peronism and the political left during the last dictatorship. And yet the class privilege, in the form of living above the poverty line and having access to institutions, was always a difference from the Qom.

The whiteness and middle-class status of people who help is not homogeneous. Visitors shape themselves as compassionate or committed, and they elide the link between their position and a nation that has privileged whiteness and dispossessed Indigenous people. The upper-middle-class helpers, with their focus on charity, constructed the Qom as a source of moral reassurance, which in turn made their own whiteness even more distant to the Qom and to all lower classes. Such a relationship generates a whiteness associated with status, for which they themselves are strong, knowledgeable, and in control, and the Qom are passive, weak, and backward. Other groups were driven by the desire to encounter in the Qom a source of knowledge that could enrich and reconnect them to their own spirituality and turn them into a different type of white, one with a connection to their "Indigenous brothers." Still others experienced their interactions with the Qom as a transformation that radicalized them politically and validated them as activists when they introduced themselves to other members of the autonomous left as doing work with the Qom. People who help, therefore, "need" the Qom as much as the Qom may "need" their help.

Visiting a Place of Authentic Indians

People who help seldom openly discussed their notion of Qom authenticity, but it was often implied. For instance, it was present in the expectation that families were coming straight from the Chaco—and in particular, the rural Chaco—and that they had lived in rural villages and not in periurban barrios, as many of them in fact had. They expected families to manifest engagement in cultural practices that match images of Indigenous identity: speaking the Qom language, making handicrafts, sharing resources communally, and engaging in reciprocal relationships with one another. In my first visits, some Qom men and women would speak to me only about forest food in the Chaco, as if that were my main and only interest in getting to know them. Moreover, there is an expectation that Indigenous people hold a specific, mysterious cultural knowledge: esoteric relations to the supernatural worlds, a mystical relation to nature, the performance of exotic shamanic healing, and so on. There is no doubt that such knowledge is indeed part of people's lives, yet its projection as an incommensurable difference veils many other dimensions of barrio life and becomes a source of fatigue for Qom families when it becomes an expectation.[5]

The Qom are infamous among the middle class for their poverty and marginalization. Media representations portray the Qom as one of the poorest Indigenous people in the country. They conflate ideas of noble savages, of people living simple lives in the middle of the bush, of people who are either outside politics or victims of political abuse, and finally, of people in dire need. The Qom themselves participate in and manage images of authenticity and assumed primitivism; they have to navigate the construction of "hyperreal Indians" but also the presumption of authenticity from people who help co-construct an indigeneity according to their own expectations.[6] People who help were influenced by periodic media reports depicting famine in the Chaco, with sensationalist images of malnourished people on the TV news.[7] Hunger is indeed a complex reality in some rural communities at specific moments, but in the barrio that is not the case. These representations have acted as affective triggers for many people who help, portraying the Qom as moral victims, physically weak and passively enduring starvation, in need of help, as good authentic Indigenous people who can prove their cultural specificity, unlike groups who are seen as politicized, "fake" Indigenous.[8] Interestingly, too, in such representations, the weakness makes the Qom an infantilized, nonthreatening group. As such, the Qom in the barrio are a focal point of interest for people who help.

Humanitarianism has been described as the sphere of intersecting reason and emotion.[9] But an analysis of a humanity is not enough, a central ethnographic question is, Who reacts to the suffering of whom? Aid implies the production of other subjectivities—in this case, Indigenous ones—that are the privileged objects of the emotional engagement of the people who help, and it also enables the actualization of white, middle-class subjectivities. Racial classifications shape both the subject providing the aid and the one receiving it. In this classification, the Qom, as compared to other groups of poor people, are innocent victims and thus subjects worthy of care. This frame establishes a moral economy that shapes people as victims without agency and as individuals with no political affiliation; victims come to be seen as more deserving of resources and care than economic migrants, organized civil society, or other ethnic groups. The relationship of help is thus shaped not around an open discussion of racial categories, but around implicit racialized attributes by which grammars of racism are made and remade.[10] Indigeneity comes to be defined as a lack of modernity and authenticity as a repertoire of cultural practices in relation to the Chaco.

In the relations of help, skin color is a marker of difference, but the Qoms' dark skin is also distinguished by middle-class people of European background from that of *negro villeros*. The Qoms' darkness is important to the visitors, for dark bodies are another mark of "purity," so lack of darkness is a problem. Ricardo, who is lighter skinned and "mixed race" but considered "fully Qom" (he was raised by his Qom mother), was viewed as "less" Qom by some visitors, and thus he made an extra effort to demonstrate his knowledge.[11] The construction of a racialized indigeneity is also achieved through ideas of culture and authenticity. Whether such projects succeed or fail, the encounters are always productive of this racial difference, by which white people become "good" people and the Qom need to remain "authentically" Qom.

When people who help approach the barrio with the assumption that it is "a piece of Chaco" in Buenos Aires, they unintentionally create distance between the barrio and the city, and they symbolically and materially detach the barrio from its location in the Conurbano by classifying it as different. This creates a paradox: Families in the barrio can connect with groups coming from the capital because they are Qom, but as Indigenous people, they are seen as distant both from the city center and from the Conurbano. Foreclosed from an identity as urban subjects, they are denied the chance to be Indigenous *and* urban at the same time. And yet, people who help also provide a way to access the city center.

In this racialized relation of help, the nature of the barrio is central. Many visitors assume that Qom families arrived in the city together, seeing them as a homogeneous group. The barrio is well located, with relatively easy access: Instead of having to enter the "dangerous and inaccessible" Fuerte Apache, people can drive to a less stigmatized impoverished area of the Conurbano. Yet at the same time, the barrio is distant enough to maintain its mystique of cultural difference. The production of the barrio as an Indigenous place, and thus as "exotic" to most *porteños*, is central to this relationship in which space contributes to constructing the identity of the people: a place of real Indigenous people, racially and spatially distinct.

When the barrio becomes "a piece of the Chaco in Buenos Aires," specific expectations are set about the place, the people, and their routines. I saw one of the groups doing charity work as they enjoyed watching Antonia produce handicrafts; one of the women later added that this was "just as they do in the Chaco." I was with Raúl when one of the charity groups had just left, and he explained that they had spent over an hour asking questions about life in the Chaco, the exotic foods that Qom used to eat there, and the plants used to cure illnesses, always locating the Chaco as home to the Qom families. In conversations between Carlos, a member of the barrio commission, and a group helping commercialize handicrafts, I noted an erasure of the families' present location in the Conurbano: It was unclear whether in fact the group considered that Carlos still lived in the Chaco and was only visiting Buenos Aires. This ambiguity was also present when Antonia collected secondhand clothes and food donations "for the Chaco," presenting the community as an extension of rural villages in Chaco province. For others who had a longer-term relationship with the barrio and had traveled to rural communities, the barrio was a "copy" of Qom barrios in the Chaco. While this idea is more complex and acknowledges links with other urban barrios, it still ignores the Qom experiences in shantytowns and the specificity of being Qom in the nation's capital.

Another example is the clay handicrafts that the Qom sell. The style and technique of these were developed in urban settings such as Buenos Aires and Rosario. But to sustain interest, the families producing them emphasized these pieces' cultural meaning, presented as "traditional" knowledge: An owl is a "Qom sign" of good luck, for instance, and an open hand "represents" prosperity. Handicrafts developed in urban contexts, then, need to be turned into a product from the Chaco.

In interactions with people who help, there is a co-construction of what it is to be Indigenous, and the state criterion of recognition is only one element of that. This construction of indigeneity is informed by the media and by old tropes of the Qom as among the last "real" Indigenous people in the country. Because displays of "culture" further allow Qom people to generate income as cultural workers, families have to follow this expectation, setting aside their urban experience and, importantly, their experience in the *villas*.

Further, the notion that families come from the Chaco gives no room for Qom youth who were born in Buenos Aires or who came to the city as children to be recognized as Qom. It limits the possibilities for young people to "do cultural work" without the experience of living in the Chaco. Many of the people who help are not interested in the youth or young adults. One young Qom, who is in her late twenties and grew up in Fuerte Apache, complained that they do not get invitations to do cultural workshops, even when she could run a workshop after having accompanied her parents so many times. This makes it almost impossible for youth to claim an identity as "authentic" Indigenous, while the possibility of an urban Indigeneity is omitted in such interactions. For visitors, the youth are closer to *negros villeros*, as one social worker implied: "Youth have been hanging out with bad company, they have friends who are the worst of the *villas* . . . they are losing their identity."

On the other hand, this is an implicit recognition of the *villeros* as Indigenous people without culture; a moment of insight into a racist structure and against the claims of Indigenous disappearance.

The movement of people who help to the urban periphery reinforces the construction of the Qom as Indigenous others and the white middle class as modern, moral subjects; it does so by reshaping spatial connections between the barrio, the Conurbano, and the capital. Help is a relationship that creates racialized subjectivities—white visitors from the modern and European-looking capital and Indigenous people—and a racialized spatiality whereby the barrio, a "piece of Chaco" in Buenos Aires, is connected to and in tension with the center and the *villas*. The recognition of the barrio as Indigenous is crucial, but expectations of a "true" identity limit urban Indigeneity; given other aspects of Qom's urban life, links with the shantytowns have to be sidelined.

Longing for the Radical Indian

There are groups from the political left (broadly characterized) who approach the Qom with a particular idea of help that is based on the expectation that, as Indigenous people, they will be involved in (and sometimes at the vanguard of) radical politics. This approach has also been a source of frustration for the groups who visit and part of the cycle of visitors who engage for a period but then do not come back to the barrio. As I mentioned, during the negotiations over land to create the barrio, a lot of non-Qom Indigenous activists living in the city enthusiastically supported the Qom families' request for land title. One of them, a Mapuche man in his mid-forties, explained to me that he and other people saw the land request as a radical claim: asking for land titles as Indigenous outside "traditional territories" and in the national capital. Many people self-identifying as Indigenous lived in Buenos Aires, and a group of them, including Lorenzo and the first Indigenous lawyer Eulogio Frites, had created Asociación Indígena de la República Argentina (AIRA) in the 1970s, a national Indigenous association based in the capital that brings together dispersed Indigenous people.[12] There had been antecedents of popular settlements composed of mostly Indigenous families of Qom and Guarani origin that, through general housing projects (for popular sectors and not only Indigenous people), had settled in the Conurbano.[13] There were also the precursors in La Plata in 1991 who had created a Qom barrio, taking the opportunity to use housing funds by the province of Buenos Aires that were not specific to Indigenous people.[14] However, as noted, this was the first claim for lands for an Indigenous community, and people engaged in it expected it would be a very important precedent for other urban Indigenous groups seeking land title in Buenos Aires. However, once the barrio was created, and as the families became more involved in cultural work and less engaged in political activism, the groups and individuals supporting them grew disillusioned.

Two acquaintances involved in Indigenous movements in Buenos Aires, activists of the autonomist left, one of them Indigenous, described to me their periods of work with the barrio. In the narrative they both described that, eventually, the relationship faded. "People there are involved in too many things; they receive too much attention," Pedro, a journalist, told me. He finished his account by saying, "I think they are a lost cause." He laughed, having meant perhaps that he had stopped trying to get them engaged in direct actions to support communities making land claims elsewhere in the country. Manuel, a friend and Mapuche activist involved in Indigenous policy in the 1990s, was more understanding. He explained to me that "people are too busy making a living; the economic need is too big." He added that people in the barrio have big families; they have a lot of care responsibilities, getting food for everyone is a big task, and any extra energy is directed to helping their relatives in the Chaco who are often living in poverty, too.

They both expressed that while they had expected the barrio to be a site for the emergence of radical political practices of Indigenous demands in the city, this potential was lost in the process of making a living and managing the amount of assistance they receive. Both people had hoped that the barrio would be a model for other Indigenous communities, but instead, its residents were caught in survival mode and, as Cristian put it, "too distracted with so many visits."

The experience of one of the more left-leaning groups visiting the barrio sheds light on their disenchantment. The non-Indigenous group I call Qom Art was formed when several art education students approached the barrio to research Qom music for a college assignment and decided to continue to visit. When I met them in winter, they had over ten members, most of them in their mid-twenties from middle-income neighborhoods in the capital. The group had links with student activism and found it easy to organize, with no institutional affiliation but a calendar of regular meetings to discuss activities and political aims. They were self-funded, and a few of them had cars that they used to get to the barrio to do art workshops.

When I met Qom Art's members, they had an intense activity in the barrio; they attended weekly to facilitate music workshops and support the people doing cultural work. The group also fundraised to buy materials for the workshops and organized a few festivals in the barrio and the capital. I started to attend their activities in the barrio and in Buenos Aires city (CABA) and learned that they aimed to travel to Chaco at the end of the year.[15]

In the early spring, after they had been working with the barrio for many months, they invited some of the Qom collaborators to one of their activist spaces in the capital, a meeting to prepare for the countercelebration of the Bicentenary Anniversary, which was held on a weekend on an independent radio station in the CABA.[16] I attended the meeting and found the young activists openly disappointed that nobody from the barrio had turned up. Even when they understood the time constraints of people in the barrio, they highlighted that neither older Qom with political experience nor young people appeared to be able to sustain a committed, activist engagement in the present. They did not have the interests or abilities to become part of a leftist, activist world that demanded a minimum of middle-class standing to have time to attend events and money to pay for the bus and the food. The student members of this group were aware of their own privilege in having time and resources to engage in activities held in the center of the city. Yet their awareness did not resolve the paradox and generated a growing distance.[17]

When the end of the year approached, Qom Art got busy planning the trip to the Chaco. Through people from the barrio, they had contacted a cultural center in a town close to Castelli in Chaco province, where they would develop a literacy program, art workshops, and a film festival.

In the Chaco, they met the group of young Qom community leaders who ran the cultural center there: Antonio, Julia, and Miguel. The three are Qom activists, journalists, and teachers, and had been part of a takeover of the cultural center, occupying the space against the will of municipal authorities and running it ever since.[18] I knew Antonio from previous work in the Chaco and met him in the cultural center they manage in the Chaco, a few days after Qom Art had finished its activities and returned to Buenos Aires. Antonio explained that the group's time there had been "very powerful"; its members had organized art workshops and activities with children. As we drank *terere* (cold mate), Antonio and Julia explained that they had made sure that Qom Art's members got to "see the reality of the Qom communities," organizing a series of visits to rural communities. So these young activists had their political aims for the group and organized a routine for them: "In the morning, we let them do the activities they had planned; in the afternoon, we visited the rural communities, introduced the group to Qom leaders, discussing local problems, including the legal battles for land, problems with non-Indigenous neighbors, and the lack of implementation of Indigenous policies. When they left, they were transformed," Antonio and Julia explained.

When I met the Qom Art group back in Buenos Aires in late summer, they explained that the trip had a profound impact on them. They learned about land conflicts and had come to see them as a priority of their work, so they would not work much more in the barrio. They perceived people in rural areas as having more urgent problems, so decided to prioritize them and support their activism.

For several months, Qom Art members dedicated most of their time to organizing the bicentenary's countercelebration, working together with other experienced leftist, activist groups, including radical Indigenous leaders in Buenos Aires and "spread out" in different barrios, as well as independent media activists. They continued to fundraise for travels and to develop activities in the Chaco. They also started a reading group on Marxism and Indigenous people at a cultural center.

The relationship between the Qom Art group and the barrio grew distant with the disillusionment that members experienced as they became more engaged in a form of activism they saw as more serious and urgent. The group stretched its relations into the Chaco, where "more serious" events were taking place; these were confrontations with the state for territory, autonomy, and services.

While the groups connected to the Chaco through the barrio, they considered both places differently: The Chaco was where more radical leaders were based and where urgent matters demanded their work, and the barrio was where people were losing the radicalness by disengaging in formal politics. While subtly detaching the barrio from the Chaco, they also reinforced a differential attribution of political relevance, as other groups of the left have done, too. This is not a unique understanding: Leftist groups have had a tendency to consider territorial struggles as core and in need of more urgent support, in contrast to the struggles of the urban Indigenous, whose territorial, political, and cultural rights are considered secondary. Paradoxically, while the families in the barrio were not radical in the way that Qom Art members expected, the barrio deeply influenced their political trajectory.

The relationship between Qom Art and the barrio demonstrates how the families in the barrio are never able to fully meet the expectations of them that visiting groups hold, even those with more critical approaches to social inequalities. Also, while families accept many projects, they are never able to participate in all activities. The disillusionment of Qom Art was not different from that of other groups. A common experience is that the middle-class groups approach the Qom with fascination and enthusiasm and find a warm welcome for their proposals. As activities unfold and encounters become more frequent, the groups grow frustrated when people do not show up for activities or do not show markers of expected improvements.

Another aspect of the disillusion in most people who help is that they ultimately find that the barrio is not the ideal community, as they had expected. Rather, families compete with each other and collaborate occasionally, and many times, resources are put to private use.

Assembling Help

To maintain relations with several groups at the same time, families in the barrio have to manage the time and energies they devote to each group. People in the barrio engage in and appropriate the help of visitors and have to manage the activities they perform in the barrio, such as by giving them access to the community center, inviting other families to a given activity, and planning and working in specific events. Families thus keep these relations active and help middle-class groups in their activities, something that I saw in the Chaco, too, where the Qom have the tendency to manage social relations with skill and deliberate effort. In the city, this becomes of particular relevance; unlike the Chaco, where there may be other economic activities such as taking care of a farm or managing patronage political relationships, help is a very relevant economic activity in the city.[19] Focusing on Qom people's management of help provides a very different perspective from considering them passive recipients of assistance.

Of all the families I met, Fernando was the busiest and most skilled at managing assistance. He was at the time president of the *comisión*, the civil association representing the barrio as a community. When I asked Fernando for an interview, he told me to come on a Saturday morning; the rest of the week he was busy delivering talks in the CABA. I found that Saturdays were long days for Fernando, given he met many visitors to the barrio then. He did not schedule visitors for strict time slots, so we often overlapped and ended up all hanging out together. One Saturday, I met a music producer who had recorded a CD "with music from the Chaco" with Fernando's relatives. Another day, a group of pharmacy students interviewed him about traditional Qom medicine; yet another a group from a Catholic parish came to consult about a bakery project. Fernando was always in a good mood, patiently answered questions, became enthusiastic about projects, and gave information about how and when to use the community center.

Fernando was also the point person for the NGO I call Aid the Qom, whose projects have an ongoing influence in the barrio. This charity NGO has been working in the barrio for the longest of all groups. Since 2005, the NGO has paid for tuition to a private Catholic school for many children in the barrio; it has created a day care in the barrio; and it regularly donates clothing, tools, and supplies for the library. This NGO has also been an important source of contacts; for example, it linked adult youth to the employment agency Manpower, which placed many in low-skilled jobs in the district, such as maintenance in the industrial complex.

Fernando explained that only his family enjoyed the full trust of Aid the Qom, expressing disappointment in other families in the barrio for lacking progress: He explained that the NGO covers tuition for many kids, but very few graduated from high school. Proudly pointing to his wall with graduation photos of his two daughters, Fernando recounted: "Last year, Juan [from Aid the Qom] asked me: Why? Why aren't other families like yours? You're the only ones seizing the opportunities we provide." After graduating from high school, Fernando's older daughter, Selena, became his "right hand" in his work with Aid the Qom, and she was also the only person in the barrio attending university. Fernando explained that he had to convince Aid the Qom to keep paying children's school tuition when staff learned that two of the funded children had dropped out of school and had "fallen in *la joda*."

This small conflict is indicative of the tensions generated between people who help and families in the barrio. The NGOs deliver assistance that is accompanied by an expectation of improvement as measured by specific indicators, in this case, obtaining a high school degree. Fernando and his family had met those expectations, but with effort. Fernando's family had to acquire specific habits; his daughters did their homework and asked for help when facing difficulties. In contrast, most Qom children are known to be "shy," which others, as Juan, explained as a reaction to the perceived racism of teachers, who "would assume Qom kids are dumb." When I had a chance to speak with Selena and her sister, Teresa, alone, she recognized that graduating had not been easy at all and that she had to swallow her rage at teachers' racist comments very often through the years of schooling. As a whole, the family had to demonstrate the desired signs of improvement, which were materialized, too, in their home, neatly painted and decorated, unlike other houses.

By showing signs of "improvement," Fernando and his family moved from being seen as just "victims" to being considered worthy, model "victims." They obtained more support and were able to mediate the assistance of other families in the barrio. For Fernando, then, managing help was about developing habits that enabled him to be regarded as trustworthy by the NGO and other institutions. Furthermore, he said that "help" was not one-sided, and he recognized that by receiving everyone who wanted to meet them as Qom, he helps visitors by sharing about Indigenous culture and providing the experience of chatting with an Indigenous leader. Thus, Fernando manages help in two directions: He distributes assistance to the families in the barrio and his relatives in the Chaco, and he allows visitors to experience "Qom culture."

While other families have not been so efficient in keeping up projects with so many groups, many families welcome the visitors and seek to maintain these relationships. Another aspect of the management of assistance is the work to incorporate the groups that help into a routine of frequent visits and when necessary, redirecting the work into other activities beyond the ones that had been initially planned. As it is for Fernando, the practice of hosting visitors in Qom homes is an important part of maintaining relations. In the visits, the new projects are planned and logistics are discussed; they are also moments for maintaining social links active. Most visits begin with questions about the well-being of the visitors' relatives and news. Visits are long, and people spend considerable time chatting while drinking mate and reflecting. Qom from the barrio also maintain relations by staying in touch through text messages, checking in and sending greetings. This intense socialization is not restricted to the barrio in Buenos Aires, and it is related to the maintenance of assemblages across space and through time, which I discuss in the next chapter.

In the barrio, families describe with sadness having lost contact with "people who help" from the capital. They describe this as an unfixable loss, because they lose their contact information (e.g., address, phone number) or because they lose a cell phone with contact numbers they cannot recover. Unlike the cities and towns in the Chaco where Qom families can trace people who help by showing up at their house or work, the relations with people who help from the capital can be lost without a trace. Different men and women explained with sadness how they had lost touch with a group or person who used to visit them frequently, and they lamented when regular contact was interrupted. The main critique of people who help is, in fact, the interrupted visits, which they see as a lack of commitment. In their narratives, they stressed how they missed the group of people more than the activities they carried out, which reinforces my analysis of the "projects" of the people who help as often secondary in importance to the relationship itself.

A final point is that these relations also shape a disconnection. Families in the barrio have actively disconnected from social movements around them. For example, the *piqueteros* (movement of the unemployed) has a strong connection to all the barrios in the area, but not to the Barrio Qom. When I took the train to the barrio and back, I often saw *piqueteros* traveling downtown for a demonstration or saw their *local* (a small shop acting as a community center) open for an activity. Even though most people from the barrio were unemployed or semi-employed, nobody I met was connected to *piqueteros.* This lack of connection with an organization that is close and accessible is also indicative of how the Qom prioritized relations with people who help over other associations.

These encounters were, therefore, affective and spatialized in that, in Spinoza's terms, they transformed the capacities of action and the possibilities of moving around the city of the people involved.[20] While middle-class people have a "default" possibility to move out of downtown Buenos Aires and go to a place of "authentic Indigenous People," the Qom are more limited in their possibilities to move around the city. The connections with the people who help significantly extended their possibilities and allowed them to visit downtown Buenos Aires; it also improved the possibility of accessing downtown when they were in the *villas*. Yet the relations are also about staying "fixed" in place because they needed to wait for visitors to show up. Encounters unfolded variations of intensity: When middle-class people arrived in the barrio, they were thrilled to "meet the Indigenous People" and enthusiastic about helping; the motivation literally moved them to continue to show up, and they stopped visiting when their excitement faded.

For both groups, the visits, being there in person, mattered and was productive of who they are. The creation of different racial subjectivities resulted, too, from these embodied encounters, which re-create difference as an embodied racial difference between brown Qom people and white, European-descent, middle-class people who help. This contact further reinforced the Qom as Indigenous and people who help as white moral subjects, even as they came out of their middle-class spaces in the city. This "racial proximity," to use Mawani's term, produced not only a dichotomy of dark-skinned rural Indigenous and white, urban, middle-class subjects but also a variation and gradation within categories.[21] White people who help became moral subjects, adventurous, helping those who deserved their care, while the Qom became recognized by them and the institutions they represented as different from the racialized, Indigenous-descent *negros villeros*. These encounters implied the construction of a common space and routine temporality, one that created a form of intimacy and familiarity while the connections lasted.[22]

The encounters with the groups who regularly visit the barrio are productive, too, in that they allow families to redirect the "help" toward activities they were not originally planning to be involved in. They thus incorporate the work, connections, and resources of the people who visit the barrio into other activities of the assemblages of families. They redirect efforts, for example, asking for rides in a car that were not initially planned, which might be related to, for example, doing a favor for a relative in the Chaco or incorporating activities into larger connections such as turning a music workshop in the barrio into a chance to request help in filling out a state assistance application. Incorporation (or composition) is different from "negotiation," as in negotiation, the parties involved make concessions and strategize. In composing relations and assembling the help, there is no compromise, but an expansion of the possibilities of action.

For example, Julio asked Qom Art, which conducted drumming classes on Saturdays, if its members could find a market fair where he and his wife could sell handicrafts. They got in touch with a market in the capital and made the arrangements to get a spot for Julio's wife. The day of the market, Natalia, a Qom Art member, picked up Julio and his wife and drove them to the market. This kind of redirection of help is common; it may involve small requests such as asking for help fixing a computer or getting a ride to the capital, but it also includes assistance with filling out government forms and performing other bureaucratic procedures. In the rest of this section, I focus on this specific form of reorienting help, deployed as a strategy against the restricted access to state institutions.

Visitors who go to the barrio frequently end up supporting Qoms' access to state institutions, including the municipal hospital and national offices in the capital. One of the most striking instances of help being redirected was when a man in the barrio had difficulties obtaining his national ID.[23] Martín, in his sixties, needed to obtain a *monotributo*, the equivalent of a social insurance number, in order to get paid for a language workshop, so I offered to go to the office with him. The day he went to the office, Martín explained that he had lost his ID, which was necessary for all state bureaucratic procedures, and police often requested it when they stopped nonwhite, working-class men.[24] As we already knew, at the agency, an employee explained to us that she could not process the request without the ID. From that moment on, a long search started. Martín talked with the social worker who assists the barrio and concluded that she was of no help because she requested his birth certificate; he explained it would be impossible to obtain. Martín contacted relatives back in the Chaco to try to get him a copy of his birth certificate, and they responded a couple of weeks later saying there was no record of him in the local registry. This is not uncommon; at the time of his birth, Indigenous newborns were completely unrecorded.[25] Martín explained that he had obtained his ID previously without a birth certificate at a documentation campaign in the Chaco, when he was a young adult. Thus, Martín asked if I had any connections at the ID office to issue a new document without presenting a birth certificate. I found it hard to believe that could be possible; it is almost impossible to do anything in Argentina without a birth certificate. However, Martín insisted, and every time he saw any new person who helps coming to visit the barrio, he asked if they had a connection.

We explored many options with other colleagues, but after one month, we were frustrated; there was no avenue for requesting the ID. Finally, one day, Martín got a visit from a woman working as an administrator at a school where he had gone to play music. She had a friend who was an assistant at a national congressman's office. She arranged a meeting directly with him. The congressman met with Martín in his downtown office and walked with him to the ID office. The congressman explained Martín's irregular situation to the ID office employees, and the agency made an exception. Martín got his ID card issued and printed that same day. With the right contact in the city, he was able to solve a problem in one day that had gone unresolved for several months. In this situation, the redirection of help solves a major problem for him: the right to an ID.

Martín's access to his ID reveals the way many people in the barrio understand their relation with institutions. To solve his problem, Martín extended networks and redirected visits, asking every new person he met for help. He knew that having been born in a Qom rural community, he was in an exceptional situation in regard to citizenship, with no access to documentation, a fundamental human right that Indigenous people were denied by inaction, negligence, and state abandonment in the communities.[26] Thus, Martín searched for a "contact" until he eventually succeeded. He appropriated and reoriented his relations with people who help by mobilizing their networks to solve his lack of access to the right to his citizenship record. When middle-class visitors had met with him for other reasons, we all involved ourselves in helping him obtain his ID card, redirecting our work to solve this problem.[27]

This experience is also indicative of urban Qom access to basic citizenship rights and to state institutions. Even when they want to follow every required step, they may find themselves in an anomalous situation, missing an ID or another document. In a similar experience, Juan, another Qom man attempting to obtain his ID, found that his birth certificate had been lost in a fire. Indeed, with time, I learned that this ID problem was experienced by many children who had been born in Buenos Aires and whose parents did not know how to register them. Parents had no idea about how to request a birth certificate at the hospital or documentation agencies. In contrast, in the Chaco, towns and offices are nearby, and political brokers often support such documentation. Because most Qom in the barrio are not registered as legally residing in Buenos Aires, and because their small numbers make them irrelevant as a group of interest to political brokers, they are not the target of patronage relations as other barrios and the Qom in the Chaco are. In the Barrio Qom in Sauces district, the people who help become key actors for Qom in accessing state institutions: They helped complete forms, drove people to offices, and accompanied those aiming to avoid bureaucrats' mistreatment (and racism).

The lack of access to basic citizenship rights situates the Qom similarly to subaltern and international migrants in the city, who need to go through complex bureaucracy to obtain a permanent residency.[28] Any bureaucratic procedure was, for the Qom, subject to uncertainty and arbitrariness: Without assistance, procedures may be very hard to follow and never-ending. Facing uncertain bureaucratic procedures full of discretionary elements that constantly defer an outcome is a regular path to access a national ID—what is at stake, too, is access to the citizenship right to identity and state assistance, an experience that Javier Auyero identifies among impoverished and subaltern groups in Buenos Aires.[29]

The Qom find themselves entrenched in mechanisms that systematically deny them citizenship rights, evident in the routine practice of enduring long waits in state offices amid bureaucratic uncertainties, what Auyero refers to as a construction of a "denizen," or denied citizen," condition. While he primarily identifies the impoverished and migrants as subjects of this predicament, it's essential to acknowledge the urban Indigenous as another subaltern group subjected to passive denial of rights through deferral, with always shifting requirements the result of bureaucratic discretion and arbitrariness. Qom experiences with state institutions also demonstrates the depth and relevance of the relationships of help, in that they expand Qom assemblages to confront mechanisms of their political subordination.

This reorientation of help compensates for the absence of political brokers, barriers to accessing state institutions, and the failure of institutions themselves to be accessible to people in the barrio. In this way, Qom in the barrio have established direct connections with people who help, replacing dependence on political brokers as a means to access citizen rights.

The expansion of assemblages through help is not restricted to commercializing handicrafts and commodifying ethnicity, as the Comaroffs have noted, but to political relations, in that people who help were also fundamental allies in the negotiations for the barrio's land. Help is thus embedded in a central but contradictory way in the possibilities of the Qom shaping an Indigenous life in the city in the wake of their recognition.[30]

Romanticizing Community

During my time in the barrio, I saw how families scarcely worked together. This was also a topic of conversation among other people. For example, one day, I joined Beatriz and Lidia in the kitchen of the barrio's community center to help them cook empanadas to sell during a music festival in the barrio. As the time came to assemble the empanadas, Beatriz sent Lidia to look for her sister-in-law to help. Lidia came back alone; she explained that her in-law was tired because she had worked all evening in an activity with another group who helps. Lidia commented, "Things are not as they used to be; people do not work together anymore." Refusing to work together, as many people explained, was because families are related to the multiple visitors in the barrio and to multiple simultaneous projects. No single project could include all barrio families, and families were drawn in different directions. Sometimes this generated tension, for as when a group of researchers offered Iván the chance to travel with them to the Chaco. Ricardo and Andrea, who had collaborated with the group intensively, felt betrayed when they were not asked to join the trip. Raúl and Andrea are a couple, so it was easier for the researchers to take Iván, a widow, and they made that decision at the last minute. For Ricardo and Andrea, missing out on the possibility of travel and to see their relatives meant that they had engaged in hours of volunteer labor without compensation. Thus, when groups that help associate with different families, they (myself too) also generated tensions among those families. Families also subtly manage middle-class groups by promoting competition between them. For example, during our workshop, we were compared with other groups that brought snacks, which was a way to ask us to do more.

Reflecting on this, Silvia explained that, initially, all families in the barrio worked together, but things had changed, and every family "was by themselves." She remembered with a tone of nostalgia that all women used to cooked together when there was a celebration at the community center, but "now everyone is busy with their own work." I was also surprised when Marcos, a man in his sixties, told me that his adult nephew had "stolen" a school workshop from him. Because Marcos did not have a cell phone and relied on his nephew to be contacted, his nephew diverted the invitations for Marcos to himself. Marcos's nephew went to the school and received payment for the workshop.

During my fieldwork, the NGO Aid the Qom facilitated the largest family gathering I observed. Each family was asked to send a representative to a meeting for planning the expansion of family houses in the barrio. Construction teams were formed at the meeting, comprising four male members from each family. The teams were tasked with rotating in the construction of each member's house, so each team member would work on the other members' houses and on their own. The NGO requested strict cooperation among team members, making it a requisite for receiving construction materials. Failure to make progress would result in the NGO withholding further materials, such as bricks and cement, needed to complete construction.

This seemingly forced cooperation was a source of major tension throughout the project. For many weeks, the topic came up in conversation, and people blamed one another for the lack of progress at particular houses. The reasons men missed a day of work were understandable, as many worked in short-term contracts. Their employment was volatile, and they needed to take every opportunity they were offered, most of which were last-minute requests for manual labor. These reasons can be considered "productive" in contrast to imaginations of the NGO workers who thought they were lazy or lacked work ethic. This also demonstrated how, to a charitable NGO, the Qom were victims waiting to be saved, idle in their daily lives, and they would adapt and commit to the NGO's suggested project. The NGO ideal of working with a "community" whose members collaborate with one another was challenged by the tensions and competition between families. Even when the NGO wanted to impose cooperation, it did not consider the complexity of the lives of the Qom, which are subjected to the demands of short-term contracts and the challenges of care. Some families did not complete the work and lost the chance to receive construction materials, which disappointed them and the NGO alike.

Another recurrent point of frustration across several groups is when resources such as a big donation of secondhand clothing are distributed in each family's specific networks instead of reaching every household in the barrio. Instead, families in the barrio tend to prioritize relatives in the Chaco and relations outside the barrio. This is seen by groups who help as mismanagement, and some suggested that it was perhaps a form of corruption, that they should trace where the donation ended up and identify specific needs elsewhere in the Qom assemblages.

The Qom in the barrio circulated resources within networks that send resources to barrios in other cities as part of larger activities, such as selling handicrafts or supporting a *piogonak* (shaman) from the Chaco in visiting the barrio, which has no active shaman among its members. While Qom assemblages separate families in the barrio along kinship lines, relations created through the church communities, and past relations in other barrios, when barrio families do not share with one another, NGOs often interpret this as a sign of mismanagement. Often, NGOs cannot avoid seeing the barrio as one community, and NGO workers expect it to function as a horizontal, harmonious group of people.

Collaboration between families in the barrio is never totally broken: Families share and support one another beyond what is typical in other sectors of society. I saw how Martín, the barrio's most recognized musician, shared his *nvike*, a one-stringed violin he built himself, with Ricardo, who is not in his networks and did not know how to play the violin, so that he could play a few chords at a school workshop. I also saw a generalized borrowing and lending of tools and house supplies. I saw several families across the barrio, many of whom are not friends or collaborators, using Lorenzo's lawn mower. I was surprised to see a washing machine being borrowed and returned weekly to Mariana, a young woman living in a shack on the soccer field. Women would show up and carry the machine on a cart across the muddy field and bumpy road into their houses many blocks away, what Mariana considered a small gesture when I asked her. This ethics of sharing shows how the resources of groups who help become intertwined with complex sharing practices and with separation, as money and food cannot be openly distributed when a family has to meet the basic needs of its members.

The restricted use of donations and other resources that groups that help consider and expect to be "common" in the barrio is seen as a form of mismanagement and is a major source of disillusionment among people who help. The expectations of people who help is to work with Indigenous people who have no individual self-interest, who work together and share the resources they provide in the manner that they imagine they will. Romantic ideas about a "primitive communism" are projected onto the Qom as part of the imaginations of them as "authentic" hunter-gatherers from the Chaco.

Furthermore, the barrio is imagined as a cohesive group, integrated by people who share blood relations and migrated together to Buenos Aires. All these are the common representations of what a community is and should be.[31] People who help avoid recognizing families as having deep relationships elsewhere, as seeing them as linked with different communities, even when they share a common history as Qom people of the central Chaco. As explored in Chapter 1, families have had different migration trajectories to the city and different settling histories.

The disappointment in not finding the romanticized community they expected, along with the perception of a supposed lack of progress as they had envisioned, contributed to a sense of tiredness among the groups that helped, leading many to discontinue their work in the barrio. For example, a social worker who was formerly involved in the barrio explained her disillusionment in detail. The social worker expressed how much they had looked forward to working with a community like the one in the Barrio Qom. Upon arriving in the barrio, they were happy and made many plans. However, as time went on, they became drained. She narrated that the community asked for a health station, so they brought in a doctor and raised funds for basic equipment; but the equipment was stolen (probably by a local gang from a neighboring area), and the doctor refused to continue working. The community also requested a school, and the social worker helped establish a high school annex in the barrio, but students kept dropping out every term. The social worker had set up an office at the community center, but people failed to show up, and instead asked them to visit their homes, one by one. For the group helping, this was the final straw. Its members felt they had "given everything" but saw no improvement in return, and as a result, they gave up and decided to work only from their office from then on.

The efforts of this social worker are not to be disregarded. However, in this initiative, there is also a series of problematic expectations. It is a simplified expectation to believe that the structural problems of the Qom people regarding the educational system can be solved by creating a school closer to the families' homes, or that frictions with state institutions, such as being denied the right to an ID, can be overcome in the relationship of this social worker with the Qom. In this example, we see the type of deterioration of the relationship when people who help maintain their expectations, unchanged, and romanticize the Qom as an Indigenous ideal throughout their work.

Groups that help tend to value specific signs of collective transformation and progress. They expect a full cohort to graduate from high school, or for families to organize collectively and selflessly forget other work opportunities to expand. Even people from activist circles had specific expectation about what it is to be politically engaged and active. In short, families are expected to demonstrate efforts toward self-improvement, proving themselves deserving of assistance and deserving engagement.[32] Meanwhile, other groups expect them to become vanguard activists and be at the center of activities in the agenda of reputable leftist organizations, which the families in the barrio also "fail" to become (in the eyes of activists).

The Qom in the barrio maintain long-term relationships with people who provide concrete assistance in specific projects and who develop personal relationships through time. These visitors often show genuine enthusiasm for any progress made, exemplified by Laura, a dedicated school administrator who fundraised for a water pump for a Chaco village and then traveled with a family to install it. I met her after her trip, which she narrated as full of adventures with transporting and installing the pump, something she had no experience doing. For her, the obstacles had become anecdotes; she felt proud to have worked together with urban and rural Qom families to solve every problem in installing the pump. Numerous researchers, especially one team organizing language workshops over four years, sustain long-term commitments and connections. Researchers often involve their families, who visit the barrio alongside them, including their children, partners, and parents, which for the Qom is a more meaningful form of socializing in which people engage their kin relations in larger collaboration.

Apart from this exception, the families in the Barrio Qom are expected to embody these conflicting imaginations about what Indigenous people should be, representations affected by images of the Chaco as "primitive" societies of hunter-gatherers, as classical anthropology described.[33] Under this, the encounter with Indigenous people in the city generates shock and befuddlement in people who help as they get to know this group of people they see as radical others. And yet people who help are immersed too in the larger dominant media concerns that infuse constant fear of the city and the nation becoming "dark," the French architecture of downtown Buenos Aires being taken over by the brown and Indigenous bodies of Peronists, migrants, and shantytown dwellers. This fear is of Indigenous people remerging as "malones"—Indigenous raiders from the past who are today embodied by the politicized negros.[34] The barrio is perhaps a place where it is possible to imagine a romanticized relationship with spiritual, radical, earnest, communitarian Indigenous people by shaping it as a different place, one detached from the Conurbano and shantytowns. As mentioned, when groups that help find there is not a community in whichever way they expected, they leave the barrio.

Closely Distant

In 2006, a progressive newspaper published an article about the Barrio Qom. The article plays with images of modernity (e.g., the city, rock music) and tradition (e.g., the Chaco, "real Indians") and portrays the Qom as embodying this tension. What I found even more interesting is how these tensions are spatialized by the author, who, describing his arrival in the barrio as an adventure, wrote: "One has to go more kilometers than one thinks to get there. We are in the outskirts of the city looking for a Qom community that someone told us is around here. We are looking for a settlement of pure aboriginal people. [When we find them, we see] the Qom Indians were sent behind a garbage dump in the middle of nowhere. Even more: they have no nearby river like the Bermejo [in the Chaco]."[35] This is another example of the images that shape the Barrio Qom as an exoticized place. The author highlights that he traveled "more kilometers than one thinks"—the barrio is a few blocks away from gated communities. There is a sense of adventure—"We are . . . looking for a Qom community someone told us is around here." There is also a sense of connection and contrast to the Chaco and a reference to poverty that permeates media representations of Qom people as proximate to the garbage dump. In the narrative, the dump appears in place of the river, as if the urbanization of Indigenous people inevitably leads to poverty and a loss of their original harmony with nature and the river. The barrio's assumed exoticism is thus not restricted to the groups that work in the barrio and is fed by media representations about the Qom, and in this particular article, about the barrio as spatially distant and exotic.

While the article (one of around four mainstream media journalistic reports about the barrio) is dominated by observations about how heterogeneous the space of Conurbano is and how close the highway takes one, the journalist is interested only in separation and distance. In this exaggerated distance from downtown Buenos Aires, something authentic and revealing is to be found—namely, "pure aboriginal people." We can sense the excitement: This interview is not just with another suburban group, but with "pure aboriginal people." These paragraphs condense the idea that, to clearly define a group as a target of "help," its members must be grounded in a specific place: the barrio as a place of difference, more connected to the Chaco than to Buenos Aires, and not fully belonging to the city.

In this article, the journalist presents himself as a middle-class professional and a sensitive person who physically moves outside the city's comforts to encounter the Qom. Furthermore, in this commuting, he reveals what "Argentina is really about," and he transforms himself by finding a specific, supposedly new truth about the city and urban indigeneity: In this case, the barrio has youth who are Qom and listen to rock music. This is a narrative line that, with variations, underlines many of the groups that help when they explain their work.

This chapter has highlighted aspects of the everyday relation between Qoms and the people from the urban white middle classes who visit the barrio. These relations take place out of the spatial possibilities the barrio enables: The barrio is a place where these groups meet and constitute themselves as racially different in a long tradition of charity and humanitarianism. The encounter of Qom and groups that help produces specific racialized subjectivities, one that follows tropes of contemporary humanitarian relations but results from specific tensions of the city's racial formation and one in which indigeneity is either erased or romanticized, denied yet feared as ubiquitous in the figure of the *negros villeros* that implies an Indigenous continuity.[36]

If transnational humanitarianism creates relations where a generic, economically advanced West helps a third world that is also dark and experiencing an eventful crisis, humanitarian encounters re-create racialized subjects whose distinction from one another is emphasized. Furthermore, in these relations, aid workers become "good" white people, and victims are understood as "culturally backward" people unable to control the events they suffer.[37] The relation produces a moral imperative to save certain victims. In their everydayness, the projects allow the groups to shape themselves as specific types of white and dark-skinned people. This approach is socially and affectively productive, as both groups mutually benefit in the encounter, but it also defines the conditions of subsequent disillusionment. The Qom more often than not cannot meet the different expectations set by the groups, and the latter end up leaving their work in the barrio. The affective arch from intensity to disintegration re-creates the groups but also introduces some variations in what each can do.

These relations start from unequal possibilities of moving through the space of the city. Since their arrival the Qom have had a hard time accessing the city center and have experienced a policing of their bodies in downtown

Buenos Aires, while the white middle class has the privilege of living in downtown Buenos Aires and access to fast methods of travel; they can get in their cars and drive to the barrio in forty minutes. Once more, white subjectivities in this relation are shaped through movement and exploration, whereas the Qom are expected to be in place, in the barrio, waiting for a visit.

Schematically, the barrio is a piece of the Chaco in Buenos Aires; the Buenos Aires city center is produced as a place of modernity, inhabited by white Argentineans (who police the movement of nonwhite bodies in it) who reach out to help those in need, while the Chaco becomes a distant and mysterious place that still hosts authentic Indigenous people. In these encounters, both groups transform the possibilities of moving through space. Qom families access schools, market fairs, government offices, and cultural centers; they become authentic Indigenous in the city. For their own part, middle-class groups access a barrio of "pure Indigenous people," "save" people with their food donations, teach them how to cooperate to build their own houses, and travel to the Chaco to meet Indigenous leaders engaged in "serious" land struggles.

In this relation, both groups produce variations of the simplified racial distinction between white and nonwhite. The Qom are re-created as "authentic Indians from the Chaco," a form of nonwhiteness that, as I argued in Chapter 3, is more valuable in the city than being a *negro villero*. At the same time, the "people who help" reinforce their whiteness in their contrast to the Qom and produce a variation of it. They perform work on themselves and become sensitive, charitable, and progressive—"people who do good." A politics of contact allows focusing on the encounter itself, the changing intensities of the relation, and the effects of continuous collaborations. In the next chapter, I extend an exploration of contact into the networks that link the Barrio Qom with multiple other locations.

CHAPTER 5

Subaltern Assemblages

Extending Spatial Control Through Multiple Associations

Connecting Heterogeneous Elements

The families who donated clothes and food for "the starving Indigenous people of the Chaco" during Miguel and Leandro's visit to a public school in a lower-middle-class neighborhood in Buenos Aires were probably expecting the donations to end up in a distant rural village in the Chaco. A few months earlier, the TV news had been full of images of flooded houses in the Chaco, with sick adults and malnourished children under headlines of "nutritional emergency." An NGO report claimed that half a dozen Indigenous people had died of hunger in the province.[1] As we carried bags of secondhand clothes, canned food, and blankets, among other things, to a small truck parked by the sidewalk, the headmaster confirmed this: "As soon as we heard it was for the Chaco, every family gave as much as possible." But the distribution of these objects followed complex trajectories. I estimated that half the items stayed in the area of the Barrio Qom in Buenos Aires, a few were sent to other Qom barrios in Rosario, and around 40 percent ended up in rural villages in the Chaco. This was not the product of the "mismanagement" of donations, but a distribution that went beyond what humanitarian action shown on the TV news could anticipate.

This chapter examines how people, objects, and relations in the Barrio Qom in Buenos Aires get entangled with others in distant locations. I draw on the concept of assemblages to trace how Qom people create networks of social and nonhuman relationships that get entangled nearby with distant communities and places beyond. For Deleuze and Guattari, "the first concrete rule for assemblages is to discover what territoriality they envelop."[2] I have thus followed this provocation. These connections link heterogeneous agents, objects, and relations from diverse sites associated with activities such as the distribution of donated resources or the production of handicrafts. The Barrio Qom in Buenos Aires was a privileged site from which to trace the associations, as I could see, for example, how resources obtained from the urban middle class circulated to multiple communities in the Chaco. Traveling with people from the barrio to other barrios, in cities such as Rosario and Castelli, and to rural areas, such as Bermejito and Espinillo, further allowed me to trace associations across space to see how this subaltern spatiality is repeatedly remade across distance.

While Qom assemblages build on the ethnic connection of the Qom and networks of kin, community, or church relations associated with their recreation of indigeneity, I employ the concept of assemblage to highlight the heterogeneity of the elements that are brought together and connected in novel arrangements. The Qom connect with other Qom, but their connections also extend beyond the specific boundaries of their group or what is agreed on in formal community organizations. In assemblages, an element gets a new purpose when it is put in connection with another for a specific activity; the emergent territoriality of an assemblage refers to the reach of an activity emerging from the location of the participating components.[3] Here, assemblages construct an Indigenous territoriality within and beyond recognized territories, communities, and organizations, including Qom and non-Indigenous people in Buenos Aires, periurban barrios in Santa Fe and the Chaco, and the forest and marshlands.[4]

In this work, a specific ethnic group organizes the connections. This therefore constitutes an ethnic network that fits the literature on diasporas that highlights the translocal cultural production generated beyond state jurisdictions. Assemblages are one modality of Indigenous diaspora, a perspective from which rural-urban Indigenous links are examined and where Indigenous urban experience is regarded as a form of diaspora with respect to traditional territories.[5] By using the term *assemblage* instead of *diaspora*, I draw attention to the links that include but also transcend the specific ethnic relationships of Qom with other Qom people and leave open the possibility to discuss the activities that emerge in these connections.

The assemblage created with Leandro's and Martín's visit to the school had at its center Qom families spread out in different locations, but it also involved images circulating in the mass media, a school, and families in the Chaco who collected *totora* leaves in the bush and marshlands to produce baskets. Through such assemblages, people not only distribute objects but also collaborate to undertake bureaucratic procedures, solve problems (e.g., dealing with a teenager dropping out of school), and, in a few cases, build steady control over space. Assemblages reshape the spaces whose elements they connect, and in doing so, they create subaltern Indigenous spatiality: a form of control over space shaped by Qom relationships that re-creates a territoriality within and against the expropriation of their territory. This Indigenous Qom territoriality unfolds from a subaltern position of relative exteriority from formal politics and economy, generating connections beyond exclusive Qom ethnic relations.[6]

To trace the organization and productivity of assemblages that traverse the barrio, I first follow how, through these assemblages, people distribute goods. Second, by analyzing a trip to an Evangelical church event, I trace how relations re-create assemblages across time and space.[7] Finally, I analyze a case where one extended family constitutes an assemblage that coordinates activity across a wide area that links the barrio, Buenos Aires's city center, a town in the Chaco, and several farms, among other locations. I draw on my experience participating in workshops that people from the barrio deliver in the capital and on my travels with the Qom to the cities of Rosario (Santa Fe province), as well as Castelli and Sáenz Peña in Chaco province, including two rural localities in the area of Bermejito (north of Castelli).

Moving Packages: Activating Assemblages

Packages regularly circulate between the Barrio Qom and other Qom locations. Qom people from rural areas in the Chaco send packages of handicrafts and raw materials to the Barrio Qom in Buenos Aires for production and final assembly. Meanwhile, packages of secondhand clothing and canned food donated to the barrio are sent to the Chaco. In both directions, boxes are sent as *encomiendas* (a delivery service provided by bus companies) to and from towns and cities within and beyond the Chaco. When Martín and Leandro, the men in charge of the workshop mentioned earlier, received the items collected by the school, they embarked on the careful labor of distribution. First, they kept a portion of the food for themselves and took the clothes that would fit Leandro's four sons and daughter. Martín's family is not the poorest in the barrio; he and his son Leandro are recognized musicians who regularly perform music at events in the capital. But neither has a steady income, and they are often paid in donations. There are months in which they barely make ends meet, they eat only once a day, and Leandro's children lacked shoes at the start of the school year. Keeping part of the donated food, therefore, allowed them to eat for several weeks. After setting some of the items aside for their families, then, they distributed the other clothes and food, placing donated objects into smaller boxes and earmarking them for recipients outside the nuclear family. Their answers were brief and elusive when I asked about the distribution, revealing that this distribution generates conflicts, because anyone who does not receive something feels left out.

Martín told me they had immediately given many of the clothes and some of the food to a neighbor, a widow living outside the Barrio Qom with five children. She is neither Qom nor a relative, but her children regularly ask around for food and money. They decided they needed the items the most and gave them a large amount of them. When I asked Leandro about the distribution, he explained he was going to send two boxes to the Barrio Qom in Castelli (Chaco) where he used to live. Two cousins were taking care of his house there, and they would distribute the items among people in the community. "In the Chaco, everyone is in need. Everything is hard to get: clothes, blankets; everything is useful," Leandro explained to me. He also mentioned he was considering moving back to the Chaco, and so the cousins taking care of his house would have to move out. By sending them a package, he could make himself present and smooth potential future tensions. Two weeks later, Leandro's wife Carolina went to the bus station to send an *encomienda* to her mother in a rural village a few kilometers west of Castelli to reciprocate the handicrafts her mother regularly sends from the Chaco and that Carolina sells in the city. That day, Carolina also sent a package to a brother living in town, who was helping her get a provincial subsidy in the Chaco (where she was still registered as a resident) through a local *puntero*, a political broker (another strategy within the assemblage). Finally, a month later, a prestigious shaman visited the barrio and performed healing sessions for Martín to cure his headaches. On another visit, I saw a small box Martín had packed for him with the last of the donated items.

The packages sent to Castelli and the villages were carefully packed and moved on. The goods were put into cardboard boxes that were taped up; names of recipients were handwritten on the boxes; and the packages were taken to the bus station and sent as *encomiendas* directly to towns in the Chaco (or to the Qom barrios in Santa Fe). In my travels to the Chaco, I saw the other end of this circulation: Relatives pick up the packages at the bus station and take them home. Some recipients, such as Leandro's relatives, lived in the town where the package was delivered so biked the goods home. Others (like Carolina's mother) lived in villages a distance from town and needed to take boxes by motorcycle. When packages were bigger or more numerous, people in the villages either made several trips or needed to hire a rental car or truck.

This is one example of the habitual movements of objects back and forth, connecting the barrio in Buenos Aires with other Qom communities and locations where these connections spread out still further, such as downtown Buenos Aires. This is not unique to this particular Qom barrio, in that handicraft production with materials sent by relatives from rural areas is a generalized economic activity, in particular for landless Qom people or Qom migrants to the city who need cash income. Diasporic activity based on the circulation of goods from home to the location of migration is, moreover, widely documented.[8] In Argentina, Bolivian and Paraguayan communities likewise send home consumer goods from Buenos Aires and receive, in turn, food for personal consumption and to sell in fairs. However, the generalized production of "ethnic" handicrafts is less central in other communities, where the emphasis is on participating in popular economies and sending remittances.[9] Studies also show how migrants to the city use consumer items to generate narratives of success when they go back to their hometowns.[10]

To account for the complexity of the connections, diasporas have already begun to be conceptualized as assemblages.[11] A particularity of the Qom exchanges is that they do send resources not simply from one place to be consumed in another but also to enable active coproduction across space. For example, instead of finished handicrafts, many families send materials to produce the handicrafts elsewhere. More significant is the support Carolina receives to request a subsidy as a Chaco resident. Seeing this circulation and these activities as assemblages highlights coordinated actions that go beyond merely sending and receiving. Deleuze and Guattari show that elements of an assemblage are fragments that have unfolded from other arrangements. These arrangements are also spatial. Qom assemblages stretch outside the Chaco and connect heterogeneous places: rural communities, the bush, towns, and cities in the Chaco and Buenos Aires. The specificity of the elements and their organization is what shapes the assemblage. In this case, the specificity of the objects donated mattered, as the canned food was saved for consumption or shared with others who needed it.

Moreover, the assemblages created through sending packages activate both the spatial connections between locations and specific relationships that are not only a matter of ethnic identity. The connection with the neighbor in need is one example of the way distribution does not follow only norms of reciprocity defined by kinship and ethnicity. The assemblages were also organized around unpredictable and specific circumstances.

The assemblages' activity is not predictable or regular, either. The distribution described earlier was not part of a regular event or seasonal rhythm; it was in response to conjunctural events. The people in the barrio had no control over the floods in the Chaco or the fact that, at that moment and not others, the media would draw attention to the ongoing predicament of malnourishment in the Chaco. When the mass media disseminated images of hunger in the Chaco, and the school contacted Leandro and Martín to organize a donation campaign, what started to take shape was an assemblage of objects distributed from Buenos Aires to the Conurbano and on to the Chaco. However efficiently the unfolded connections redistributed the goods, there was no guarantee that this assemblage would endure or be re-created in the same way in the future.

All these elements and relations are fragments extracted from other forms of relation (e.g., the middle class's out-of-date fashion, the mass media construction of news about crisis, a school's effort to learn about Indigenous people) and given new functions, generating new activity—in this case, the distribution of clothes and items that are unaffordable for the widowed neighbor or in rural communities. The elements in circulation reorganize the place from which they were extracted and, if only slightly, also reorganize the school, the barrio, and the villages in the Chaco where the boxes arrive. The assemblage also reorients people's actions in these places. For example, people in the Chaco who receive the packages will go on to redistribute the items and be ready to reciprocate when asked, as when Martín needed his birth certificate.

But what linked the elements together in this assemblage was not a smooth confluence or a frictionless "flow" of objects from place to place. The workshop required preparation: A teacher got Leandro's phone number from a friend and called him to arrange the visit; Martín and Leandro had to travel to the school in the Buenos Aires barrio of Flores, lugging a big box of handicrafts and baskets. When people from the Chaco send materials for handicraft production, the connection is not easy, either. Because the vegetable fibers used to weave baskets are found in the countryside, people in the villages send large quantities to the Barrio Qom in Buenos Aires and send baskets they have already made. *Totora* and palm-tree leaves are heavy and do not fit neatly in a box, so palm leaves are packed in square packages and wrapped in cloth, tied with string, and *totora* leaves are tied together in cylindrical packs. Women who make handicrafts need the leaves to be long to weave strong baskets. So people in the Chaco make sure the *totora* leaves are not broken or damaged in the trip when sent as *encomiendas* to Buenos Aires.

In the Chaco, people take the *totora* packages to the bus station, often balancing huge packages on the back of a bike. At the bus station, they face another problem. Andrea explained that when a bus company first takes the packages, there are often complaints that they are too dirty, too big, or too oddly shaped, and bus drivers may refuse to carry them. But there are now bus companies where drivers know about these exchanges and have made a habit of carrying them. When the packages arrive at the Retiro bus station in Buenos Aires, there is still over an hour of travel to get to the barrio. *Remises* in the train station near the Barrio Qom are also used to transport handicraft materials, and they are not known to complain about them. They have a standard fee for the packages, charging each large package as an additional passenger.

Connecting Buenos Aires and the Chaco is, then, not effortless "work" in which two elements simply converge to generate an action. Deleuze and Guattari argue that desire is the force that put bodies in motion, connects them to other bodies, and produces new connections: "The question posed by desire is not 'What does it mean?' but rather 'How does it work?'" They continue: "It represents nothing, but it produces. It means nothing, but it works."[12] Here they are thinking of desire not in its psychoanalytic or even personal, emotional vein, but rather as a force that sets relations in motion. Here, too, I am interested in the activity that constructs connections between the Barrio Qom, the school, and rural communities. Indeed, the Qom call this general disposition to activate relationships, to find solutions to economic precarity, and to solve problems *tener ganas* (to be willing): a driving force that produces a life despite the multiple structural challenges of impoverishment, ongoing displacement, racism, and so on. They worry when a person lacks such a drive, or when *se le fueron las ganas*, that is, when a person's will abandoned them. In such cases, there is a collective effort to push the person to get active again. Indeed, many parents of teenagers were constantly looking for ways to *dar ánimo* to the kids. One mother explicitly asked me to try to bring back *ganas* to his son, who had dropped school after being a very good student.

Connection poses the question of how elements come together in the first place. In this case, connecting is not just an easy meeting up. Instead, it implies effort and some determination, just as it requires effort to move packages across space. The dynamics of connection are social but also material and nonhuman. To transport handicrafts, Qom families take particular care to establish good relations with bus drivers, bus companies, and *remise* owners. Connections, therefore, always imply effort and friction. The material qualities of *totora* and palm leaves imply that these elements do not "flow" from rural villages in the Chaco to the Barrio Qom in Buenos Aires, but travel in rough conditions, on bike racks across dirt roads. The characteristics of the packages require people and vehicles to move despite the frictions that slow them down. Efforts to overcome those frictions that impede movement have a limit, and when packages are too heavy, or when bus drivers are not in the habit, friction may stop movement altogether.

While some connections that are activated when an assemblage distributes packages can be partially expected because of kinship obligations, others are more circumstantial or the product of spatial proximity. For instance, Martín and Leandro had no reason to share donated clothes with the widow. She was not a relative, nor was she Qom, and she was not a fellow church member. But she lived close by and sent her children around to ask for food because she had no other options. This connection, therefore, extended the assemblage beyond the extended family members working together. Unexpected lines of connectivity both extend and threaten the assemblage's activity. There was some risk in sharing with the neighbor widow, as Martín and Leandro could have ended up not having enough to give to Carolina's mother, which could have resulted in potential conflicts for not having shared. In fact, Martín felt indebted to the shaman and paid him with his own cell phone, since he considered the box of donations not enough. The ad hoc and conjunctural nature of the networks shifts the emphasis of relations and the spatiality of distributed packages.

For every element in the assemblage, the circulation of secondhand clothes and handicraft materials is productive and has an important role in families' economic subsistence. At one end, it allows families in the Barrio Qom in Buenos Aires to produce the handicrafts they sell and generate much-needed cash income. At the other end, it gives families in rural areas access to valuable goods.[13] In the Chaco countryside, people wait expectantly for packages of donations. While food can be partly obtained in many rural villages through subsistence agriculture or gathering, fishing, and hunting, in contrast, clothes, supplies for the house, and bicycles are expensive and hard to obtain in the Chaco, even for families with cash income. At both ends, the circulation of goods between the Barrio Qom in Buenos Aires, other barrios, and rural areas offers an alternative to unemployment and low-paid jobs.

In the case of donated clothing, color, texture, and style matter. Most people in the Chaco value a nice baseball cap or a fashionable silky shirt. In the Chaco, such items cannot be found easily or at an affordable price. The circulation of packages allows access to such "nice" things for families in the city and the countryside, and it enables participation in consumption habits they could not access otherwise. People in marginal barrios in cities and towns, and even in remote villages, regularly watch TV and see shop windows in towns and city centers: They have seen what they cannot afford to have. Donations enable people living in a "faraway" village to participate in the globalized desire for certain goods. These distributions networks, in sum, are outside the formal economy yet connected to it: Handicrafts generate cash for people who sell them in the city, and secondhand goods allow people who receive them to access consumption practices from which they are otherwise excluded. This is a form of inclusion through consumption identified as one of the modalities of "neoliberalism from below," a means by which popular sectors participate in global economies and global consumption trends.[14]

But these spatial networks through which objects circulate do not level inequalities among Qom families in a barrio or village. In many cases, they reinforce a family's relative affluence and their power over a particular location. When a family manages the distribution of a large donation of secondhand clothing, they also re-create their position as redistributors and as more affluent and influential than others. Because families seek to concentrate resources within their networks and often compete with one another, in the barrio and in most Qom locations I visited, information about donations or the arrival of handicrafts or raw material for handicrafts is kept secret. Secrecy wards off pressure from other neighbors to share materials or donations.[15] Families bring boxes of donated clothes to the barrio as discretely as possible, which can be quite difficult considering the quantities of boxes they receive and the proximity of the houses in the Barrio Qom. Gossip about another family receiving a donation or materials may prompt people to show up to ask for something. Silvia made this clear: "I know my uncle received more than ten boxes of clothes from a school. But he keeps everything for himself or sends it to his in-laws in the Chaco. He even sells the clothes! But I'm going to go and ask him. I don't have money so he should give me some." Later she told me that, at her request, her uncle gave her two big bags of clothing, saying that was all he had, but she suspected he was hiding more.

In her feminist examination of gossip, Karen Adkins argues that gossip is a connected and relational form of knowing, a form of situated knowledge production where the person narrating, the recipient of the message, and the object of knowledge all become intertwined in discussions of a theme that concerns the people involved, forming an intimate engagement.[16] In her example, the gossip creates a boundary and spreads distrust of an institution, the CIA, that has similarly functioned by spreading misinformation as a political strategy. For Adkins, gossip thus creates knowledge among people for whom that knowledge is relevant; presupposing narrative creates an emotional engagement with that information and builds from and extends an intimacy that re-creates connection. In her analysis, gossip is associated with disempowered groups, yet it is not all that distinct from the dominant knowledge of state and science.

Gossip in the barrio follows these characteristics, implying and extending information for people who find that information relevant if they have a relationship to it. Gossip creates intimacy and reinforces communities. But here, instead of perpetuating groups, gossip reshapes assemblages and can challenge some families' boundary-making attempts. Gossip is a factor shaping circulation—in this case, the circulation of information. Information about families receiving donated clothing enters into the tension between connection and disconnection in assemblages, which Strathern notes in her critique of assemblage and network theories. Through gossip, families monitor one another, and the extension of connections within an assemblage may be put in tension when a family with more resources is forced to share what it would rather not. Gossip, though, also establishes a separation.[17] If a family has not shared and others find out, then other families in turn will not share with that family. Secrecy keeps the movement of objects within certain relations, and gossip about families who keep things for themselves may create pressure to share or even social rupture. There seem to have been ruptures among families in the barrio who used to work together. Thus, gossip can both reproduce relations between networks and create a disconnect between families previously connected through relations of sharing.

The barrio is not one unified assemblage, but a point of convergence of various assemblages. Instead of collaborating, people in assemblages may compete and be in friction with one another, so Qom villages and barrios are not homogeneous, tightly connected, ethnically defined groups, but rather entangled places traversed by superimposed (dis)connections. The barrio is a point of convergence of multiple assemblages that function autonomously and only occasionally come together as one (as when families came together to make the legal claim for the barrio itself). Leandro and Martín connected with their family in the Chaco, and with a widow and a shaman, yet the assemblage they activated disconnected them from the rest of the Qom barrio: I saw no packages shared within it. Yet the separation between assemblages is never absolute: Families in the barrio continue to share valuable items with one another.

Connections in assemblages, in sum, extend beyond ethnic specificity. The heterogeneity of relations, the trajectory of the distribution of objects, and the ways different assemblages converge and separate all problematize the notion of ethnicity as a default commonality. While being Qom is significant and makes for shared experiences and practices, ethnicity is not the only component in the activity of assemblages. The work of reconnecting people, keeping relations active, and creating new connections responds to political dynamics that are not guaranteed with the articulation of Qom identity and result instead from activating some kinship relations and not others, and from spatial associations, such as meeting neighbors in the city. Another relation reconnecting these assemblages is the Iglesia Unida, the Qom Evangelical church. This church's religious encounters are central to reconnecting the elements of many assemblages and to extending their connections in time and in space.

Iglesia Unida: (Re)creating Associations

The Iglesia Unida is a Qom appropriation of Pentecostalism that originated in the activity of American missionaries, in particular the work of John Lagar in the 1940s in the central Chaco region, and the emergence of a new type of leadership among the Qom. Former shamans became leaders of a new religious movement that was soon institutionalized as the Iglesia Unida. In it, Pentecostal notions of a direct connection with God combined with forms of Qom spirituality and healing to become, in the 1950s, a mass movement that spread across Qom communities.[18] In the barrio, Iglesia Unida not only is an active institution but also has a central role in helping Qom people move between distant places and getting people together several times a year. The Unida organizes large meetings in different Qom locations almost every month. Meetings can be in a barrio in a big city like Rosario, a small town, or a remote village in the Chaco. Invitations are sent by text message and advertised in *Nuestro Mensajero*, a newsletter that Mennonite missionaries (who have worked with the Iglesia Unida for decades) publish and distribute monthly to most Qom churches.[19] Unida churches help their followers to travel to and attend the encounters. For smaller meetings, a church might pay bus fare for a few members, and for bigger events, it might rent a bus for people to travel together. Some larger encounters are funded by international Evangelical organizations and religious NGOs. During my fieldwork, an international encounter took place in the area of Bermejito, which brought together Indigenous people from the Chaco with Indigenous people from New Caledonia in the South Pacific. During these encounters, Unida buildings become accommodations for travelers and places where large meals are prepared and shared. But the biggest seasonal encounter is the annual anniversary of the Iglesia Unida in Sáenz Peña, the town in the Chaco province where the church was founded.

Toward the end of my fieldwork, Iglesia Unida in the Barrio Qom organized a trip to the annual encounter. The church commission arranged for a bus to transport residents from the barrio to the event, and I joined them for the journey to Sáenz Peña and back. In recounting the trip and the encounter, I emphasize two aspects of how assemblages work. First, I expand on the effort required to integrate diverse elements within an assemblage. Second, I illustrate how church encounters, by assembling heterogeneous relationships in moments of intense connection, re-create associations and reconstruct assemblages over time. The Iglesia Unida is another component of assemblages that, alongside kinship relations, connects and reconnects elements and keeps them working overtime, bringing together families who do not usually cooperate.

On the day of the departure to the annual Iglesia Unida encounter in Sáenz Peña, my colleague Mariana, also a researcher, and I arrived at the preacher's house in the Barrio Qom in the late afternoon. Family members were making last-minute preparations for the trip: A woman was packing, older children were finishing handicrafts, a woman was feeding her baby, and people came in and out of the house, while the preacher constantly checked his cell phone. "Juan just came home from work. He is having a shower and will be on his way," he updated us. The charter bus parked in a side street around eight o'clock at night, but since many people were arriving from other Qom barrios and had a long commute, we did not leave until after midnight. As we waited, we visited other friends and saw the whole barrio actively preparing. People walked with bags, boxes, pillows, and comforters. Children who would stay behind in the barrio hung out with the ones who would travel, who were wearing their packs hours in advance. This collective effervescence anticipated the intensity of the encounter. At midnight, everyone had arrived, and we gathered around the bus, anxious to start the trip.

The preacher and his assistant Emanuel had made the travel arrangements. Through some women in the barrio who regularly went to the popular clothing fair La Salada in Greater Buenos Aires, they rented a charter bus for the weekend.[20] They had advertised the trip, asked passengers for a deposit, and organized the departure through text messages. Text messaging, once again, was the main technology through which people coordinated how objects and people moved from one place to the next. Tickets were very inexpensive: less than a third of what commercial bus tickets would cost. When we gathered around the bus, we could see why it was such a cheap trip: The bus seemed to be poorly maintained. Emanuel and the preacher had a list of passengers from which they called out names and invited the people to board. The bus capacity was forty, but there were soon over fifty passengers. With everyone on board, Emanuel gave us instructions: "Children have to sit on parents' laps. Make sure they aren't standing in the aisle or we may have problems with the police." Emanuel sat on the floor and told the drivers we could leave. He did not have a seat.

As we left, Emanuel said he would message "the van" to let them know we were on our way. We learned "the van" was a group of six people from a middle-class Catholic parish traveling to the encounter with a vehicle full of items to be donated to the church for distribution in the area. One young woman from the group later explained to me: "We want to know the Chaco and the Qom's reality firsthand, exchange experiences." As soon as the bus got going, several people grabbed guitars and started singing religious songs, and everyone joined in. Meanwhile, the two drivers talked about which detour to take to avoid a police check. An hour into our trip, we got stopped by the first police check. The officer requested the bus's documents from the driver, who handed them over. When the officer read them, he started shaking his head. After a long conversation, inaudible from inside the bus, the driver came back and said he had to "arrange" things with the officer. He had paid some money so that the officer would overlook the bus's illegal transport of unseated passengers. Soon we were on our way again.

At around three in the morning, the singing stopped, and we all fell asleep. At six, the sun was coming up, and we could see out the windows the fluorescent green fields of genetically modified soy, the lucrative agribusiness crop in the province of Santa Fe. We arrived at the first Gendarmería checkpoint, near the city of Rafaela.[21] A female officer asked for the bus's documents and shook her head as she read them. She stepped on the bus and explained in a loud voice that there were many irregularities, including that the commercial license had expired. The drivers insisted they were taking "Qom people" and food donations to the Chaco, implying that this was a worthwhile trip. The officer said we would have to go to an office to sort things out.

An hour later, we were all hanging out next to the bus in a field, while the preacher, Emanuel, and the men from the van spoke to the authorities in the Gendarmería. It was a surprise when a female officer took the women and children aside and started asking us questions: Where were we going? Where were we coming from? Finally, she asked us directly if the men were taking us against our will. Were we going to work in cotton fields in the Chaco? Were the men taking us to Paraguay? We replied that we were voluntarily going to a religious encounter, and the officer relaxed. She explained that they were worried we were "being trafficked," especially because there were so many women and children on the bus.[22] After two hours of waiting, the drivers, the preacher, and the men from the van came back with the news that an officer had given the bus a special permit, valid for three days only, to continue the trip and return to Buenos Aires. They made an exception because we were going to a church encounter and taking donations to the Chaco.

Traveling to the encounter was not effortless. In their discussion of assemblages, Deleuze and Guattari describe already-constituted assemblages and avoid analyzing the process of their constitution as part of social systems.[23] The connections I observed in the field were not effortless processes of coming together. Rather, connecting Buenos Aires with the Chaco implied working against frictions that slowed the connection. Friction also indicates that movement needs not smooth surfaces, but rough ones that create grip. The grip needed for an encounter implies an adjustment and a transformation of elements so that they can generate traction that sets elements in motion.[24] In this case, this was the church organization, the pooled money to pay for the bus, the charter bus itself, and the road. The frictions faced by travel to the Chaco were many: the lack of resources to rent a bus in good conditions, the need to travel side roads to avoid police checks, and the fact of carrying passengers beyond the bus's capacity. Traveling on a national road on an old bus created further friction as we tried to advance, friction that stopped our trip and almost ended it. We were granted an exception based on the donations we were carrying and the fact that the bus was taking "Qom people" to the Chaco, as well as that a group of people who help from a parish were with us and corroborated what the preacher explained to the police. In this incident, recognition of indigeneity smoothed the way. The trip to

Sáenz Peña, in short, implied a collective effort against the "roughness" of the travel, where the relationships established on the road were part of the friction and grip of the travel.

What Qom people call *ganas*—which I translate as "willful desire" and can be connected to the notion of *conatus*, the impulse to persevere in being—played a crucial role in persuading the officers of the Gendarmería to allow us to proceed.[25] Women were also assertive and dispelled any suspicion that they were being trafficked. The effort and determination necessary for this travel implied that desire, as the connecting mechanism, is not completely "beneath" rationality but able to work with it. There was a degree of willful determination added to the desire necessary to get us to the Chaco. A combination of willful determination and the argument that we were traveling to aid rural Qom people put us back in motion. Desire, determination, and friction both slowed our movement and enabled it to continue.

As we continued our trip, the landscape changed from soy farms with sophisticated machinery to more modest-looking cattle farms with pastures. By sunset, we entered the Chaco province and were surrounded by cotton fields. Older people on the bus commented that the harvest would start soon and recalled their time working in cotton fields. When we arrived in Sáenz Peña, a city of seventy-six thousand people, it was almost dark. The bus took us straight to the Qom barrio, one of the oldest Qom urban barrios in the province and the place where the first Iglesia Unida was founded.[26] We stopped at one of the churches and were immediately surrounded by relatives of the people on the bus. People greeted one another with hugs and glowing faces, while our hosts began picking up bags and packages and walking them to their houses. People with no relatives in town stayed in other Evangelical churches, which had been turned into fields of mattresses and sleeping bags. We had been invited to sleep in another smaller church, near the house of a large family from the barrio, where only two families were staying, to be more comfortable.[27] Mariana and I spread our sleeping bags by the church altar and soon met our host family around a large fire.

There were religious services every day, starting in the late afternoon outside the main church. On the first night and day, the encounter featured a series of musical performances. Religious music groups came one after another for hours, with only brief introductions in between, no praying or preaching. Older men and women sat, while adults, young people, and children danced in outfits they had made: colorful beaded jackets and aprons with long strips of fabric, part of a syncretic dance practice incorporated into the structure of the Qom service.[28] With these music performances, religious groups gave their best, people danced eagerly for hours, and then the following morning, preachers gave impassioned sermons, to which people responded by praying aloud in the Qom language. Evenings were full of children running around in groups and teenagers walking and chatting, while mornings had reflective services in the Unida church, attended by adults and elders only. On Sunday morning, there was a debate about splitting the church into two branches: schisms and the creation of new churches has been a common and well-documented part of the dynamic of expansion and continuation of the Unida (and is not a sign of crisis).[29] The sermons' calls to maintain unity made the audience respond even more energetically. People in the room uttered loud prayers and cheered "Amén" in response to the speakers. There was a call for unity; preachers from all over the country gave sermons quoting the Bible, arguing to remain as one, and sons and daughters of the founding preacher were invited to speak. Religiosity made people feel intensely and intimately connected to one another, to God, and to past generations, and in this event, people appeared to be renewing their engagement to God, to the Unida, but also to one another.[30]

The meeting also generated social intensity beyond the religious services. We all shared days of living in intense proximity, which created an unusual and intense sociability. The everyday rhythm was reorganized for locals, too, as their "homes" became crowded places, and we were all meeting new people and renewing links with old acquaintances. Hosts shared food and mate with visitors almost constantly and kept feeding the fire—it was the end of the winter and still chilly. There was hardly any space or time to be alone, and the intense coexistence generated opportunities to share stories, make plans, or just get to know others. Homes had turned into extroverted places as people came and went or sat in doorways to chat. I met many people I knew from my past travels to Qom villages and barrios, some of whom were active Evangelicals but also many who were not avid church members.

Spatial proximity and the chance to reconnect with relatives and acquaintances allowed people to arrange logistic issues. Beyond lively talk and catching up about life, joking and passing information, we saw people engaged in pragmatic activities, such as handing over packages of handicrafts to be sold in Buenos Aires, updating one another about land conflicts, and making plans to send secondhand items to remote villages, among other activities. Being there physically, moving around randomly, being open to put aside plans, stop, say hi, and make new plans—these things were central to the encounter. People who had been out of touch had time to catch up and plan future collaborations. This happened, for example, when Nicanor from the barrio in Buenos Aires made plans with his schoolteacher sister, Leticia, to send supplies to the school where she worked in a rural village not far from Sáenz Peña. People who had tensions with others could drift apart, give some air to the relationship, and form new connections. This happened, for example, when Octavio, a musician from Rosario I met on my first trip and saw again the first night of the encounter, left one musical group and was invited to join others. This musical group brought together people from different Qom communities who were planning on getting together and touring in the summer. These meetings thus allowed for new collective bodies to emerge. Meeting up is, in sum, an action that re-creates existing connections and creates new ones.

The meeting in Sáenz Peña was a gathering not only of people but also of assemblages coming together. The families on the bus do not regularly work together; in fact, they compete with and gossip about one another. In addition, in the encounter, there were several collaborators, such as the people from the van who traveled with us, Mennonite missionaries who lived in the Chaco and worked alongside the Iglesia Unida for decades, and anthropologists such as Mariana and myself. In the intense sociability, we all hung out with one another, and new relations emerged between us. The encounter was effective because it joined heterogeneous elements and different assemblages in relatively horizontal relations, in rhizomatic associations. Other than the connections between preachers, there were no specific rules or hierarchical agents coordinating the encounters, and each element during the encounter could connect and reconnect with any other. For example, there was no restricted or exclusive use of places, and everyone could walk in and out of most locations. Everybody circulated in and out of the churches, the soccer field, and the fair that surrounded the main area. The only forms of separation were when preachers met inside the building of the first Unida church to decide the future of the institution.

These new connections do not just re-create assemblages as stable formations through time. Rather, by enfolding new elements or changing the relations between elements, they change the type of activity an assemblage could perform. For example, Nicanor and Leticia have always been in touch as siblings, but in this encounter, they decided that Nicanor would start collecting school supplies (instead of only clothing and food) from workshops in Buenos Aires and send them to Leticia's school, instead of sending everything to their mother. Leticia offered, in turn, to take care of Nicanor's teenage son, Julián, who at the age of fifteen had dropped out of school in Buenos Aires because he thought there was no point in studying. Leticia would try to motivate Julián, who had always been a good student, and encourage him to consider postsecondary studies. They were thus reshaping their relationship as adult siblings into more complex forms of collaboration, and by doing so, they were reshaping the assemblage created when objects are distributed. Now Nicanor would help children in Leticia's school to access school supplies, and their meeting at the encounter would extend, among other things, what the children in Leticia's school could do by having new pencils and books. These (re)connections were possible because the religious meeting united multiple, heterogeneous forms of relations, including religion, kin sociability, and youth socialization.

Another level of heterogeneity unfolded around a soccer tournament. The day after our arrival, I noticed that a group of youth on our bus had traveled not to attend the religious event but to play in an annual tournament celebrated in parallel to the church meeting. The tournament took place just beside the church and brought together many teams of young and middle-aged Qom men from different villages and barrios.[31] The tournament attracted fans who, instead of attending the religious services, hung out watching the games. The teams came from Qom barrios and rural villages: Every Qom village and barrio I have visited has a soccer field and regular matches between local Qom teams. While I had seen intense activities when neighboring teams played one another, I had never seen a tournament bring so many teams together from so many distant areas. But it was not just the size of the event that caught my attention. The Iglesia Unida openly condemned soccer. Most Evangelical people in the church say that *creyentes* (believers) cannot play soccer, because it is connected with *vicios* (vices). Indeed, during most matches, people around the field were gambling, drinking beer, and smoking, all activities that Unida members are expected to avoid because they are not conducive to service to God.[32] Therefore, most Iglesia Unida members argue that soccer is associated with the *joda* (partying) and a transgression of religious life that believers should avoid. Only a few people active in the Unida played soccer; they explained that they never engaged in the after-sport activities and distinguished the sport from "partying."

Yet the tournament was openly connected to the religious event, creating a peaceful tension between the two. We learned that the tournament was not new but a regular event planned along with the church anniversary. The soccer tournament was openly accepted, yet when I asked about it, nobody wanted to discuss the contradiction openly. The silence implied that while the tournament was accepted (and helped to attract youth and nonbelievers to the encounter), it was in tension with some fundamental religious ideas.

Most people agreed it had been going on for over a decade, bigger each year. When I discussed the tournament with the youth, they talked openly about how fun, competitive, and large it was.

Overall, the coexistence makes sense in light of the general relation that the Qom church has with people who are not part of it. While *la joda* is against church mandates, people are not judged for it and everyone is accepted in the church—even while they are in *la joda* and then when they decide to quit that life for good. In fact, during the weekend, the two events coexisted peacefully and were integrated with each other. The tournament's importance as part of the encounter was clear, for example, when religious people from the barrio commented to me how important the tournament is, for it is the biggest encounter of soccer teams from Qom communities where there were famous Qom players in action.

One afternoon as I walked past a very religious family by the field, they stopped me to point out the best players. Others commented on the fact that Qom players were barefoot, so tougher than other players. In addition, I learned that some families had been able to drag their teenagers to the religious encounter only because of the tournament. Parents were pleased with this coexistence of activities and preferred that the youth hung out close by and under their attentive eyes, rather than not having them there at all. Parents did not stop the youth from getting drunk or "hooking up" with one another, and they intervened only if there was a fight. The soccer event thus did not create major spatial or social tensions with the church meeting, and in fact, it added to its social intensity by creating a parallel form of socialization entangled with it.

The subtle tensions were expressed to me in minor complaints about the amount of alcohol sold and consumed around the field and the disturbing rhythms of the soccer tournament taking place beside the main events. Because many players were sleeping in the smaller churches around the main one, players shared space with families attending the religious meetings. One group of women, cousins of women from the barrio, explained that players were partying all night and disrupting everyone's sleep. Players had woken up the children several times while drunk and talking loudly, and the children got scared. To avoid problems, the lights in the church beside the soccer field were kept on all night, which made families sleeping there feel safer but also made it harder to sleep. I noticed the care that had been put into where Mariana and I were sleeping. We were close enough to the event but farther from the soccer activities, in a quiet church where fewer than ten people were staying, and the lights were off at night.

The coexistence between the soccer tournament and the religious encounter indicated that what was actualized in this event was not a single type of sociability, religious participation, or kin relations; rather, it was multiple connections that could emerge when people came together in one place. The coexistence of religion and sport amplified the possibility of connection and reconnection, bringing Evangelicals together with youth and people engaged in "party life" in one weekend. In this event, a sense of being Qom and Indigenous, and of working against impoverishment, land loss, and unemployment, was actualized as well.

The event brought together Qom from different generations, city dwellers and rural folk, religious and nonreligious, political leaders and preachers, in a single moment of intense socialization. Ester explained that, despite the efforts to get there, "we are happy, we are all together, we get the strength to keep going." Ester highlighted a dimension of identification as Qom and Indigenous that goes beyond struggles over representation. Stuart Hall stresses the articulation of racial self-identification at moments of key political significance in confronting colonial misrecognition and subordination. In his work on Caribbean identities, he examines the emergence of Rastafari culture in his natal Jamaica as a challenge to the aspiration to Britishness among Black Jamaicans through expressing pride in Afro-Caribbean culture.[33]

While Hall is concerned with the relationship between historical experience and identity, and in the potential of identity in collective organization against structural and economic subordination, his emphasis on the processes of signification leaves moments of socialization underexamined. He is aware of the affective transformations of gathering (beyond articulation), where the power of Rastafari irruption is generated in the vitality of music, the coming together in music events, the creation of a type of life different from that of British rule and British culture and morality. Yet Hall is more interested in the meaning-making process, the content of lyrics, and the generational redefinition of what it is to be Black. While affective resonances are present when he discusses his shock upon returning to Jamaica from his time in the metropolis, seeing the Rastafari vitality and its call to emancipation, when he is confronted by his anxious mother not to identify as Black and honor his Scottish ancestry, he does not make this affective dimension the main focus of analysis. While the notion of articulation focuses on the coming together of groups, people, and relations that are heterogeneous, for Hall, heterogeneity needs to be "resolved" through setting aside differences into one dominant form of representation that generates commonality.[34]

His double notion of articulation involves, first, coming together around common meaning about the historical experience that "overcomes" particularities (as if they needed to be resolved) and, second, a form of expression of this commonality that has to be legible in a particular social context. The religious encounter gathers heterogeneity but does not homogenize; it reconnects not to communicate but to solve beyond language (and of course discourse acts and has effects). The encounter is thus not simply articulation as meaning making and is effective in organizing collective activity after the event.

In this encounter, what is at stake is not so much a coming together of heterogeneous elements and relationalities around common signification (what Hall identifies), but a material coming together that remakes associations. Being Qom and Indigenous in this coming together is not so much about what commonality defines the group, but about what assemblages can do. Recomposing assemblages challenge political subordination through other means; it is not a challenge to the state on the formal field of politics, but a recomposition of Qom relations through organizing specific activity.

Indeed, at the encounter, I got a different perspective on the barrio, not as an isolated, marginalized place subjected to political and economic pressures, but as an element in the larger configuration of heterogeneous relations and places that Qom people build. While the possibility of claiming indigeneity and Qomness and redefining the devalued signifier of being Indigenous has been significant for people in the barrio, gathering to recompose these associations puts in motion the possibilities that are present in that given moment: for example, in the meeting up of adult siblings to work together or in the management of youth partying with indirect supervision. Here, Qomness is not an identity defined in a rigid boundary-making action; it is actualized in the connections it creates. These links join Qom families together in a particular activity, such as making Julián return to school, but may also involve other non-Qom churchgoers, people who help in Buenos Aires, Mennonite missionaries in the Chaco, and anthropologists.

Accepting the soccer tournament is thus a central dimension of the heterogeneity that is accepted and brought together. It was only because of this tournament, for example, that Julián, fourteen years old and a dropout from the barrio in Buenos Aires, agreed to travel with his family. While he told me that he traveled "to party," his parents explained that they were discussing with Leticia, his aunt (and an accomplished schoolteacher), the possibility of sending him to live with her in a rural village and attend the school where she works, so he could go back to school. Allowed to party alongside the religious meeting, Julián was also mingling with other youth from Leticia's village and getting to know his cousins better. Thus, the soccer tournament helped him socialize and be willing to move in with his aunt. Enfolding *la joda* into the religious encounters extended the spatial and social traction of the religious encounter. If the youths had been reprimanded for playing soccer, prevented from hanging out, or disciplined for drinking alcohol, they would have likely not traveled, and the encounter would have probably missed a large part of the demographics of young people and nonbelievers. If soccer became exiled from Qom life, this likewise could become a point of generational rupture, where people could get lost from family and kin relationships. The soccer tournament between Qom teams extended the reach of the encounter, and conversely, the multiplicity of relations converging in the encounter allowed assemblages to extend their reach, too.

Extension and reconnection also had a temporal dimension. By fueling people's determination to arrive in Sáenz Peña, allowing people living apart to (re)connect, the assemblages created by Qom families endured any tendency to dissolution. The Iglesia Unida maintained people's adherence and was a single institution joining multiple communities, barrios, and churches across space. What matters is that families were willing to help one another across locations (rural and urban, Chaco and Buenos Aires, among others), that youth played soccer and partied close to adults.

However, these spatial and temporal extensions created by bringing together heterogeneous elements, some of which are in tension with each other, also implied a risk. The line of deterritorialization created by the soccer tournament was also a threat to the encounter's joyful atmosphere. As I mentioned, many people were uncomfortable with the amount of alcohol being sold and the people getting drunk, and indeed, drunken people can get into fights with one other and disrupt others. The soccer tournament was thus also a potential threat to the peaceful gathering and to the Evangelical commitment to being part of the church. Churchgoers could potentially stay up watching soccer all night long and "fall" into *la joda*. Or soccer players could fight and break the safe environment in which parents were allowing groups of older children to play by themselves around the church. This coexistence had points of tension that could become a threat to connections and even bring about their dissolution. If too many people get annoyed with the soccer tournament, or if drunk people were to start fighting, the tournament could potentially be separated from the encounter, and then youth and adults engaging in *la joda* would not be part of the gathering.

The Iglesia Unida and the meetings it organizes are a central component of assemblages, which work by (re)connecting people, objects, and relations, bringing them together and reproducing them over time. Intense and direct contact with God, but also a chance to see relatives, provided a strong motivation for people to attend every service and stay up at night. The encounter was also intense because it was a time for the heterogeneous relations to reconnect in one place, organized around horizontal relations promoting unregulated meet-ups of people. Assemblages were reconstituted through time with variations.[35] The elements connected together changed in accordance with specific needs and circumstances, as with Nicanor and Leticia trying to get Julián back into school. What was maintained was a collaboration across space and across relations that link Qom people and collaborators.

At the end of the religious meeting, on Sunday afternoon, the sleepy atmosphere revealed how physically demanding the encounter had been and how tiring the process of reconnecting was. By late afternoon on Sunday, we were ready to go back to Buenos Aires. We said goodbye to our hosts, hugged and headed to where the bus was parked. This time, there was no need to call people out as we got on the bus. Relatives waved goodbye as the bus drove out of the barrio. When the bus pulled away, there was an immediate silence all around us. A few minutes later, people were murmuring prayers or asleep.[36]

Controlling Multiple Places: Extensive Associations

Most of the connections created between Qom villages, urban barrios, and the people who collaborate with them are temporary arrangements. They can be activated according to specific needs, such as the distribution of donated items and may then become inactive for some time. Families work to maintain activity across space and relations through keeping communication active, such as by sending messages just to say hi or sending a Bible quotation for reflection. Most families keep relationships in a state of latency, to be activated when necessary, and they engage on and off in activating relationships at specific times. A few families, among them the ones that concentrate major possibilities, build assemblages that connect places across space and are almost constantly active, mobilizing resources, distributing people and goods and solving problems across space.

Families create networks through which people can access multiple places simultaneously. An example of this is Andrea and Antonia's extended family, which has created an assemblage organized around Gustavo and Laura, Andrea's parents, and their eight adult children (all the children's

FIGURE 5.1. The central fire on the farm. Andrea and her family enjoying their time in the Chaco. Photo by the author.

names start with an *A*, something unusual among Qom people that marks this family as different). These adult children are spread across different places where they live or own properties, and all are closely in touch with one another across distance. The spatial reach of their network includes several farms in and near Bermejito, the Qom barrio in Resistencia, the Barrio Qom in Buenos Aires, and, for a few years, Brussels, Belgium, when one of the brothers married a Belgian missionary and moved there with her. In what follows, I give an account of how this assemblage operated during a trip when I joined Andrea on a visit to her parents' farm in Bermejito.

The trip from Buenos Aires to Bermejito started with last-minute travel arrangements on my part. I was initially going to travel to Bermejito with Antonia and her husband on a trip they had planned with a school from Buenos Aires to "help Indigenous communities." I would then stay with Andrea, who was also traveling that week to visit her family (it was winter break and thus a popular time for travel). Because the middle-class school was canceled at the last minute, I made my own travel arrangements and traveled with an ethnohistorian colleague, Patricia, who worked in the area. While on the bus, I messaged Andrea to tell her that our bus was arriving the next morning, and in a sequence of messages, she told us what to do the next day. What

I first saw as an obstacle to my fieldwork, because I would not get to travel with people from the barrio, ended up being an enlightening experience, as I could see how they organized my trip to the farm. In her text messages, Andrea explained that when we arrived by long-distance bus in Castelli, we would have to take a second bus to get to the town of Bermejito. But that bus leaves only in the late afternoon and arrives in Bermejito after sunset. Because traveling to the farm at night is very difficult, Andrea instructed us to spend the night at her parents' house in town. One of her brothers, whom we had never met before, would be waiting for us.

We did as we were told, and when we arrived in Bermejito, we looked for the house (as she put it) "close to the town hall" by asking around for her family's name. Andrea's brother, Javier, and his wife were waiting for us and had everything organized. We had a bed to share; there was mate and bread for the evening and a bucket of water for us to bathe. Javier had also arranged with a *remise* driver to take us to the family farm the following day and had contacted one of his brothers who needed a ride to come with us (as an alternative to taking the bus). We had dinner and went to bed, and early the next day, we were on our way to the farm. From the start of my trip, I was able to see the coordinated work of the family. Andrea did not just leave it up to me to get to the farm; she calculated the timing of the buses and asked her brother to host us. Her brother, who lives on a farm, was sent by his family to receive us (and use the trip to get his pregnant wife to a medical checkup). Andrea had also coordinated with another brother to use our trip to get him to the farm. They planned all this mobility in an incredibly efficient manner with detailed instructions to the *remise* driver, his brother, and myself through complex text messages. This contrasted with the relationship Andrea has in the barrio with people who help, who seem to want to believe that Andrea could not manage without their help.

On the farm we were happy to meet Andrea, her partner, and their children, who told us with huge smiles that they were "having an amazing time." Her parent's farm was a plot of for hectares. There was a small Evangelical church out front, close to a dirt road, and four one-bedroom houses, each an adobe-brick house, except for one of red brick (the one Andrea was living in). Andrea's father was the church's preacher. He built the church with the help of his followers. Behind the church, the biggest house was of adobe, where Gustavo and Laura, Andrea's parents, lived. "They could have a brick and cement house but prefer the mud one," Andrea explained to me. As on most Qom farms, the kitchen was a separate and open construction, consisting of a hay roof with no walls and a big table. Beside it, there was a big fire that

FIGURE 5.2. Crossing the Bermejito River. Photo by the author.

was almost always lit, for heating water or cooking food for all the people in the different houses. The fireplace, surrounded by chairs, was also the meeting place where we all socialized at the end of the day and had conversations that lasted hours. The rest of the farm was a bushy field with goats and a small vegetable garden for their own consumption that Laura took care of. The farm was located in semiarid forest, with sandy soil and low trees, and the land divided into a series of small farms organized around several dirt roads. Hardly anybody owned a car, and people moved around on bikes and motorcycles. Biking fifteen minutes toward the Bermejito River, everything became greener, and the bushes and trees were denser and higher. The banks of the river were open to everyone, and people went there to hunt and fish.

The weekend of our arrival, Gustavo was awaiting the arrival of a big donation of used clothes from Buenos Aires that Antonia had coordinated. On the Saturday, families from the area gathered around the church, waiting for the arrival of the boxes. Gustavo was thus in charge of the other end of managing the "help" I discussed in the previous chapter by distributing objects in the rural Chaco coming from middle-class houses in Buenos Aires. Some families had arrived from afar, and it had taken them all morning to walk to Gustavo's church. They settled in at the school and waited a day and a half for the boxes. In the meantime, Gustavo shared food with them. Once the boxes arrived, the distribution was quick: Gustavo divided items in smaller bags, handed each family a couple of bags, and then people quickly dispersed back to their homes.

These were not the only actions they coordinated. When we arrived on the farm, everything was organized there, too: A brother had moved out of his house into a cabin in the bush on the other side of the river to give space to Andrea and her family, while Patricia and I slept inside the church. Andrea's mother, Laura, baked bread and asked one of her sons to look for wild honey in the bush, which we had for breakfast every morning. A day later, Andrea's brothers looked for one of their cows in the bush and butchered it so we all had fresh meat, which was a big offering, given that food was scarce. The day after our arrival, they lent us bikes to move around, and by drawing on the dusty ground, they explained to us the locations of places to visit during our stay. Arturo, Andrea's thirteen-year-old brother and the youngest sibling, guided us on his bike while other children, including Andrea's son, who was a visitor from the city like us, joined us in exploring the area. We visited the bush, the high school founded by Belgian missionaries that Andrea and Antonia attended when they were young, and the river. In our explorations, we followed some of the connections this family maintains to different places: a fire station where, Arturo explained, Gustavo is a collaborator; the river that delimits one of the boundaries of the 140,000 hectares of land obtained after long struggles by the Qom Land Association, which Gustavo advised; the high school built by Belgian missionaries that Andrea and Antonia attended; and an area of forest where a cow belonging to one of Andrea's brother had been lost and that everyone in the family helped to look for.[37]

Laura contacted another of her sons, Aníbal, living on the other shore of the Bermejito River so that we could visit *el monte* (the bush), see the goatherds, and learn about the history of the land.[38] The following day, we left early in the morning. More children than usual joined us, most of them Andrea's young cousins. Arturo guided us to the river, where Aníbal was waiting for us with a small rowboat, and after hiding our bikes under some bushes, we crossed in three groups. On the other side of the river, Aníbal and Julia, his wife, were waiting for us, by a big and well-kept pen with over thirty goats. Beside it was a small shack and an outside kitchen. Everything was recently built, and the vegetation around the buildings was thick. On their side of the river, everything was "wilder": There was no road, only trails. Construction material had to be brought by boat and then foot. Houses were temporary shacks; Aníbal stayed for a few days while tending the herds, and there was no presence of the state or any other institution.

While Aníbal took the herds to feed, Julia and their daughters showed us around and walked with us to a second shack and pen deeper in the bush.

FIGURE 5.3. The children from Buenos Aires and cousins posing by a skull in the ruins of a *criollo farm*. Photo by the author.

The bush was dense, and at points, Julia skillfully used her machete to open up the path. On our way back, we traversed the bush instead of walking by the river so we could see more of the place. We passed a lagoon where the older children told me they usually fish, and we ended up at an abandoned *criollo* settlement with an old pen and a ruined shack. The soil there had been much more eroded by goats and people, showing longer occupation than the newer structures Aníbal and Julia had built. The place had a ghostly atmosphere. The children told me about an old man who had died there, and they insisted I take a photograph of them beside a goat skull hung on a spike that, they said, they found strange.

Walking around the area and seeing the new homes and fences that Aníbal and another brother had built revealed how the family had had shaped and occupied that place. On the small tour, Julia seemed to make a point in showing us the *criollo* settlement in ruins, which contrasted with their lively pens. This place across the Bermejito River was, therefore, a spatial extension of the assemblage that the family had created over the years, an extension they had only recently created but had very efficiently incorporated into their control. Also, Laura had made a strong case that we had to go there and see the land. Aníbal and Julia were clearly proud of their work as they showed us around and highlighted what they had built. By walking around the paths, opening the trails with the machete, and showing the area to two researchers from Buenos Aires, they were also claiming the place as their own. They were reaffirming their control over an extended spatiality as this nuclear family lives simultaneously in the town of Bermejito, the more settled farm, and in the shack in the bush.

We met with Gregorio back at the first pen to drink mate and chat. He explained the history of how the Qom Land Association obtained the titling of 140,000 hectares (including the land across the river) in the 1990s. During the land struggle, the Indigenous leaders had made agreements with the *criollo* population of the area. Both groups had agreed to fight for land titles together, but the *criollos* consented to relocate elsewhere so that the Qom could have one unified common parcel. However, the relocation of the *criollo* families had not been easy, for (as the ruins showed) they had lived in the area for many decades, and the families on the other shore did not want to leave. Aníbal was one of the people who gradually occupied the lands, building pens and bringing the family's own cattle while pressuring the remaining *criollos* to move out. Only that year, in 2010, and after almost fifteen years of land titling, had the *criollo* families moved out and handed over occupation to the Qom.

Aníbal also gave us an overview of the Qom Land Association. The association has the legal status of an Indigenous association and is the entity that owns the land, registered as Indigenous under one communal land title. This legal status is the same as the Barrio Qom in Buenos Aires, with the difference that the association is registered in the province of Chaco and is a complex political unity managing a vast extension of land for more than twenty Qom villages whose leaders administer the land together. All twenty leaders meet periodically to decide, for example, whether to give permits to lumber companies for forest exploitation, a topic that, at the time of my visit, divided leaders. Another topic was the paradox of communal Indigenous land. On the one hand, that legal status guarantees the land will never be expropriated (e.g., by a bank as payment for a loan), but this makes it impossible to get credit to make the lands productive.

The process of land titling in the early 1990s was possible thanks to the support of a Catholic NGO and Belgian Evangelical missionaries.[39] These organizations helped in legal negotiations with the state and in measuring the land for titling, and they had funded the school Andrea attended. These organizations were still connected, and in the early 2000s, the Belgian missionaries had developed a big education project with international funding that trained Indigenous youth as journalists and created a local radio station. In that collaboration, one of Andrea's siblings had met a missionary who would later become his wife, with whom he would move to Belgium. Such activities spurred other ongoing collaborations; for example, in Bermejito I met a young Qom man who was receiving help from a Belgian association to go and study medicine in Cuba and then come back to work as a doctor in the area. Finally, a group of young journalists was trained around a radio project, the same young leaders who organized the takeover of the community center in Bermejito.

Carmen, one of the older sisters, liked to live on the farm and had house and cattle across the river. But she also had a house in the town of Bermejito, where they spent the weekdays so that her children could go to school. Many days a week, her husband biked for two hours to the plot on the other side of the river to take care of the goats, staying overnight and returning when he could take a break and some family member had arrived to cover for him. Other times, he spent the week there and waited for the weekend, when his wife and children could join him. All of them, even those living in the city, had plots of land with pens and cattle in the area. The brothers who lived in the villages took turns caring for their siblings' plots and animals, as family members living in town were not able to attend to their cattle every day. But even nuclear families, such as Carmen and Gregorio's, lived between different houses, moving on a daily basis from one to the other. While Carmen and Julia lived mostly in town so their children could attend school, they also spent many nights on the farm and in shacks in the bush. During our visit, we saw siblings and in-laws coming and going on their motorbikes and bikes, text messaging, taking turns caring for the herds, and helping with lost cattle or building fences. Kids often ran from home to home, taking messages and other items, such as flour for bread. I also saw how a big jar of honey one of the siblings obtained was quickly subdivided, and various kids were sent in all directions to take honey to different family members. They also coordinated taking everyone's cell phones every two days to charge their batteries, given that none of the farms had electricity. The men especially moved constantly between the town, the farms, and the bush. They were in constant communication and coordinated their work with one another.

Connections were constantly re-created and activated through meetings, text messages, and sending siblings to help out. While Gustavo had a key role in coordination, decisions were carefully considered, and at night, we gathered around the fire, drinking mate and talking for more than two hours. These gatherings were opportunities to share what we had done but also to make plans and discuss what would happen the next day. The gatherings were neither a moment in which everyone provided random opinions nor a moment of autocratic instruction from Gustavo. Instead, people listened according to their experience and engagement, and I saw situations where one of Gustavo's sons or daughters insisted on an action against Gustavo's advice and were allowed to go ahead. These were perhaps moments of key political relevance, given that this is how lands had been distributed, how the church was maintained, and how the farms were kept.

A few days after our arrival, Antonia, her husband, and one of their teenage daughters arrived by car from Buenos Aires. After spending the day with us on the farm, they went back to sleep in Bermejito, where they owned a house occupied by another of Andrea's siblings. When Antonia and her family were on the farm, they visibly presented themselves as urban people, wearing carefully ironed and very clean light-colored clothes, in contrast with the soiled work clothing of their rural relatives. Their embodied demeanor seemed to make clear that they would not engage in rural work, unlike Andrea and her husband, who had "blended in" with the farm and its rhythms and helped with cooking and the fire, helped with the cattle, and had gone hunting. Andrea's children were also happily integrated into the farm, carrying baby goats (and convincing their parents to let them sleep with them) and playing in the bushes with their cousins the whole time. In contrast, Antonia, her husband, and teenage daughter seemed to embody a stereotypical urban subjectivity that rejected the idea of getting dirty, working with animals, and smelling like firewood. But none of this was a topic of conversation, and, for example, Andrea and her mother, Laura, never criticized her sister for being "urban." This was another moment at which difference was enabled, and people were allowed to be themselves and expected to contribute from their position.

Through my participation in the coordinated work of Andrea's siblings in different places, I began seeing how this assemblage was organized. The coordinated work is organized around the extended family spread out across rural Bermejito, other towns and cities in the Chaco, and the Barrio Qom in Buenos Aires. The assemblage also connects heterogeneous social relations such as missionary work from a Belgian NGO, Qom Evangelical practice, farming, the educational system, and land struggles in the legal domain. It includes a multiplicity of objects and nonhuman living forms, such as cattle, the bush, the river, and secondhand clothes. That weekend, the emergent actions this family managed included hosting Andrea's and Antonia's family and their different needs, hosting me and my colleague and making sure we had access to "relevant" experiences, managing the boxes of donations arriving from Buenos Aires and a religious service on Sunday, making plans about the use of the "new" lands on the other side of the river, taking care of goats and cows on different farms, finding a cow that had been lost in the bush, managing houses in town and adults so that school-aged children could attend school, and making it possible for older children to attend the mission high school, in addition to other activities I probably missed. All these actions brought together an assemblage formed by adults and children; houses, shacks and fences; boats and goats; traveling boxes of secondhand clothes; motorcycles and bikes; cell phones; religious teaching; help from middle-class groups in Buenos Aires, and land titles, among other elements. It was in the interconnection of these elements that the diversity of actions I described was produced.

The assemblages connected different places and incorporated the simultaneous different relations coming together in each place. In Buenos Aires, Antonia and Andrea had linked up with middle-class people who approach the barrio "to help" and had worked with researchers. Further, Andrea was involved in multiple projects and had been trained as a health assistant, as a Qom-language workshop coordinator, and as an agrarian extension agent. Antonia was mostly dedicated to Indigenous handicrafts and developing workshops in schools. In the Chaco, their father, Gustavo, was a preacher, a leader in the land association, a fire department member, and a farmer.

The assemblage's spatial organization extended over multiple relations, resonant of what Massey calls spatial multiplicities.[40] These are the spatial arrangements that result from the multiple simultaneous relations unfolding over several places, shaping and being shaped by the relations. Massey explains: "We understand space as the sphere of the possibility of the existence of multiplicity in the sense of the contemporaneous plurality, as the sphere in which distinct trajectories coexist; as the sphere of coexisting heterogeneity. Without space no multiplicity; without multiplicity no space."[41] This multiplicity is fundamental for the spatiality of this Qom assemblage and the assemblages discussed so far. One of the strengths of these connections is that Gustavo, Laura, and their eight children owned many properties over different locations: houses in the town of Bermejito, forest lands with cattle, and houses in the Barrio Qom in Buenos Aires. The relevance of these properties was not only about accumulating land in rural and urban spaces. While property is relevant in positioning this family as affluent in comparison to most other Qom families, the houses were not homogeneous spaces (i.e., Indigenous land); rather, diversity was crucial. Houses and land spread out in different locations were heterogeneous resources as relations unfolded. A house in town was good for kids attending school or for young people working with a radio station, but not as productive units. The farm was productive and fed all the families, but it was a bad place for a pregnant woman if she did not have access to a health clinic, as was the case with Andrea's sister-in-law, who waited for us in town. Accessing and connecting these different places simultaneously, and enfolding, or bringing into the assemblage, resources from each of them, was how this assemblage could generate activity in one place or domain by activating relations from another. And the members of the assemblage did this as a constant activity.

Simultaneous access to a multiplicity of places increased family members' capacity to generate actions. Activities across space took place not simply because Gustavo masterminded them. Rather, activities implied careful organization but also leaving people and events unmanaged. Most of the time, siblings had not been forced to act in a specific way and were allowed to follow what they wanted while staying connected to the others. The extension over multiple places and relations was, therefore, the result of these lines of deterritorialization created by some of the siblings moving far. Allan is Andrea's sibling who fell in love and married a Belgian missionary woman while she was working in the Chaco. She asked him to come back to Brussels with her, and they moved in the early 2000s. While Allan's family could have tried to make him stay, since he was a respected schoolteacher with a job who could, for example, help his nieces and nephews access education, and he could share his salary with the rest of the family, the family presented no opposition to his moving far away. During his time in Belgium, their younger sibling Nicolás did very well in high school and was motivated to go to university. From Brussels, Allan helped him apply to the agronomy program at a university there. Nicolás moved in with them, learned French, and started to study, although he did not settle down and returned before finishing his studies. Allan then divorced, moved back to Argentina, and took a job in government education programs in Resistencia. Thus, while his move could have meant that the family would lose a valuable member, that siblings would spread out and lose touch, instead it extended their connections to Europe, a very unusual link.

The point made by Massey on the simultaneity of spatial multiplicity is relevant, as this family managed multiplicity by creating and re-creating connections. In that, there was no given plan but a constant use of the conjunctural possibilities present. Heterogeneity was not a problem and rather was used as a possibility, and spatial difference and distance were forms of extending the capacities of all people in the assemblage that Andrea and Antonia integrated. Difference, for example, that was created with Allan's move enabled Nicolás access to a university in another country, which is quite rare among Qom people. Over the weekend, I met most of Andrea's eight siblings, who converged at their parents' farm for a visit.

Over conversations by the fire, Andrea and her partner insisted on what a good time they were having there, how happy the children were, and how much they missed the bush and the river when in Buenos Aires. She and her partner continuously expressed a desire to move back to Bermejito. A few days after my arrival, Andrea told me her father was arranging to give them title to a plot of land in the newly recovered area on the other shore of the river, "so that she could have a place to return to." Andrea and her husband were very excited. They planned to start spending the children's school holidays there and move permanently when the children finished school (their younger child was only seven months old).[42] Andrea's desire to move back could extend the family's presence over the newly recovered land, but there was also a risk if she moved back that the assemblage in Buenos Aires would become weaker, since she would not be coordinating help there. Andrea was already anticipating that some of her children would probably prefer to stay and could continue their work in Buenos Aires, and if some of her soon-to-be adult kids stayed, all would be sorted. But this made her move impossible at that time, and Andrea lamented but also accepted the impossibility of a move. She did not like to live in Buenos Aires but had to wait, not as a form of subordination, or even sacrifice, but for the balance of her family of origin and for her children's chance to attend a good school in Buenos Aires with a scholarship.

Andrea's and Antonia's family was therefore an example of an assemblage that is constantly generating actions, re-creating its connections and extending over new relations and places. This assemblage connects all these relations, people, and objects together to produce something that cannot be explained in terms of only one of the elements, one space alone, or one type of relation (e.g., subsistence economy, religion, ethnicity, kinship). This assemblage had at its center family relations, and specifically the relations between adult siblings and their parents, yet the assemblage also enfolded people who help, several educational institutions, a land association and legal struggles over land, a fire department, and all the relations created in those places. The logistics of organizing in the assemblage were complex but always simultaneous. When Andrea arranged my trip to the farm, she also connected my arrival with a sibling, and when the siblings went to hunt for a lost cow, they took Andrea's children from the city so they could learn about the bush and forest, and they took everyone's cell phones to charge at a local school with electricity. During my stay, many activities were taking place at once. The networks connect heterogeneous relations and elements by generating stable access to different places, on the farms and in the bush, towns, and cities, but also across the specific forms of farming, their role in religion, and Indigenous leadership. These connections allowed for the emergence of activity across relations and space and created a specific territoriality linked by activity, some of which was extended in reach, such as Gregorio's occupation of the other side of the river or Diego's move to Brussels, but that needed to be remade to be effective. The extension of Andrea's siblings in space in sum was not orchestrated but not completely random either, for it followed the rhythm of specific needs, desires, and activities and involved a multiplicity of elements that had to be cared for.

The Spatiality of Assemblages

The notion of assemblage allows us to think about the heterogeneity and emergent activities that these Qom families create across space, and it shows the Barrio Qom in Buenos Aires in a new light. Rather than as a unified community, the barrio should be thought of as a place where multiple assemblages are activated in connection and disconnection from one another and at the same time. Leandro and Martín's musical performance, described in Chapter 4, cannot be fully understood as only a relationship between them and the staff at the school who invited them. The performance was part of a larger set of connections that went beyond the barrio and beyond Buenos Aires. It was separate from other assemblages, such as the one Andrea, Antonia, and their families constitute with a center on a Chaco farm. Yet the disconnection is not permanent. The Iglesia Unida meetings bring assemblages together and allow for the re-creation and reconfiguration of connections. Paraphrasing Doreen Massey's understanding of multiplicity and spatial simultaneity, new associations emerge when people come together in the intense socializing of religious events, soccer games, and multiple meet-ups with open-ended possibilities, with "no warranties" as to what the outcome may be.[43]

The reconnection established in the encounter links Qom families with one another and thus re-creates the relationships that make the Qom a distinct group with an identity as one Indigenous people. Yet they do more than re-create cultural practices from the Chaco or elsewhere, more than create one translocal form of sociability as a diasporic indigeneity. Assemblages extend through the Evangelical church and through other interactions, such as with people who help, informal associations with bus drivers who agree to take *totora* leaves, and the partying life of *la joda*. The connections are established in unexpected ways, according to specific circumstances and the coming together of people with different needs and capacities, and thus do not follow one single rationale or norm. The only expectation is that of reciprocity and the intention to work together.

The fact that these connections are not one form of social relation does not mean that they are chance occurrences. In all cases, there were frictions alongside connections, and so effort and some determination were needed for the connection to take place. If one important form of connecting is the movement of people, objects, and information, this was not effortless. Movements between the Chaco, Buenos Aires, and other cities encountered many forms of friction that threatened to stop connections from forming completely on many occasions.

Lines of deterritorialization extend assemblages in their capacities and in the spatial reach of their activity, but the tensions that these lines of deterritorialization generated also threatened the rupture and dissolution of the action they generate. For example, the extensions created in Buenos Aires with the middle-class groups that wanted to help the Qom cyclically dissolved because the Qom were not productive, as the groups helping expected, and because the groups helping did not persevere and were not committed to the open-ended relationships that the Qom suggested. Another example is the reoccupation of lands Gregorio had recovered across the Bermejito River as part of long-term legal struggles that had required considerable effort in the family: building pens and taking cattle, rotating family members to take care of things. Thus, even without a rupture, expansion generated friction and new efforts in the whole assemblage.

Another way assemblages expanded was in the spontaneous creation of new associations. Family members could shift their associations and choose whether to emphasize collaboration specific members or to include people such as an unrelated neighbor. The re-creation of associations with variations was therefore one way that assemblages extended through time. Each new association changed the spatiality of the assemblage by connecting different elements together—for example, a sibling living in Buenos Aires and his schoolteacher sister living in a remote village. In their activity, such as sending school supplies or trying to get Nicanor's son back in school, this assemblage entangles places in new ways. When Allan moved to Brussels, he did not just leave; he also affected the potentialities of his siblings back in rural Chaco. In sum, when assemblages are re-created, heterogeneous places are connected and reconnected together, emphasizing that assemblages link heterogeneity together. In the territoriality of the assemblage, the space over which a group has some relative control that emerges out of the connections is characterized by multiplicity, against an isomorphic association of place, group, and culture.[44] The assemblage cuts across (even when it does not escape) forms a territorial control over space, including private lands where forests are located, roads and train stations, the barrio and public schools in downtown Buenos Aires, among others. This heterogeneity, while not outside it, is not fully subordinated to the neoliberal form of value extraction that reaches popular economies and generates profit from their activities.[45] Heterogeneity as the basis of the territoriality that Qom assemblages shape is activated each time people in the Barrio Qom in Buenos Aires contact a new school or when a new religious musical group is created at the annual Iglesia Unida revival. However, extension over space also happened when relatives spread out across multiple places while keeping them engaged in collaborations, as Andrea's family did.

Assemblages are therefore a form of re-creating political and economic control over space through actual daily occupation and use of the space in a way that transcends the notion and special order of a state territory in its politico-legal domain as a system of jurisdiction. Yet it also importantly includes titled Indigenous lands that enable forms of occupation, use, and organizing that would not be possible with private lands. In these assemblages, communities are centers of action. Territoriality is thus shaped in actions corresponding to what Milton Santos calls used territory, or the control of space that emerges from active engagement with space.[46]

Assemblages were efficient because they did not have a prefigured aim and served instead to expand the possibilities of reproduction of families based in different places. The networks that allow the circulation of packages work not only at an economic level. The network created by the Unida church encounter, and Andrea's family does not only connect relatives; rather, it generates connections to access multiple places in regard to specific needs. Recreating a Qom identity or culture was not the main purpose of the exchange of goods, the religious encounter, or the family activity; it was extending people's actions in a given assemblage. These actions contribute to re-creating identities and cultural practices, but not as one homogeneous set of practices or a unified meaning around identification. Instead, Qomness and indigeneity are expanded in the variation, in their heterogeneous forms, in remote villages, in town or in Buenos Aires, in the church, and in *la joda*. People's capacities are extended within the assemblage by incorporating (enfolding) heterogeneous elements from different places (e.g., a farm in Bermejito, a barrio in Buenos Aires, a house in Resistencia), different institutions (e.g., school, religion, transport), and assembling heterogeneous practices (e.g., taking care of cattle, helping children attend school, sharing Evangelical teachings, redistributing donated items from Buenos Aires).

While not outside the state or value production, assemblages are both Indigenous and subaltern. Assemblages are Indigenous in that Qom relations, including kin and church relations, political relations between leaders, land claims, and community formation shape these associations that cut through colonial, unfolding space built by the state by means of Indigenous, and specifically Qom, dispossession. But the indigeneity and subalternity of assemblages do not simply oppose the state, as Indigenous legislation and land titling are a part of the assemblages and territoriality, too. Assemblages are thus also subaltern in that they extend beyond relations of Indigeneity and include associations generated from segregated urban areas that are economically impoverished and politically subordinate. An Indigenous subalternity in this analysis is not exterior to "civil society" (regulated by law and rights), but a social location of generativity, one that always partially escapes regulation without being fully outside it. Another moment in which the assemblage is subaltern is when women hire the run-down bus to take them to the Unida encounter or to the La Salada fair every week, even with its expired permits and having to evade police checks. Following Milton Santos, who identifies space as simultaneously immersed in hierarchies and in solidarities, subaltern assemblages are not completely outside or a form of fugitive flight; they are connections that escape the hierarchies of space while inhabiting it.

The spatial connections created by these assemblages do not form a subaltern spatiality that is external only to dominant political regulation.[47] I have shown that these assemblages are not inside or outside of government institutions, discipline, or governmental control. In them, there is no "pure" resistance, resilience, or escape. There are lines of subordination that transverse these assemblages, such as Martín and Leandro's position as part of the urban unemployed class, which pushes them to carefully administer the donations they receive. Assemblages extract elements from those relations and turn them into something different, even if only temporarily, by making them work together. This takes place in the context of major social and political constraints, including unemployment, land displacement in the Chaco, encroached farms in the Chaco, and institutional racism in towns and cities. In Martín's encounter with his widowed neighbor, the assemblage works beyond help, kin, and Qom relationships, producing a form of solidarity that is invisible to people who help and to state institutions engaged with Indigenous issues. The assemblages Qom people create do not resist or subvert power; rather, they enfold resources, redirect relations and institutional practices, and spatialize them in newly productive ways. In doing so, they actualize relations as Qom people and Indigenous but also traverse the boundaries of ethnicity, making a life from all the possible relations in each place.

CONCLUSION

Assemblages and Rethinking Indigenous Territorialities

One afternoon, while sitting in his yard in Buenos Aires, Lorenzo told me about the time when, as a teenager, he got lost in the bush in the area of Las Palmas, Chaco. He was looking for firewood and got disoriented. He knew the forest well, so he kept walking and looking for familiar landmarks. He finally encountered the river, but when he reached the riverbank, instead of finding a familiar shoreline, he was confronted with something that made him shiver. Through thick fog he saw a gigantic metal bridge crossing the river that was unlike anything he had seen before. It was in the middle of nowhere, far from any roads or villages. "I could feel there was something wrong. . . . It was a phantom bridge!" he explained. Overcoming his surprise, he walked away and somehow made it back home.

He went on to tell me that several years later, on one of his first days in Buenos Aires, he went for a walk around Isla Maciel, near the *villa* where he was living. When he reached the Riachuelo River, he saw it again: "There it was! The bridge I had seen in the Chaco years earlier was there!" He was referring to the iconic bridge called the Transbordador Nicolás Avellaneda, which connects the barrio of La Boca with Isla Maciel. Although the bridge shut down in the 1960s, its massive structure is still a salient feature for La Boca and a postcard image of Buenos Aires. It is indeed an unusual engineering construction: a transporter bridge composed of two towers and a high connecting structure for a suspending cart (big enough to carry several buses and cars) that moved from one shore of the river to the other. It was inaugurated in 1914 and is one of the few bridges of its kind in the world. It

FIGURE C.1. Puente Transbordador Nicolás Avellaneda. By Andrzej Otrębski. Creative Commons. CC BY-SA 4.0.

was another attempt by the Argentinean elites to turn Buenos Aires into a European-like, civilized, modern, and white city. For Lorenzo, the bridge was one of the amazing features of the city that soon became part of his experience, for he, too, had to take it to cross the river every day to go to work in the port of Buenos Aires.

The apparition of the bridge many years earlier in the Chaco was therefore anticipatory and part of shamanic forms of knowledge that shape the bush as a site of encounters with nonhuman beings, encounters that have a specific intensity and can harm or kill or alternatively empower the person experiencing them.[1] In the Chaco, the bridge represented an image of his future in Buenos Aires and revealed an entanglement of temporalities and trajectories: Lorenzo searching for firewood, his uncle waiting for him to cook dinner in the village after a long day of work on the sugar plantation, the forest, the river, and the bridge from Buenos Aires. In this apparition, space became a new multiplicity, bringing together the forest in which Qom people are still in relative control and an industrial structure made to connect both sides of a river, both untouched by agro-industry, and the ongoing advances of settler and *criollo* occupation and Argentine state regulation. This was a ghostly bridge in the middle of the bush, with no roads or trails connecting it to other places, and as an apparition, it was only available to Qom people like himself. The vision disconnected the bridge from Buenos Aires and the mobility of *porteños* and anchored it in the Chaco; it suggests that in the Chaco, too, indigeneity is entangled with urban areas, industry, and its technological infrastructure, which are also animated. The bridge creates, in a ghostly form, a spatial multiplicity and an assemblage that brings together very different types of objects, producing a new activity and an emergent territoriality.

Lorenzo's memory of that apparition condenses this book's three main themes: urban space and indigeneity as entanglement and multiplicity, the racialized dimensions of indigeneity and space, and the productivity of Indigenous subaltern assemblages.

I have suggested that the space the Qom shape from the position in the city and beyond is multiple, not because the spatiality that the Qom create is a mosaic-like collection of discrete places (rural, urban, periurban) to which people are connected by choice or by power. Rather, space is multiple, as Massey has provoked us to consider, because of a continual and simultaneous unfolding of relations.[2] State hierarchical organization of space, territory as property, and multiple relations, including the regulation of kin relations that Andrea's father generated and forms of a life in common, unfold at the same time in different places. Places, and in particular, the urban Barrio Qom, are therefore shaped by multiple and superposed spatialities produced by patterns of mobility and connections. Multiplicity means that there is always an excess of relations that remain outside the entangled and layered forms of regulation of people in space, as there is never any one technology or one habit that could control all space simultaneously or any place completely. Multiplicity is also about hierarchical and horizontal relations coexisting and being in tension with each other.[3] Thus, for example, while perceptions of authenticity have shaped how white, middle-class people of European background perceive the Barrio Qom, there is much in the barrio that escapes those relations. In space, therefore, relations overflow macro or reticular regulation, and their inevitable entanglement also makes it impossible to escape entirely or to create a "pure" alternative space. There are always elements that escape, but there is no outside time or space to be found beyond the spaces that the Qom inhabit.

In the same way that it is not possible to understand places in isolation, I found that it is not possible to conceive of absolutely "free" or unconditioned mobility. Historically, the movements of Qom people have been regulated by the Argentine state and by market pressures, as in the evictions and displacements generated by the expansion of the agricultural frontier. But Qom people's movement to visit relatives, search for alternatives to exploitative jobs on sugar or cotton plantations, or escape difficult life situations were lines of flight, enabling them to expand and move away from conflict. But flight was not effortless. The patterns of movement examined in this research imply frictions created by modalities of Qom subordination that slowed or prevented people's access to particular places, such as the lack of access to formal housing in the city because of being nonwhite.

Some of these frictions produced new relations and collaborations. For instance, the trip on an old bus from Buenos Aires to a religious meeting in Sáenz Peña faced interruptions that led to productive collaborations between Qom people in the barrio, bus drivers, police officers willing to be flexible with formal regulations, and middle-class people who gained traction and enabled movement to continue in spite of the obstacles. But friction was also created in the disruptions of those regulations, as when some Qom people, together with other residents, resisted eviction from shantytowns. Movement implied effort, and there was always the possibility it would fully stop the activity, as when police saw Qom men as *negros* and requested ID.

Thinking of Qom people's aboriginality as produced through movement within and beyond the city of Buenos Aires has implied recognizing that Indigenous people have always been part of Buenos Aires. While the Qom were not there at the city's foundation, they had connections with the Guarani people and early encounters with elites who shaped the city. The traces of a nonwhite Buenos Aires are not difficult to find. The city, after all, was built on Indigenous land and with Indigenous labor, and autonomous Indigenous people lived in their own territories not far from Buenos Aires until the late eighteenth century.[4] While the presence of self-identified Indigenous people was largely erased in the twentieth century as a result of the efforts to Europeanize and whiten Buenos Aires, the migration of Qom people from the Chaco added yet another component to the presence of the nonwhite poor (the *cabecitas negros*) in the spatial makeup of the city.

When the Qom arrived in Buenos Aires, it was far from white and was already a heterogeneous city made up of Afro-Argentines, Indigenous people, and mixed-race populations who had migrated from rural areas. The Qom presence became regulated in regard to the divisions between these groups, and their experience became immediately entangled with the forms of spatial organization of nonwhite bodies in Buenos Aires. They, too, became nonwhites and "throwntogether" in the *villas*. The racialization of the Qom people and their exclusion from the spaces of the formal city, as I have argued, was not a misrecognition but the product of a racialized national project whose purpose was to erase these others and "whiten" the population and city space.[5] While the Qom sustain their identities as a people, language, and knowledge, they were racialized together with other nonwhites, including mixed-race people and people who do not want or cannot trace their links to a specific community or nations, yet know their ancestors are nonwhite and are likewise racialized as *negros* (and very recently also articulated as *marrón*, or brown).[6] By examining racialization as an entry point for understanding the aboriginality that these people created in the city, I have explored the potentialities of thinking of Buenos Aires as a city also shaped by the nonwhite. While the Qom came from outside the city, their urban aboriginality became entangled with *negros* and with nonwhite experiences, as well as with the traces of the past history of a nonwhite Buenos Aires that is evident across its urban space. For some Qom, those connections became so significant that they chose to stay in a *villa* and inhabit that space of encounters to claim that as both Qoms and as people from the *villa*, they, too, are part of Buenos Aires.

I have also shown that Qom people push to redefine how they were racialized in the city. One way they do this is by shaping what I have called "a different shade of nonwhiteness," that is, using to their advantage exotic images of "Indians" cherished by the *porteño* white middle classes. In doing so, they fulfill the expectations of a neoliberal multiculturalism seeking to grant special rights to authentic groups. Qom families moved from being racialized as nonwhite *negros* in the shantytowns, a category including recognition of constitutive "traces of Indigeneity" (now also *marrón* identities), to embodying an aboriginality of exemplary authenticity that the government and the middle class can "save." It was in interactions with teachers, professionals, researchers, the Catholic Church, and NGOs that the Qom shaped their *porteño* aboriginality. In these interactions, Qom men and women learned to select from their experience what was seen as constitutive of their authenticity as "Qom Indians." They learned that their experience as workers in the port and union members in Chaco cotton farms, their long decades in the *villas*, or the desire of the youth to become professional soccer players like Carlos Tévez, was beyond the criteria of authenticity established in government recognition and cultivated by the Buenos Aires middle class. Qom people tended to silence those dimensions in their public depictions of themselves and in their interactions with institutions and researchers arriving to the barrio to meet Indigenous people. These interactions restricted the options of Indigeneity available to them but also enabled new encounters and new ways of accessing the city.

Perhaps a more subtle but profound way of challenging racism is the action in the assemblages, whereby white middle-class people are brought to work on a particular issue to solve a problem. In these relations, the definitions of difference are folded, incorporated into the assemblage organization, against their hierarchies. It is in the moments of teasing one another about being Indigenous, as when Julia, who was about to marry a non-Qom neighbor, was teased by her friends about him "marrying an Indian," and the laughter demanded no more explanation, we all joined in. It is also in the moments in which I got teased for my inability to walk the muddy roads in the barrio without stepping in the mud puddles, or when Carlos, the president, asked if I wanted to move into the barrio for good. It is in the long-term relationships that can be established, where difference is not erased but can be openly incorporated, and when the links remain active in spite of changing circumstances. These grammars of anti-racism shaped in relationships, intimacy, and humor rebuild affective relations outside racial hierarchies and can be sustained in commitment through time to generate deeper and more profound effects.[7] Anti-racism dynamics, mobilized in assemblages, unfold in everyday interactions such as the playful banter and jokes that make us all laugh about race, cultural, and class differences.

Thinking about aboriginality from the city, and the links that assemblages generate for this location, as I proposed here, does not mean seeing the Chaco as the source of an Indigenous essence that was then displaced and re-created in Buenos Aires. To consider the city itself in terms of Indigenous, nonwhite, and subaltern groups with whom the Qom are part and entangled implies that the Qom experience was also shaped by their connection to forms of indigeneity already present in the city. For the Qom people, developing a *porteño* aboriginality implied creating a new conviviality with "people from everywhere" in the *villas*, a process that created an urban subjectivity at odds with notions of authenticity that restrict indigeneity to the re-creation of connections to the Chaco. For the Qom youth, their urban indigeneity was shaped in original and new ways by their engagement with youth culture in the *villas*, in the experience of young women developing entrepreneurial practices through the sale and resale of clothes, and by some young men's embrace of hip-hop, among other new developments.

To regard Buenos Aires as a site of indigeneity implies thinking about how people in the Barrio Qom shape the space of the Chaco, too, and problematizing the notions that continue to take for granted rurality as a source of Indigenous identity, organization, and cultural creativity. People who ended up in the city were moved by chance but also by a desire to be part of the vibrant and rich city they had heard about. Later, through the flow of donated clothes that reached villages in rural areas, the city also contributed to the re-creation of life and the extension of consumption habits in the Chaco, as well as to the idea that Buenos Aires overflows with attractive objects to consume. Interactions with middle-class people, in turn, also affected such people's perceptions of themselves as white subjects and agents of humanitarianism helping out Indigenous "others." The making and recognition of Qom urban aboriginality is, in sum, not a side product or an acculturated version of indigeneity but is relevant to the understanding of larger racial and ethnic formations in the country, the city, and Argentina as a whole.

This analysis has highlighted that the experience of Qom people in and beyond Buenos Aires is not reducible to their indigeneity, as it has components that I have explored through the notion of subalternity. Their positioning as Indigenous and subaltern actors reveals forms of domination and subordination that also involve other marginalized populations. In particular, I have drawn on the concept of Indigenous subaltern assemblages to examine from a spatial perspective the way that people living within multiple forms of constraints re-create life out of seemingly disjointed objects, relations, and places. The notion of Indigenous subaltern assemblages helps explain how people connect heterogeneous elements and places in ways that are not reducible to the logic of aboriginality or ethnicity, as diaspora studies tends to imply. While many connections I have examined are indeed part of a Qom diaspora that connects Qom women and men across space, these connections transcend the boundaries of an ethnic specificity and a circumscribed cultural formation. The notion of assemblages enabled me to trace the work emerging out of this heterogeneity. In this way, assemblages created from the Barrio Qom extracted elements from their original uses and settings and put them to work in new relations elsewhere. This "elsewhere" often involved other Qom places in the Chaco but also included places mobilized by the Iglesia Unida, which is itself linked to a transnational Evangelical association of churches, or places such as the schools that the children of the middle-class *porteños* attend. A spatial analysis and the notion of assemblage allow us to observe the emergence of new configurations producing a "newness" within, but also beyond, the constraints faced by Qom families.

The concept of assemblage has been criticized for "flattening" asymmetrical relations of power, but it can actually contribute to understanding the multiple dimensions and layers in which subordination is (re-)created and to understanding its complexity.[8] Assemblage does not need to erase the simultaneity of hierarchies and horizontality, in Santos's terms, or the spatial multiplicity created by what escapes power, representation, and institutional arrangement.[9] In my analysis of assemblages, I placed the forces that connect, orient, and regulate those connections at the center of my investigation. The notion of Indigenous subaltern assemblages I have suggested takes into consideration the layers and entangled forms of subordination that shape the practice of Qom families. It also traces the extensions and connectivities through which Qom people and their neighbors overflow and can, in some situations, move past their subordination. Indigenous subaltern assemblages superimpose new multiplicities that open up new forms of life in common (including conviviality and the encounters of trajectories) and allow new capacities and variations in the making of subjectivities.

The phantom bridge that appeared in the Chaco is, therefore, not just a manifestation of a Qom cosmology that extends reality into visions of the future or a metaphor for the advancement of capitalist relations over the Chaco. From a spatial perspective, the vision can also be seen as a spatial reconnection: the opening of a potentially different future, one in which the bridge is on land that is still under Qom control and the *transbordador* is another link in a Qom assemblage in the Chaco. This work has contributed to the understanding of Indigenous subaltern territorialities and the creation of urban Indigeneities in Latin America. It has also shown how Indigenous people in a subaltern position produce extended and multisited control over space to re-create their life across space within and in spite of multiple constraints. The action of assemblages produced from these subaltern positions shows that forces identified as "inevitable," such as the economy and systems that re-create matrixes of inequality, have effects that overflow this re-creation and can be redirected to other locations and connected to other relations. Assemblages are thus another way of challenging one-dimensional explanation of politics of space and the social.

Inspired by Doreen Massey's understanding of space as a multiplicity, my analysis of the people from the Barrio Qom in Buenos Aires shows that something always falls outside of forms of domination and structural inequalities, but also of organized resistance. The patterns of mobility and connectivity created by the people I met reveal that there are always multiple forms of conviviality emerging from unplanned encounters that have not been fully enveloped within the layers of spatialized governmental regulations of bodies in space, bodies in themselves, and bodies with things. My ethnographic fieldwork has shown the specificity and variations of this multiplicity. Ethnography allows us not just to "test" explanations but to generate new forms of understanding. I have engaged with theoretical approaches to produce the best possible map of these Indigenous subaltern spatialities I was tracing in the field. I expect this map to offer potential points of entry for engagement in the unfolding of these and other subaltern entanglements.

If there is a political message in this work, it is not just a call for recognizing Indigenous people's presence and mobility within and from the city. As I have shown, shantytowns and Qom barrios are already a part of the city, creating forms of relating that go beyond divisions and regulations. The political sensibility that this research advocates is one that engages more radically with the extension of spatialities that re-create forms of horizontal conviviality that enfold multiplicity in common activity. I am therefore not suggesting that to oppose forms of power and domination the Qom people should create places of resistance, for both are already interconnected and mutually constituted. This work instead suggests that the Qom people's shifting Indigenous subaltern assemblages may bring to light forms of extending capacities and mobilities that challenge the private appropriation of what was previously shared freely. Understanding these assemblages and patterns of mobility can, through common action and laughter, hopefully help all of us create, and extend, forms of life in common.

NOTES

INTRODUCTION

1. The Malón de la Paz initially got a very positive response from the Peronist national government, which supported its claims against a "landowning oligarchy." But the government never followed through on the promise of land grants, and after a few weeks in Buenos Aires, Indigenous participants were evicted from the hotel where they were staying and had to go back empty-handed. See Diana Lenton, "The Malón de la Paz of 1946: Indigenous Descamisados at the Dawn of Peronism," trans. Beatrice D. Gurwitz, in *The New Cultural History of Peronism: Power and Identity in Mid-Twentieth-Century Argentina*, ed. Matthew B. Karush and Oscar Chamosa (Duke University Press, 2020).
2. In 1778, 60 percent of the population of the city of Cordoba was of African descent. See Erika Denise Edwards, *Hiding in Plain Sight: Black Women, the Law, and the Making of a White Argentine Republic* (University of Alabama Press, 2020), 1–10.
3. See Ezequiel Adamovsky, *Historia de la clase media argentina: Apogeo y decadencia de una ilusión, 1919–2003* (Planeta, 2009); Chisu Teresa Ko, "Making Identities Visible and Invisible: The Uses of Race in Argentine National Identity" (PhD diss., Columbia University, 2009); Ezequiel Adamovsky, "El color de la nación argentina: Conflictos y negociaciones por la definición de un ethnos nacional, de la crisis al bicentenario," *Jahrbuch für Geschichte Lateinamerikas (Colonia)* 49 (2012): 343–64.
4. This was a moment before the (trans)feminist movement erupted in the political center, and my identity as a woman (never fixed), positioned me among the female researchers, volunteers, missionaries working with Indigenous Nations (but not yet as part of a transversal feminist movement).
5. As the Indigenous group advanced, there were new groups joining in; with their legitimizing presence, the Mothers of the Plaza de Mayo marched alongside the Nobel Peace laureate Adolfo Pérez Esquivel.

6. Milagros Sala was jailed in 2016 on charges of mismanaging state funds. Her prosecution by the conservative provincial government can be considered a move to stop the leader of one of the strongest social movements in northern Argentina. The UN Human Rights Council has called hers an "arbitrary" detention. See UN Human Rights Council, Working Group on Arbitrary Detention, "Opinions Adopted by the Working Group on Arbitrary Detention at Its Seventy-Sixth Session (22–26 August 2016): Opinion No. 31/2016 Regarding Milagro Amalia Ángela Sala (Argentina)," UN Doc. A/HRC/WGAD/2016/31, November 2, 2016, https://docs.un.org/en/A/HRC/WGAD/2016/31.
7. Inside the presidential palace, Indigenous leaders took a petition to President Cristina Fernández de Kirchner, who welcomed them with a speech congratulating Indigenous people for "feeding national popular identity" but asked them to "consider that discrimination and suffering are not a monopoly of *pueblos originarios*." The petition handed to her was likewise ambivalent, emphasizing a need to take care of nature and have a "plurinational" state but silencing conflicts over land. The leaders of the march and the government were producing a specific Indigeneity, as part of a popular sector, that did not push too much for the implementation of Indigenous law, reparation through redistribution of resources, or resolution of land conflict. "Cristina habla a los pueblos originarios," TV Publica–Canal 7, May 20, 2010, https://youtu.be/jJa805H9C50?si=Bd94Wr8_lbx5dcab.
8. Charles R. Hale, "Does Multiculturalism Menace? Governance, Cultural Rights and the Politics of Identity in Guatemala," *Journal of Latin American Studies* 34, no. 3 (2002): 485–524; Elizabeth A. Povinelli, *The Cunning of Recognition: Indigenous Alterities and the Making of Australian Multiculturalism* (Duke University Press, 2002), 56–67.
9. See Paulina L. Alberto and Eduardo Elena, eds., *Rethinking Race in Modern Argentina* (Cambridge University Press, 2015), 10–22.
10. During my fieldwork, most people referred to themselves as Toba and said they felt comfortable with that term. However, recent land conflicts in the province of Formosa have created a stronger assertion of Qom as an ethnonym. See Lorena Cardin, "Entre realidades y simulacros: El proceso de relevamiento del territorio qom," in *Campos de interlocución y políticas de reconocimiento indígena en Argentina*, ed. Morita Carrasco (Antropofagia, 2018). For this reason, I use the terms *Toba* and *Qom* throughout this work. The names cover a multiplicity of groups that share local variations of the same language and were largely located in the central and eastern Chaco at the time the Argentine military occupied the region from the 1880s to the 1920s. See Elmer S. Miller, ed., *Peoples of the Gran Chaco* (Bergin & Garvey, 1999).

11. Cristina Messineo et al., "Lingüística y etnografía: Un proyecto de investigación colaborativa en a comunidad Qom (Buenos Aires)," *Signo & Seña* 17 (2007): 229–45; Héctor Vázquez and Graciela Rodríguez, "Socio-Ethnic Interaction and Identity Formation Among the Qom-Toba in Rosario," in *Beyond Multiculturalism: Views from Anthropology*, ed. Giuliana B. Prato (Ashgate, 2009).
12. Liliana E. Tamagno, *Nam qom huetáa na doqshi l'ma: Los qoms en la casa del hombre blanco: Identidad, Memoria y utopía* (Al Margen, 2001).
13. Gilles Deleuze and Félix Guattari, *A Thousand Plateaus: Capitalism and Schizophrenia* (University of Minnesota Press, 1987), 3–25, 351–423; Bruno Latour, *Reassembling the Social: An Introduction to Actor-Network Theory* (Oxford University Press, 2005).
14. See Marisol de la Cadena, *Indigenous Mestizos: The Politics of Race and Culture in Cuzco, Peru, 1919–1991* (Duke University Press, 2000).
15. See Nancy Postero, *The Indigenous State: Race, Politics, and Performance in Plurinational Bolivia* (University of California Press, 2017), 1–24; Philipp Horn, *Indigenous Rights to the City Ethnicity and Urban Planning in Bolivia and Ecuador* (Routledge, 2019), 21–48; Olivia Casagrande, "Towards a Tuwün Wariache? Place-Making and Creative Acts of Traversing in the Mapuche City," *Journal of the Royal Anthropological Institute* 27, no. 4 (2021): 949–75.
16. James Clifford, *Returns: Becoming Indigenous in the Twenty-First Century* (Harvard University Press, 2013), 68–90.
17. Milton Santos, "The Return of the Territory," in *Milton Santos: A Pioneer in Critical Geography from the Global South*, ed. Lucas Melgaço and Carolyn Prouse (Springer International, 2017).
18. Glen Coulthard and Leanne Betasamosake Simpson, "Grounded Normativity / Place-Based Solidarity," *American Quarterly* 68, no. 2 (2016): 249–55; AbdouMaliq Simone, *The Surrounds: Urban Life Within and Beyond Capture* (Duke University Press, 2022), 1–58.
19. Diego Sztulwark, *La ofensiva sensible: Neoliberalismo, populismo y el reverso de lo político* (Caja Negra, 2019), 43–90.
20. Juan Manuel Engelman, "Etnización de políticas públicas al sur del Área Metropolitana de Buenos Aires, Argentina," *Anales de Antropología* 53, no. 1 (2019): 121–31.
21. Pablo Wright, "Histories of Buenos Aires," in *Peoples of the Gran Chaco*, ed. Elmer S. Miller (Bergin & Garvey, 1999).
22. Messineo et al., "Lingüística y etnografía"; Ana Carolina Hetch, *"Todavía no se hallaron hablar en idioma": Procesos de socialización lingüística de los niños en el barrio Qom* (Lincom Europa, 2010), 56–92; Tamagno, *Nam qom huetáa*, 1–43.

23. Elmer S. Miller, *Los qoms argentinos: Armonía y disonancia en una sociedad* (Siglo Veintiuno, 1979), 50–101.
24. The Iglesia Unida is the main and largest Evangelical church but not the only one. Part of the religious movement implied the emergence of Qom-run Evangelical churches of other denominations. Evangelical churches work together; for example, preachers of non-Unida churches attended the anniversary of the creation of the first Unida church, and this is a national event with people traveling from most Qom communities (see Chapter 5). When I speak of "Qom Evangelical church" and not Unida, I mean this larger movement.
25. See Susan Lobo and Kurt Peters, eds., *American Indians and the Urban Experience* (AltaMira, 2001); de la Cadena, *Indigenous Mestizos.*
26. Horn, *Indigenous Rights to the City*; Sarah D. Warren, "Indigenous in the City: The Politics of Urban Mapuche Identity in Chile," *Ethnic and Racial Studies* 40, no. 4 (2017): 694–712.
27. Lorena Cañuqueo and Laura Kropff, "MapUrbe'zine: Los cuerpos de 'la lucha' en el circuito heavy-punk Mapuche," *E-misférica* 4, no. 2 (2007): https://go.exlibris.link/tY9YgVyD; Dana Brablec, "Indigenising the City Together: Ethnic Place Production in Santiago de Chile," *Journal of Ethnic and Migration Studies* 49, no. 3 (2020): 892–908. https://doi.org/10.1080/1369183X.2020.1814711; Casagrande, "Towards a Tuwün Wariache?"
28. See Miriam Álvarez and Laura Kropff Causa, "La diáspora puelche en la obra de teatro Tayiñ Kuify Kvpan," *Cadernos de Arte e Antropologia* 11, no. 1 (April 2022): 48–65; Warren, "Indigenous in the City."
29. See Sian Lazar, *El Alto, Rebel City: Self and Citizenship in Andean Bolivia* (Duke University Press, 2008), 61–143; Postero, *Indigenous State*, 1–22.
30. Alejandro Frigerio, "'Negros' y 'blancos' en Buenos Aires: Repensando nuestras categorías raciales," *Temas de Patrimonio Cultural* 16 (2006): 77–98; Lea Geler, "African Descent and Whiteness in Buenos Aires: Impossible Mestizajes in the White Capital City," in *Rethinking Race in Modern Argentina*, ed. Paulina Alberto and Eduardo Elena (Cambridge University Press, 2016), 213–40.
31. Paulina Alberto and Eduardo Elena, "Introduction: The Shades of the Nation," in *Rethinking Race in Modern Argentina*, ed. Paulina Alberto and Eduardo Elena (Cambridge University Press, 2016), 1–22; Ezequiel Adamovsky, *Historia de las clases populares en la Argentina: Desde 1880 hasta 2003* (Penguin Random House, 2012), 18–73.
32. Gastón Gordillo, "The Savage Outside of White Argentina," in *Rethinking Race in Modern Argentina*, ed. Paulina Alberto and Eduardo Elena (Cambridge University Press, 2016), 241–67; Adrian Gorelik, "Buenos Aires Is (Latin) America

Too," in *City/Art: The Urban Scene in Latin America*, ed. Rebecca E. Biron (Duke University Press, 2009), 61–84.

33. Ignacio Aguiló, *The Darkening Nation: Race, Neoliberalism and Crisis in Argentina* (University of Wales Press, 2018), 141–65.
34. Ignacio Aguiló and Ana Vivaldi, "Race and the Shantytown in a Race-Less Country: Negros Villeros, Whiteness and Urban Space in Argentina," *Latin American and Caribbean Ethnic Studies* 18, no. 4 (2023): 551–73.
35. Deleuze and Guattari, *A Thousand Plateaus*; Latour, *Reassembling the Social.*
36. Deleuze and Guattari, *A Thousand Plateaus*, 3–25, 351–423.
37. With a similar logic, Gago analyzes the assemblage of heterogeneous regimes of labor and the spatiality over which they extend among Bolivian immigrants in Buenos Aires. She finds that an economy of inside-outside is not enough, because the space of the textile workshop is interconnected to that of the market and the *villa* in an organization of space that exceeds any single space. Verónica Gago, *Neoliberalism from Below: Popular Pragmatics and Baroque Economies* (Duke University Press, 2017), 78–107.
38. Silvia Rivera Cusicanqui, "Ch'ixinakax Utxiwa: A Reflection on the Practices and Discourses of Decolonization," *South Atlantic Quarterly* 111, no. 1 (2012): 95–109.
39. Henri Lefebvre, *The Production of Space* (Wiley-Blackwell, 1991), 68–167; David Harvey, *Justice, Nature and the Geography of Difference* (Wiley-Blackwell, 1996), 210–48; Milton Santos, *The Nature of Space* (Duke University Press, 2021), 34–53.
40. See James Ferguson and Akhil Gupta, "Spatializing States: Toward an Ethnography of Neoliberal Governmentality," *American Ethnologist* 29, no. 4 (2002): 981–1002, https://doi.org/10.1525/ae.2002.29.4.981; Audra Simpson, *Mohawk Interruptus Political Life Across the Borders of Settler States* (Duke University Press. 2014), 115–46.
41. Jared Sexton, "The Vel of Slavery: Tracking the Figure of the Unsovereign," *Critical Sociology* 42, nos. 4–5 (2016): 583–97, https://doi.org/10.1177/0896920514552535; Coulthard and Simpson, "Grounded Normativity / Place-Based Solidarity," 249–55.
42. Coulthard and Simpson, "Grounded Normativity / Place-Based Solidarity"; Lorena Cañuqueo, "El territorio relevado, el territorio disputado: Apuntes sobre la implementación de Ley Nacional 26.160 en Río Negro, Argentina," *Revista de Geografía Norte Grande* 62 (2015): 11–28.
43. Ileana Rodríguez and María Milagros López, *The Latin American Subaltern Studies Reader* (Duke University Press, 2001), 1–35; John Beverley, "The Im/possibility of Politics: Subalternity, Modernity, Hegemony," in *The Latin American Subaltern Studies Reader*, ed. Ileana Rodríguez (Duke University Press, 2001), 47–63.

44. Ranajit Guha, *Elementary Aspects of Peasant Insurgency in Colonial India* (Oxford University Press, 1983), 220–332.
45. George Reid Andrews, *The Afro-Argentines of Buenos Aires, 1800–1900* (University of Wisconsin Press, 1980), 178–208; Jacqueline Sarmiento, "Indias urbanas en el Buenos Aires tardocolonial: Familia y grupos domésticos," *Anuario del Instituto de Historia Argentina* 11 (2011): 27–41.
46. Lea Geler, *Andares negros, caminos blancos: Afroporteños, estado y nación, Argentina a fines del siglo XIX* (Prohistoria, 2010), 55–89.
47. Adamovsky, *Historia de la clase media*, 240–365.
48. Adamovsky, *Historia de la clase media*, 240–365.
49. Urban racial-spatial separation is described, with multiple differences but in a related process of spatial racialization, by Saidiya Hartman, regarding the creation of exclusive Black urban spaces to separate white European urban poor. Saidiya Hartman, *Wayward Lives, Beautiful Experiments: Intimate Histories of Social Upheaval* (W.W. Norton, 2019).
50. Aguiló and Vivaldi, *Race and the Shantytown.*
51. Sergio Caggiano, *Lo que no entra en el crisol: Inmigración boliviana, comunicación intercultural y procesos identitarios* (Prometeo, 2005), 179–96; Natalia Gavazzo, "Jóvenes migrantes e hijos de inmigrantes latinoamericanos en una generación en movimiento," *Confluenze: Rivista di Studi Iberoamericani* 10, no. 1 (2018): 131–65; Brenda Canelo, *Fronteras internas: Migración y disputas espaciales en la Ciudad de Buenos Aires* (Antropofagia, 2013), 117–70, https://doi.org/10.1093/jsh/shu132; Sergio Caggiano, "Racismo, fundamentalismo cultural y restricción de la ciudadanía: Formas de regulación social frente a inmigrantes en Argentina," in *Las migraciones en América Latina: Políticas, culturas y estrategias*, ed. Susana Novick (Catálogos-CLACSO, 2008), 31–52.
52. Natalia Gavazzo and Débora Gerbaudo Suárez, "Desigualdades generacionales y prácticas políticas en las juventudes migrantes paraguayas en Buenos Aires," *Migraciones: Publicación del Instituto Universitario de Estudios sobre Migraciones* 48 (April 2020): 133–60, https://doi.org/10.14422/mig.i48y2020.006.
53. Benjamin Bryce follows the organization of European immigrant associations in Argentina. While these have had a role in organizing services, they have not created ethnic enclaves, where people spend the majority of their lives in community institutions. By contrast, Argentina has had a high degree of assimilation, by which people developed "Argentine" identities relatively quickly. See Benjamin Bryce, "Paternal Communities: Social Welfare and Immigration in Argentina, 1880–1930," *Journal of Social History* 49, no. 1 (Fall 2015): 213–36; Canelo, *Fronteras internas*.

54. Aguiló and Vivaldi, "Race and the Shantytown," 551–73.
55. Warren, "Indigenous in the City."
56. Brablec, "Indigenising the City Together"; Casagrande, "Towards a Tuwün Wariache?"
57. Álvarez and Kropff Causa, "La diáspora puelche."
58. Jérémie Voirol, "Assembling 'Indigeneity' Through Musical Practices: Translocal Circulations, 'Tradition,' and Place in Otavalo (Ecuadorian Andes)," *Popular Music* 40, nos. 3–4 (2021): 428–49.
59. Xavier Albó, "El Alto, la vorágine de una ciudad única," *Journal of Latin American Anthropology* 11, no. 2 (2006): 329–50; Lazar, *El Alto, Rebel City*, 1–25; Angus McNelly, "Baroque Modernity in Latin America: Situating Indigeneity, Urban Indigeneity and the Popular Economy," *Bulletin of Latin American Research* 41, no. 1 (2022): 6–20.
60. Claudia Briones, *Cartografías argentinas: Políticas indigenistas y formaciones provinciales de alteridad* (Antropofagia /GEAPRONA, 2005), 9–38.
61. Florencia C. Tola, *Yo no estoy solo en mi cuerpo: Cuerpos-personas múltiples entre los qoms del Chaco argentino* (Antropofagia, 2012), 21–49; Pablo Wright, *Ser-en-el-sueño: Crónicas de historia y vida qom* (Biblos, 2008): 2–36; Miller, *Los qoms argentinos*.
62. Doreen B. Massey, *For Space* (Sage, 2005), 130.
63. Anna Lowenhaupt Tsing, *Friction: An Ethnography of Global Connection* (Princeton University Press, 2005), 213–38.
64. John Urry, *Mobilities* (Polity, 2007), 17–52. *Mobilities* is generally paired with *immobilities*, a term I do not use because I prefer to focus on frictions, variations in speeds of movement, or impasse, given that mobility is always modulated and changing in degree. See Noel B. Salazar and Alan Smart, "Anthropological Takes on (Im)Mobility," *Identities* 18, no. 6 (2011): i–ix; Paul Virilio, *Speed and Politics: An Essay on Dromology* (Columbia University Press, 1986), 27–48; Tsing, *Friction*, 21–80.
65. Tim Ingold, *Being Alive: Essays on Movement, Knowledge and Description* (Routledge, 2011), 20–36, 200–225.
66. I paraphrase Latour, *Reassembling the Social*.
67. Gastón Gordillo, "Places and Academic Disputes: The Argentine Gran Chaco," in *A Companion to Latin American Anthropology*, ed. Deborah Poole (Blackwell Publishing, 2008), 447–65.
68. Laura Kropff, "Debates About Politics Among Young Mapuche in Argentina," *Revista Latinoamericana de Ciencias Sociales, Niñez y Juventud* 9, no. 1 (2011): 83–99.

CHAPTER 1

1. Andres Solimano, "Globalizacion y migracion internacional: La experiencia latinoamericana," *Revista de la CEPAL* 80 (2003): 55–72.
2. For in-depth analysis of these processes, see Valeria Iñigo Carrera, "Sujetos productivos, sujetos políticos, sujetos indígenas: Las formas de su objetivación mercantil entre los tobas del este de Formosa," *Cuadernos de Antropología Social*, no. 32 (2010): 229–31; Carlos Salamanca, "Deslizándose en las fisuras de la utopía: Los qom en las fronteras del estado nación argentino," *Corpus: Archivos Virtuales de la Alteridad Americana* 5, no. 1 (2015): 1422, http://corpusarchivos.revues.org/1422.
3. Noel B. Salazar and Alan Smart, "Anthropological Takes on (Im)Mobility," *Identities* 18, no. 6 (2011): i–ix.
4. In this chapter, I follow only people (and not objects or communications).
5. In the typification of migration theories, all three moments involve a degree of rationality and choice: people moving as a search for better life (modernization theory), as an escape of negative conditions and neocolonial inequalities (dependency and world system theories), and as processes in which culture and community mediate larger economic factors (articulation theory). See Elizabeth Horevitz, "Understanding the Anthropology of Immigration and Migration," *Journal of Human Behavior in the Social Environment* 19, no. 6 (2009): 745–58.
6. Mimi Sheller and John Urry, "The New Mobilities Paradigm," *Environment and Planning A* 38, no. 2 (2006): 207–26; Salazar and Smart, "Anthropological Takes on (Im)Mobility," i–ix.
7. Pierre Bourdieu, *Outline of a Theory of Practice* (Cambridge University Press, 1977), 72–95, 159–97.
8. Clifford, *Returns*, 68–90.
9. Glen Sean Coulthard, *Red Skin, White Masks: Rejecting the Colonial Politics of Recognition* (University of Minnesota Press, 2014), 1–78; Patrick Wolfe, *Traces of History: Elementary Structures of Race* (Verso, 2016), 43–75.
10. It is important to note connections between the creation of political power and economic power in the Chaco and the relationship of both to Indigenous mobilities. Given that the government distributed lands to the elite families and military personnel who participated in Chaco's colonization, those people also became responsible for policing where Indigenous groups would be placed as workers and during their "free" time.
11. Santos, "Return of the Territory," 25–31.
12. Nicolás Iñigo Carrera, *Violence as an Economic Force: The Process of Proletarianisation Among the Indigenous People of the Argentinian Chaco, 1884–1930* (IWGIA, 1982), 1–50.

13. Indigenous populations in the Chaco are recognized as ethnic groups organized into six linguistic families—Mataco-Mataguayo, Guaycurú, Maskoi, Zamuco, Lule-Vilela, and Tupi-Guarani—but this does not fully reflect the complex and fragmented multiplicity that existed before colonization. See José Braunstein and Elmer Miller, "Ethnohistorical Introduction," in *Peoples of the Gran Chaco*, ed. Elmer Miller (Bergin & Garvey, 1999), 1–22.
14. M. A. Palermo, "Reflexiones sobre el llamado complejo ecuestre en la Argentina," *Runa* 16 (1986): 157–78; Lidia R. Nacuzzi, "Los grupos nómades de la Patagonia y el Chaco en el siglo XVIII: Identidades, espacios, movimientos y recursos económicos ante la situación de contacto. Una reflexión comparativa," *Chungará (Arica)* 39, no. 2 (2007): 221–34.
15. Edgardo J. Cordeu and Alejandra Siffredi, *De la algarroba al algodón: Movimiento mesiánico de los guaycurú* (Juárez Editor, 1971), 57–63.
16. Nicolás Iñigo Carrera, *La colonización del Chaco* (Centro Editor de América Latina, 1983), 2–41.
17. Miller, *Los qoms argentinos*; Wright, *Ser-en-el-sueño.*
18. See Gastón Gordillo, *Landscapes of Devils: Tensions of Place and Memory in the Argentinean Chaco* (Duke University Press, 2004), 109–57.
19. Melitón González, *El Gran Chaco argentino* (Comp. Sud-America. de Billetes de Banco, 1890), 1–95. The territory was initially a "national territory" under federal control. In the 1940s, two provinces were formed: Chaco and Formosa. In the 1940s, reservation and mission numbers declined and Indigenous people were regarded as "incorporated."
20. Las Palmas was established in 1887 as the province's first and main industrial unit. It was founded with British capital. In 1914, it employed three thousand temporary workers, of which it is estimated that 70 percent were Indigenous. The *ingenio* went bankrupt in the 1970s and was bought by the state. In 1994, it sold its last properties. INAI granted a portion of the lands to Indigenous communities in the area. Daniela Mariotti et al., "Fronteras en tensión," *Revista Eletrônica Associação dos Geógrafos Brasileiros Secao Três Lagoas*, no. 12 (2010): 7–37.
21. Mariotti et al., "Fronteras en tensión."
22. Óscar Ernesto Mari, "La transición entre dos ciclos y sus efectos sociales en un territorio argentino: Conflictos de convivencia en el Chaco ante una nueva etapa colonizadora (1920–1940)," *Revista de Geografía Norte Grande* 42 (2009): 21–40; Iñigo Carrera, "Sujetos productivos," 229–31.
23. Mariotti et al., "Fronteras en tensión," 7–37; Tamagno, *Nam qom huetáa.*
24. Iñigo Carrera, "Sujetos productivos," 229–31.

25. Cordeu and Siffredi, *De la algarroba al algodón*; Carlos Salamanca, "Revisitando Napalpí: Por una antropología dialógica de la acción social y la violencia," *Runa* 31, no. 1 (2009): 67–87.
26. Elmer S. Miller, "The Argentine Toba Evangelical Religious Service," *Ethnology* 10, no. 2 (1971): 149–59; César Ceriani Cernadas, "Fronteras, espacios y peligros en una misión evangélica indígena en el Chaco argentino (1935–1962)," *Boletín Americanista*, no. 67 (2014): 143–62.
27. Miller, "Argentine Toba Evangelical Religious Service"; Cernadas, "Fronteras, espacios y peligros."
28. Wright, *Ser-en-el-sueño*; Pablo Wright, "Colonización del espacio, la palabra y el cuerpo en el Chaco argentino," *Horizontes Antropológicos* 9, no. 19 (2003): 137–52.
29. Morita Carrasco and Claudia Briones, *La tierra que nos quitaron* (IWGIA, 1996), 91–148. I traveled to this area with a family from the barrio, a trip I describe in Chapter 5.
30. Tamagno, *Nam qom huetáa*, 1–44.
31. The provinces of Formosa and Chaco were among the first in the country to have Indigenous legislation in the 1980s, before the constitutional change in the 1990s. The "historic reparation" that law mandated was implemented through land titling for Indigenous occupation. See Morita Carrasco, *Los derechos de los pueblos indígenas en Argentina* (IWGIA, Vinciguerra Testimonios, 2000), 11–48.
32. Iñigo Carrera, "Sujetos productivos," 229–31.
33. Vivaldi, "'If I Have a Job in the City.'"
34. Carrasco, *Los derechos de los pueblos indígenas en Argentina*.
35. The media portrayal of Qom people associates them with extraordinary famines, with many in a state of deep malnutrition, as victims of flooding that destroys homes and scarce property, and as objects of extreme forms of political subordination, as when whole communities take political candidates hostage before elections to guarantee their votes. See Gastón Gordillo, "The Crucible of Citizenship: ID-Paper Fetishism in the Argentinean Chaco," *American Ethnologist* 33, no. 2 (2006): 162–76.
36. See Silvia Citro, *Cuerpos significantes: Travesías de una etnografía dialéctica* (Editorial Biblos, 2009), 243–97.
37. Citro, *Cuerpos significantes*, 297–322.
38. See Mariana Gómez, *Guerreras y tímidas doncellas del Pilcomayo: Las mujeres tobas (qom) del oeste de Formosa* (Biblos, 2016), 290–385; Tola, *Yo no estoy solo en mi cuerpo*, 133–50.
39. Often a male partner in the girlfriend's community.

40. The women were not employed in the cotton field or the sugar plantation by themselves as the men were. They did not travel by themselves to participate in the harvest as young men do.
41. *Auxiliar docente aborigen* (in Chaco province) or *maestro de modalidad aborigen* (in Formosa) refer to aboriginal teacher assistants. The position was created as part of national multicultural education policies. Aboriginal assistants are trained and employed in provinces with a high percentage of Indigenous residents, such as Chaco and Formosa, but not in Buenos Aires. While they are not allowed to teach, they are expected to translate and tutor Indigenous students.
42. For a full development of missionary impositions of a Christian gender system, see Gómez, *Guerreras y tímidas doncellas del Pilcomayo*.
43. Citro, *Cuerpos significantes*, 297–322; Miguel Chase-Sardi et al., *El gateo de los nuestros: Narrativa erótica indígena del Gran Chaco* (Ediciones del Sol, 1992), 15:10–47.
44. Adrienne Rich, *Compulsory Heterosexuality and Lesbian Existence* (Only Women Press, 1980): 225–52; Michelle Zimbalist Rosaldo et al., *Woman, Culture, and Society* (Stanford University Press, 1974), 1–42.
45. Rita Laura Segato, "The New Forms of War and Women's Bodies," *Sociedade e Estado* 29, no. 2 (2014): 341–71; Silvana Sciortino and Mariana Gómez, "Mujeres indígenas, derechos colectivos y violencia de género: Intervenciones en un debate que inicia," *Revista de la Carrera de Sociología* 5, no. 5 (2015): 37–63.
46. In becoming adults, affective mobilities become affections, which are the embodied trace of an affect that reshapes a body.
47. Ingrid Spennemann, "Migración y proceso político identitario: La comunidad indígena qom de la provincia de Buenos Aires" (thesis, Universidad de Buenos Aires, 2006).
48. Qom barrios in Rosario were created in the 1960s and include the biggest concentration of urban Qom and of Qom people outside the Chaco. In the 2010s, and according to Indigenous leaders' estimations, close to twenty thousand Qom lived in Rosario. See Fabiana A. Fernández and Matías A. Stival, "Políticas, sentidos y vulnerabilidad sociocultural asociados al VIH-Sida en las poblaciones qom de Rosario, Argentina," *Desacatos* 35 (2011): 29–40.
49. Jon Beasley-Murray, *Posthegemony: Political Theory and Latin America* (University of Minnesota Press, 2010), 125–73.
50. Beasley-Murray, in *Posthegemony*, argues that "politics is no longer a matter of consent and negotiation, implied by the hegemonic contract; it is a (non)relation or incompatibility between processes of capture and affective escape" (139).

51. Stuart Hall, "Negotiating Caribbean Identities," *New Left Review* 209 (1995): 3–14.
52. The opposite of being strong is to be *flojo* or *floja*, a category used for both men and women and closely related to a physical state of having neither strength nor *ánimo*, energy, initiative, or will. Gómez, *Guerreras y tímidas doncellas*, 350–80.
53. For Andrea's generation, social mobility meant getting a high school degree with an orientation in health care or teaching and then obtaining a job in one of these areas.
54. Spennemann, "Migración y proceso político identitario."
55. Tola, *Yo no estoy solo en mi cuerpo*, 33–37.
56. *Colimba* is the nickname both for the military draft and for the men who were doing it.
57. Santiago Garaño, "Entre el cuartel y el monte: Soldados, militantes y militares durante el operativo independencia en Tucumán, 1975–1977" (PhD diss., University of Buenos Aires, 2012).
58. Being a *colimba* was recognized as a hard, even traumatic, experience for many men, especially during the dictatorship (1976–83), when *colimbas* had to participate in or try to avoid participating in the military dictatorship, including confrontations with armed leftist movements and the illegal kidnapping, torturing, and killing of civilians. Further, in 1982, thousands of *colimbas* were forced to fight in the war in the Falklands/Malvinas with the United Kingdom. Undertrained and underequipped, thousands of Argentina's casualties were *colimbas*. Nowadays, *colimba* is generational marker: The last men to be drafted were in the class of 1976; the last *colimbas* are now in their fifties.
59. I am thinking in the terms set by Marcel Mauss in his notion of techniques of the body, forms of training the body to impart specific capacities. Mauss stresses something different than Bourdieu does: Rather than re-creating a socially structured disposition for acting, it was the trained body and its capacities of tracing, running, and shooting that became a source of status. Under the stressful conditions of military training, Qom's trained bodies had capacities that others did not. Marcel Mauss, "Techniques of the Body," *Economy and Society* 2, no. 1 (1973): 70–88.
60. Gordillo, *Landscapes of Devils*, 158–66.
61. Lynn Stephen, *Transborder Lives: Indigenous Oaxacans in Mexico, California, and Oregon* (Duke University Press, 2007), 35–62.

CHAPTER 2

1. See Wright, "Histories of Buenos Aires," 137–57.
2. Doreen B. Massey, *For Space* (Sage, 2005), 149–62.

3. Verónica Gago has identified this constitution of urban collective subjects that emerge out of a popular and vitalist pragmatic combining the skills and relationships of different trajectories as a form of neoliberalism from below. See Verónica Gago, *Neoliberalism from Below: Popular Pragmatics and Baroque Economies* (Duke University Press, 2017), 17–23.
4. Other families had lived in Ciudad Oculta, another infamous *villa*. Their experiences have a lot in common with that of families in Fuerte Apache.
5. Karl Marx, *Capital: A Critique of Political Economy*, trans. Ben Fowkes and David Fernbach (Penguin Books, 1981), 877–94, 931–42.
6. Frantz Fanon, *The Wretched of the Earth*, trans. Richard Philcox (Grove Press 1963), 38–41.
7. Especially Aníbal Quijano, "Coloniality of Power and Eurocentrism in Latin America," *International Sociology* 15, no. 2 (2000): 215–32.
8. Nancy P. Appelbaum, *Muddied Waters: Race, Region, and Local History in Colombia, 1846–1948* (Duke University Press, 2003), 1–31; Peter Wade, "Rethinking Mestizaje: Ideology and Lived Experience," *Journal of Latin American Studies* 37, no. 2 (2005): 239–57.
9. Brodwyn M. Fischer, introduction to *Cities from Scratch: Poverty and Informality in Urban Latin America* (Duke University Press, 2014), 1–8.
10. Saidiya V. Hartman, *Wayward Lives, Beautiful Experiments: Intimate Histories of Social Upheaval* (W.W. Norton, 2019), 10–29.
11. Daniel M. Goldstein, *Owners of the Sidewalk: Security and Survival in the Informal City* (Duke University Press, 2016), 18–42.
12. Cadena, *Indigenous Mestizos*, 272–330.
13. Albó, "El Alto, La vorágine," 329–50; Horn, *Indigenous Rights to the City*, 17–32.
14. Lazar, *El Alto*, 25–55; Postero, *Indigenous State*, 25–40.
15. Silvia Rivera Cusicanqui, "Ch'ixinakax Utxiwa: A Reflection on the Practices and Discourses of Decolonization," *South Atlantic Quarterly* 111, no. 1 (2012): 95–109.
16. Alberto and Elena, *Rethinking Race*, 1–22; Rita L. Segato, *La nación y sus otros raza, etnicidad y diversidad religiosa en tiempos de políticas de la identidad* (Prometeo Libros, 2007), 15–35, 37–70.
17. Segato, *La nación y sus otros*, 23. My translation and emphasis.
18. Ramiro Segura, "Elementos para una crítica de la noción de segregación residencial socio-económica: Desigualdades, desplazamientos e interacciones en la periferia de La Plata," *Quid 16*, no. 2 (2012): 106–32.
19. Gago, *Neoliberalism from Below*, 153–77, 178–217.
20. *Malón* specifically refers to the Indigenous attacks on *criollo* towns and cities during the colonial era. Diana Lenton analyzes the limits of Peronism in

incorporating Indigenous identities in Buenos Aires in the 1946 protest of the Malón de la Paz (peaceful raid). Lenton, "The Malón de la Paz," 85–112.

21. Currently, for example, some white middle-class people talk about having an *alma de negro* if they display a behavior associated with being *negro*, which adds complexity to the correlation of the notion of *negro* as simultaneously a class marker, perceived nonwhite phenotype, and particular set of behaviors. Frigerio, "'Negros' y 'Blancos' en Buenos Aires," 5.
22. Frigerio, "'Negros' y 'Blancos' en Buenos Aires," 18–22.
23. Domingo Faustino Sarmiento, *Facundo, civilización y barbarie: Vida de Juan Facundo Quiroga* (Editorial Porrúa, 1966).
24. Alberto and Elena, *Rethinking Race*, 1–22.
25. Ezequiel Adamovsky, *El gaucho indómito de Martín Fierro a Perón, el emblema imposible de una nación desgarrada* (Siglo XXI, 2019).
26. Geler, "African Descent and Whiteness," 40–55.
27. Ricardo D. Salvatore, *Wandering Paysanos State Order and Subaltern Experience in Buenos Aires During the Rosas Era* (Duke University Press, 2003), 3–45.
28. Richard Gott, "Latin America as a White Settler Society," *Bulletin of Latin American Research* 26, no. 2 (2007): 269–89; Ricardo D. Salvatore, "The Unsettling Location of a Settler Nation: Argentina, from Settler Economy to Failed Developing Nation," *South Atlantic Quarterly* 107, no. 4 (2008): 755–89.
29. Lucy Taylor, "Four Foundations of Settler Colonial Theory: Four Insights from Argentina," *Settler Colonial Studies* 11, no. 3 (2020): 344–65.
30. Adamovsky, *Historia de la clase media*, 240–365.
31. Adamovsky, *Historia de las clases populares*, 1–43; Hugo E. Ratier, *El cabecita negra* (Centro Editor de América Latina, 1972), 40–95.
32. Alejandro Grimson, *Racialidad, etnicidad y clase en los orígenes del peronismo, Argentina 1945* (Kompetenznetz Lateinamerika, 2016), 26–48.
33. Ratier, *El cabecita negra*, 31–32.
34. Brodwyn Fischer, in her introduction to *Cities from Scratch*, makes a fundamental point about informal cities in Latin America: "[Urbanization] demands that cities recognize the needs and interest that poor informal cities serve, the multiple ways in which they are embedded in urban life and that they expand the limits of the formal city to incorporate what informality does best" (7).
35. Javier Auyero, *Poor People's Politics: Peronist Survival Networks and the Legacy of Evita* (Duke University Press, 2001), 45–80; Eva Cameli, "Politicidad villera: El movimiento villero peronista, 1973–1976," *Quid 16: Revista del Área de Estudios Urbanos* 7 (2017): 231–34.

36. See María Cristina Cravino, *Los mil barrios (in)formales: Aportes para la construcción de un observatorio del hábitat popular del Área Metropolitana de Buenos Aires* (Universidad Nacional de General Sarmiento, 2008), 45–65.
37. Eduardo Blaustein, *Prohibido vivir aquí: La erradicación de villas durante la dictadura* (Editorial Punto de Encuentro, 2006), 53–108.
38. Cameli, "Politicidad villera," 231–34; Adriana Massidda et al., "'Villas miseria' en Buenos Aires hacia mediados del siglo XX: Tensiones políticas y primeras conceptualizaciones estatales," *EURE* 49, no. 147 (2023): 1–21.
39. Cravino, *Los mil barrios*, 45–48.
40. Aguiló and Vivaldi, "Race and the Shantytown," 556–59.
41. Aguiló, *The Darkening Nation*, 1–38.
42. David Theo Goldberg, *Racist Culture: Philosophy and the Politics of Meaning* (Blackwell, 1993), 185–295.
43. Cravino, *Los mil barrios*, 13–44, 45–65; Gabriel Kessler, "Las consecuencias de la estigmatización territorial: Reflexiones a partir de un caso particular," *Espacios en Blanco, Serie Indagaciones* 22, no. 1 (2012): 165–97.
44. Kessler, "Las consecuencias de la estigmatización," 165–97.
45. Aguiló and Vivaldi, *Race and the Shantytown*, 551–73.
46. Adamovsky, *Historia de la clase media*, 240–365.
47. Gordillo, *Savage Outside of White Argentina*, 243.
48. This experience could also be a symptom of what Adamovsky presents in his history of the middle class, *Historia de la clase media argentina*. He found that in Argentina, many people who could be economically characterized as working class assume a middle-class identity nonetheless. Classifying a perceived poor as other can be an act of class distinction between working-class and unemployed poor.
49. The experience of white, working-class immigrants arriving in the city is different from the Qom experience. Significantly, white immigrants are not likely to get stopped by the police in the city.
50. Segato, *La nación y sus otros*, 23–25.
51. Goldberg, *Racist Culture*, 185–205.
52. Ramiro Segura, "Segregación residencial, fronteras urbanas y movilidad territorial: Un acercamiento etnográfico," *Cuadernos del IDES* 9 (2006): 3–24.
53. In the Chaco, Qom are part of a typology that distinguishes *aborígenes* ("Indigenous people" who live in communities), *criollos* (mixed-race rural population, often settlers), and whites (of European descent). In the Chaco, being recognized as *aborigen* implied being the poorest of the poor and regarded as backward, lazy, deceitful, and dependent on state assistance,

among others. However, being seen as a violent criminal was not a part of this racialization.

54. Daniel James, *Resistance and Integration: Peronism and the Argentine Working Class, 1946–1976* (Cambridge University Press, 1988), 213–49; Eduardo Elena, *Dignifying Argentina: Peronism, Citizenship, and Mass Consumption* (University of Pittsburgh Press, 2011) 3–35.

55. Borges and Bioy Casares, under the pseudonym "Bustos Domecq," paradigmatically presented these negative images of *negros peronistas*. Borges and Bioy Casares, "La fiesta del monstruo," *Nuevas Crónicas de Bustos Domeq* (Emece, 2004), 14–20.

56. Grimson, *Racialidad, etnicidad y clase*, 26–48; Albertina Carri, *Los rubios: Cartografía de una película* (Ediciones Gráficas Especiales, 2007).

57. Eva Camelli, "'Atención, atención . . . ¿Los villeros se preparan para la revolución?' Convergencias y divergencias entre el movimiento villero Peronista y Montoneros," *Páginas (Rosario): Revista Digital de la Escuela de Historia* 13, no. 31 (2021): 1–27.

58. Blaustein, *Prohibido vivir aquí*, 33–53.

59. The Hotel de los Inmigrantes (Immigrants' Hotel) was a residence in the port where all foreign immigrants arriving in Argentina were forced to stay until they got legal permission to reside in the country. Lorenzo ended up in the same place as immigrants from overseas. At the hotel, Lorenzo made friends with other men who helped him to obtain a job in the port and get a legal permit to work there.

60. Paul Gilroy, *Postcolonial Melancholia* (Columbia University Press, 2005), 121–52.

61. In 1955, Perón's second presidency was violently interrupted by the self-proclaimed Revolución Libertadora (Emancipating Revolution) military coup. Military officers took over the presidential palace and bombed Peronist supporters who had regrouped in the Plaza de Mayo. Lorenzo also remembers this event and escaping the bombings that day: He was able to board the last boat, from downtown Buenos Aires to Dock Sud on the Riachuelo's other bank. He had a very clear understanding of the political event and the bombings as part of the overthrow of Perón.

62. Lorenzo knew who Perón was, as this was his second presidency, and according to his accounts of the first trip to Buenos Aires back in 1955, all Buenos Aires was permeated with signs of Peronism, such as Peronist songs.

63. On another occasion, Lorenzo vividly narrated the arrival of the boats with immigrants to the hotel, where people were received with the Peronist march: "The people were escaping wars and famine in Europe." At that point, he sang the whole Peronist march to me. I was surprised to see he knew all the

lyrics in spite of not identifying as "a Peronist." Furthermore, in this account, he revealed that in the mid-1950s, white immigrants were poor Europeans escaping war and living in the same place in the city where Qom families did. The racial categories were thus not developed over preexisting class divisions but were employed to generate that class differentiation.

64. See James, *Resistance and Integration*, 249–64.
65. This march was a year earlier than Perón's first election as president, when he held the roles of vice president and minister of labor, the role in which he gained union support. He was jailed because of a dispute with a high-command military officer in an attempt to prevent his presidential candidacy. The mass protest generated his release and has since become the Día de la Lealtad Peronista (Peronist Loyalty Day), commemorated every October 17 with marches and events by the Peronist party. A month later, Perón was running for president.
66. The number is too high. According to a Spanish newspaper, the people on strike numbered six thousand, so the people hired to continue port activities numbered probably five thousand at most. "Paro portuario," *La Vanguardia*, March 18, 1966, 22.
67. "Paro portuario."
68. In the Chaco and Formosa provinces, Indigenous people were incorporated into politics through Peronism but in a very different manner, they are incorporated in the 1980s, as Indigenous populations and through political patronage relations. The experience of Peronism in the Chaco thus contrasts highly with mass mobilization and union politics in the city. See Iñigo Carrera, "Sujetos productivos"; Gordillo, "Places and Academic Disputes."
69. Beasley-Murray, *Posthegemony*, 125–40.
70. Lawrence Grossberg, "Identity and Cultural Studies: Is That All There Is?," in *Questions of Cultural Identity*, ed. Stuart Hall and Paul du Gay (Sage, 1996), 87–107.
71. Lefebvre, *Production of Space*, 1–67.
72. Lefebvre, *Production of Space*, 352–461.
73. Massey, *For Space*, 12.
74. Jon Beasley-Murray analyzes how Peronism captures the force of what he identifies as a multitude. Beasley-Murray, *Posthegemony*, 15–66.
75. Cravino, *Los mil barrios*, 45–65.
76. Blaustein, *Prohibido vivir aquí*, 33–53.
77. Geler et al., "Afro-Argentines of Buenos Aires," 90–116.
78. Fuerte Apache continued to grow during the late 1970s, when new towers were built. The first buildings were finished at the end of 1960 during Onganía's

dictatorship. In 1973, there was a transitional democratically elected government, and as Cámpora took power, it allowed Perón to return. It was during the third Perón presidency that Lorenzo got his apartment. The third presidency ended with Perón's death in 1974, followed by the unstable government of his wife Isabel Perón and the subsequent 1976 dictatorship. By moving to Ejército de los Andes, Lorenzo avoided a wave of *villa* evictions that lefts thousands of people homeless. Cravino, *Las villas*, 17–57.

79. Elena, *Dignifying Argentina*, 18–51.
80. The escalation of unemployment in the *villas* resulted in the formation of the unemployed movement, the *piqueteros*. The *piqueteros* originated in northern Argentina, organizing around the right to work, and developed new forms of protest by blocking national roads and then urban main avenues, preventing circulation. Svampa and Pereyra, *Entre la ruta y el barrio: La experiencia de las organizaciones piqueteras* (Biblos, 2003). The state of generalized unemployment also inevitably led young people in the *villas* to become involved in gangs and the illegal economy. Míguez, *Los pibes chorro*.
81. Sibila Camps, "La historia de un barrio con 90.000 habitantes," *Clarín Diario*, October 31, 2000, http://edant.clarin.com/diario/2000/10/31/s-03101.htm; Cristian Alarcón, "El barrio Fuerte," *La Prensa Gráfica*, 2009, http://www.laprensagrafica.com/revistas/septimo-sentido/14390-el-barrio-fuerte.
82. Kessler, *Las consecuencias de la estigmatización territorial*, 165–97.
83. Alejandro Isla, *En los márgenes de la ley: Inseguridad y violencia en el Cono Sur* (Paidós, 2007), 23–47; Alejandro Isla and Daniel Míguez, *Heridas urbanas: Violencia delictiva y transformaciones sociales en los noventa* (Editorial de las Ciencias, FLACSO, 2003), 1–35.
84. I searched for news coverage of this event with no success. All journalist chronicles agree in marking this event as giving origin to the name but give no specific date to the naming.
85. Camps, "La historia de un barrio"; Alarcón, "El barrio Fuerte."
86. The 1981 movie *Fort Apache, The Bronx* is about the adventures of a policeman in an African American and Latinx neighborhood.
87. Gordillo, *The Savage Outside*, 241–67.
88. Michel Foucault, *Society Must Be Defended: Lectures at the Collège de France, 1975–76*, ed. M. Bertani et al. (Picador, 2003), 239–62.
89. I did not find a press article reporting the presence of the Qom in Fuerte Apache.
90. Axel Lazzari, "Autonomy in Apparitions: Phantom Indian, Selves, and Freedom" (PhD diss., Columbia University, 2010), http://gradworks.umi.com/34/47/3447981.html.

91. Michael T. Taussig, *Shamanism, Colonialism, and the Wild Man: A Study in Terror and Healing* (University of Chicago Press, 1986), 51–74.
92. Javier Auyero et al., *Violence at the Urban Margins* (Oxford University Press, 2015), 1–19; Loïc J. D. Wacquant, *Urban Outcasts: A Comparative Sociology of Advanced Marginality* (Polity Press, 2008), 227–52; Didier Fassin, *Enforcing Order: An Ethnography of Urban Policing* (Polity Press, 2013), 85–112.
93. Carlos Tévez played on the Manchester City team in the United Kingdom between 2007 and 2013 and gained international recognition.
94. Judith M. Anderson, "Will the Real Negros Please Stand Up? Understanding Black Identity Politics in Buenos Aires, Argentina," *Transforming Anthropology* 23, no. 2 (2015): 69–78; Lea Geler, "Categorías raciales en Buenos Aires: Negritud, blanquitud, Afrodescendencia y mestizaje en la blanca ciudad capital," *Runa: Archivo para las Ciencias del Hombre* 37, no. 1 (2016): 71–87.
95. Don Kulick, *Travesti: Sex, Gender, and Culture among Brazilian Transgendered Prostitutes* (University of Chicago Press, 1998), 2–18.
96. *Travesti* is the term used for a particular Latin American sexual identity that is linked with a lower socioeconomic status. In Argentina and Brazil, most *travesties* who grow up in small towns and rural villages migrate to the cities, where they can find a community and access the means to transform their body. See Kulick, *Travesti*. They are the object of very strong social stigma, and in Argentina, their life expectancy is strikingly low, limited to forty-one years of age, as they cannot access the health system and are the object of systemic violence (Arístegui, Zalazar, and Fundación Huésped 2014).
97. Mario asked me of my visit: "Are you a journalist? Do you want to write about this barrio?" I explained that I was researching how the Qom have arrived to Buenos Aires and that I was an anthropologist, and he looked happy with my reply. I realized that while anthropologists are frequent in the Barrio Qom, "el Fuerte" is constantly approached by journalists who want to portray life in the "most dangerous" place in the country.
98. The Gendarmería is a force created to police borders and transit on national roads. It has both military and police functions.
99. Joaquín Zajac, "Tapando baches, apagando incendios: Las prácticas de prevención e investigación de delitos de la Gendarmería Nacional Argentina en los barrios del sur de la CABA," *Sociales en Debate*, no. 11 (2016): 1–9; Gabriel Kessler, "¿Exclusión social y desigualdad? ¿Nociones útiles para pensar la estructura social argentina?," *Lavboratorio*, no. 28 (2018): 4–18.
100. Diego Escolar, "Represión y represión: Militarización de la seguridad interior, prácticas de la memoria e imágen institucional en la Gendarmería Nacional Argentina," in *Memorias militares sobre la represión en el Cono Sur: Visiones*

en disputa en dictadura y democracia, ed. Felipe Agüero and Eric Hershberg (Siglo XXI, 2005).

101. See Zajac, "Tapando baches"; Kessler, "Las consecuencias de la estigmatización," 165–97. The cities of the "empire" have simultaneously militarized the control of the suburbs while it directed an unconstrained military violence toward its "external others." In both cases, the place of the other became a space outside the law where the other's life does not count. Derek Gregory, "The Everywhere War," *Geographical Journal* 177, no. 3 (2011): 238–50.
102. Goldberg, *Racist Culture*, 185–95.
103. Goldstein, *Owners of the Sidewalk*, 10–42.
104. Coordinadora Contra la Represión Policial e Institucional, "Archivo de Casos 2014," http://correpi.lahaine.org/?p=1342.
105. Max Weber, "The Nation State and Economic Policy," in *Max Weber: Political Writings*, trans. Peter Lassman and Ronald Speirs (Cambridge University Press, 2004); Antonio Gramsci, *Prison Notebooks*, vol. 1 (Columbia University Press, 2011), 312–69.
106. Giorgio Agamben, *Homo Sacer* (Stanford University Press, 1998), 45–67.
107. Eva Camelli, "Politicidad villera: El movimiento villero Peronista, 1973–1976," 231–34.
108. Maristella Svampa, *La sociedad excluyente: La Argentina bajo el signo del neoliberalismo* (Taurus, 2005).

CHAPTER 3

1. Massey, *For Space*, 54.
2. Canelo, *Fronteras internas*, 1–45.
3. Caggiano, *Lo que no entra en el crisol*, 1–34; Gavazzo, "Jóvenes migrantes," 131–62.
4. Juan Manuel Engelman, "Migración y acceso a la tierra, urbana en la década de 1990: El caso de la comunidad Indígena Toba-Qom 'Yape' de Bernal Oeste, provincia de Buenos Aires," *Andes* 32, no. 1 (2021): 67–79.
5. Engelman, "Etnización de políticas públicas," 121–31.
6. Laura Weiss et al., "Pueblos indígenas urbanos en Argentina: Un estado de la cuestión," *Revista Pilquen* 16, no. 1 (2013): 2–18; Juan Manuel Engelman, "Indigenous Population in the Cities: Visibility and Ethno-Political Organization in the Metropolitan Area of Buenos Aires, Argentina," *Journal of Historical Archaeology and Anthropological Sciences* (January 2018): 44–49.
7. Identidad Marrón et al., *Marrones escriben: Perspectivas antirracistas desde el Sur global* (University of Manchester, 2021), 4–21.
8. Aguiló and Vivaldi, "Race and the Shantytown," 563–67.
9. Massey, *For Space*, 130.

10. The community registries were created in the 1990s to implement Indigenous legislation developed nationally and provincially. In some contexts, national and provincial legislation overlap, creating tensions around recognition. See Briones (2005) for examples. In other cases, communities may choose between jurisdictions strategically. For example, if a group is denied provincial recognition—sometimes as part of provincial governments' attempt to curtail groups' land claims—it may apply to the national registry.
11. For other processes, see Engelman, "Etnización de políticas públicas," 121–31.
12. While most houses were given to families of more than four people, there is one house occupied by a single man. There is also a single mother who lives just with her youngest daughter.
13. Massey, *For Space*, 118.
14. INDEC, "WebINDEC - Población / poblaciones específicas / pueblos originarios," 2011, http://www.indec.gov.ar/nivel4_default.asp?id_tema_1=2&id_tema_2=21&id_tema_3=99.
15. While the highway divides the two jurisdictions, the city extends without significant division, creating one of the biggest urban conglomerates in South America. There are, of course, jurisdictional distinctions in Buenos Aires city that impact infrastructure, funding, and state services.
16. Cravino, *Construyendo barrios*, 1–36.
17. Gabriel Kessler, *El sentimiento de inseguridad: Sociología del temor al delito* (Siglo XXI, 2009), 87–112.
18. Cravino, *Los mil barrios*, 45–65.
19. INDEC undertook the *Encuesta complementaria de Pueblos Indígenas* in 2002. It was the first time that Indigenous population was measured by the nation-state. See INDEC, "INDEC Censo 2001 datos por provincia," http://www.indec.gov.ar/micro_sitios/webcenso/provincias_2/provincias.asp.
20. For Brazil, see Teresa P. Caldeira, *City of Walls: Crime, Segregation, and Citizenship in São Paulo* (University of California Press, 2000), 256–96.
21. Maristella Svampa, *Los que ganaron: La vida en los countries y barrios privados* (Editorial Biblos, 2001), 207–69.
22. By "colonizing" the suburbs, the gated communities created great tension with their surroundings. Poor and working-class neighborhoods start just outside gated communities' fences and have differential access to services. Separation has been a never-ending obsession of these gated communities, as residents there continuously reinforce security, build taller fences, and make access harder. Svampa, *La sociedad excluyente*.
23. While the number is under debate, it is estimated that around three million people travel from the province to the city to work.

24. Lefebvre, *The Production of Space*, 1–67.
25. Michel Foucault, "The Subject and Power," *Critical Inquiry* 8, no. 4 (1982): 777–95.
26. Kessler, "El sentimiento de inseguridad," 87–122.
27. Simone, *The Surrounds*, 1–54.
28. Denise Ferreira Da Silva, *Unpayable Debt* (Sternberg Press, 2022), 1–47.
29. Javier Auyero and Débora Alejandra Swistun, *Flammable: Environmental Suffering in an Argentine Shantytown* (Oxford University Press, 2009), 1–36.
30. Kessler, *El sentimiento de inseguridad*, 87–122.
31. Aguiló and Vivaldi, *Race and the Shantytown*, 556–59.
32. Aguiló, *The Darkening Nation*, 51–83.
33. People in the barrio did not mind much about the focus of my research while I was there. But when I discussed the possibility of staying overnight, they were not comfortable about it, as they are very pressed for space.
34. National legislation opens up the possibility of having land claims outside the "traditional territories" when land reparation is defined as the return of traditional lands *or* other lands that "can guarantee cultural survival." This clarification has allowed land claims in urban areas and in regions where Indigenous populations moved later. Therefore, it allows for a partial recognition of displaced Indigeneity. See Carrasco, *Los derechos de los pueblos indígenas*; Claudia Briones, *Cartografías argentinas: Políticas indigenistas y formaciones provinciales de alteridad* (Editorial Antropofagia / GEAPRONA, 2005).
35. Engelman, "Indigenous Population," 44–49; Susana Sassone, "Migración, territorio e identidad cultural: Construcción de 'lugares bolivianos' en la Ciudad de Buenos Aires," *Población de Buenos Aires* 4, no. 6 (2007): 9–28.
36. Lazar, *El Alto*, 1–53.
37. Canelo, *Fronteras internas*, 117–62.
38. For critical overview, see Pilar Pérez, "Historia y silencio: La conquista del desierto como genocidio no-narrado," *Corpus: Archivos Virtuales de la Alteridad Americana* 1, no. 2 (2011): http://corpusarchivos.revues.org/1157; Axel Lazzari and Diana Lenton, "Araucanization, Nation: A Century Inscribing Indians in the Pampas," in *Contemporary Perspectives on the Native Peoples of Pampa, Patagonia, and Tierra del Fuego: Living on the Edge*, ed. Claudia Briones and José Luis Lanata (Greenwood Publishing, 2002), 33–46.
39. Identidad Marrón et al., *Marrones escriben*, 1–43.
40. Multiple other Indigenous groups have had colonization trajectories that make it harder or even impossible for them to be recognized as such. Recognition and lack of recognition are tightly connected processes, and yet

until recently, nonrecognition was not the object of academic research. This tendency has changed with recent studies of nonrecognition across the Americas. See, e.g., Muehlemann, *Where the River Ends*; Lawrence, *Real Indians and Others*.

41. Salamanca, "Revisitando Napalpí," 67–87.
42. Iñigo Carrera, *Violence as an Economic Force*, 1–50.
43. Francis Ludlow et al., "The Double Binds of Indigeneity and Indigenous Resistance," *Humanities* 5, no. 3 (2016): 2–19.
44. Silvia Rivera Cusicanqui, "Ch'ixinakax Utxiwa: A Reflection on the Practices and Discourses of Decolonization," *South Atlantic Quarterly* 111, no. 1 (2012): 95–109.
45. Hale, "Does Multiculturalism Menace? Governance, Cultural Rights and the Politics of Identity in Guatemala," *PoLAR: Political and Legal Anthropology Review* 28, no. 1 (2005): 10–19.
46. Lenton, "Malón de la Paz of 1946," 85–112.
47. See Claudia Briones, *La alteridad del "Cuarto Mundo": Una deconstrucción antropológica de la diferencia* (Ediciones del Sol, 1998), 141–71; Carrasco, *Los derechos*, 6–38.
48. For further studies on authenticity outside Argentina, see Paige Sylvia Raibmon, *Authentic Indians: Episodes of Encounter from the Late-Nineteenth-Century Northwest Coast* (Duke University Press, 2005); Tania Li, *The Will to Improve: Governmentality, Development, and the Practice of Politics* (Duke University Press, 2007); Shaylih Muehlmann, *Where the River Ends: Contested Indigeneity in the Mexican Colorado Delta* (Duke University Press, 2013).
49. Elizabeth A. Povinelli, *The Cunning of Recognition: Indigenous Alterities and the Making of Australian Multiculturalism* (Duke University Press, 2002), 16–17.
50. Povinelli, *The Cunning of Recognition*, 6.
51. Auyero, *Poor People's Politics*, 29–74; Iñigo Carrera, "Sujetos productivos," 229–31.
52. Gayatri Chakravorty Spivak, "Can the Subaltern Speak?," in *Marxism and the Interpretation of Culture* (University of Illinois Press, 1988), 271–313.
53. Li, "Articulating Indigenous Identity," 149–79.
54. John L. Comaroff and Jean Comaroff, *Ethnicity, Inc.* (University of Chicago Press, 2009), 22–59.
55. Charles R. Hale, "When I Hear the Word Culture…," *Cultural Studies* 32, no. 3 (2018): 497–509; Peter Wade, "Blackness, Indigeneity, Multiculturalism and Genomics in Brazil, Colombia and Mexico," *Journal of Latin American Studies* 45, no. 2 (2013): 205–33.

56. Briones, "Formaciones de alteridad," 9–38; Carrasco, *Los derechos*, 1–52; Kropff Causa et al., "La tierra de los otros," 19–30.
57. Povinelli, *The Cunning of Recognition*, 1–34; Coulthard, *Red Skin, White Masks*, 25–50.

CHAPTER 4

1. Alcida Rita Ramos, *Indigenism: Ethnic Politics in Brazil* (University of Wisconsin Press, 1998), 13–87.
2. Aguiló, *The Darkening Nation*, 51–83.
3. The Indigenist movement had an important role in the 1990s supporting the creation of Indigenous legislation both at the national level and in specific provinces. See Carrasco, *Los derechos*, 10–53. The two NGOs that aided the creation of the barrio are linked with larger NGOs that have been involved in the creation of national Indigenous legislation.
4. Mary Louise Pratt, *Imperial Eyes: Travel Writing and Transculturation* (Routledge, 1992), 111–71.
5. Cultural practices including, for example, shamanic conceptions of the body are in some cases part of the experience of people from the barrio, but as has been shown in other works, these are always redefined, since the experience of colonization forcefully incorporated the groups to modernity and its regimes of knowledge.
6. See Beth A. Conklin, "Body Paint, Feathers and VCRs: Aesthetics and Authenticity in Amazonian Activism," *American Ethnologist*, no. 24 (1997): 711–37; Alcida Rita Ramos, "16. The Commodification of the Indian," in *Human Impacts on Amazonia*, ed. Darrell A. Posey and Michael J. Balick (Columbia University Press, 2006), 248–72.
7. Ana Vivaldi and Rafael Wainer, "Más acá de la representación: Imágenes de 'cuerpos del hambre' en el Chaco, producción afectiva de públicos y biopoder" (presentation), Asociación Latinoamericana de Sociología, Buenos Aires, 2009.
8. Gordillo, "Places and Academic Disputes," 447–65.
9. Didier Fassin, "Heart of Humaneness: The Moral Economy of Humanitarian Intervention," in *Contemporary States of Emergency: The Politics of Military and Humanitarian Interventions* (Zone Books, 2010); Miriam Ticktin, "Transnational Humanitarianism," *Annual Review of Anthropology* 43, no. 1 (2014): 273–89.
10. Peter Wade and Monica Moreno-Figueroa, "Alternative Grammars of Anti-Racism in Latin America," *Interface: A Journal for and about Social Movements* 13, no. 2 (2022): 20–50.

11. See Bonita Lawrence, *"Real" Indians and Others Mixed-Blood Urban Native Peoples and Indigenous Nationhood* (University of Nebraska Press, 2004), 5–29.
12. Axel Lazzari and Diana Lenton, "The Indian and 'Politics': Transgressive Indigeneities in Political Activism Before and After State Terrorism in Argentina," *Journal of Intercultural Studies* 40, no. 6 (2019): 681–99.
13. Engelman, "Indigenous Population," 44–49.
14. Tamagno, *Nam qom huetáa*, 1–56.
15. I felt a connection with the group, as my own ideas do align with their leftist perspectives; however, I did not become a part of it, and I use the engagement to reflect critically on my own and the leftist relations and expectations on Indigenous people.
16. The countercelebration was organized by groups of the left as critique to the silencing of Indigenous dispossession from the national history. The countercelebration took the form of a camp in a park close to the official celebrations.
17. For a discussion on the limits to the production of "alternative," see Arun Saldanha, *Psychedelic White: Goa Trance and the Viscosity of Race* (University of Minnesota Press, 2007), 132–52.
18. While they collaborated with NGOs and the church, they are also critical of both institutions and of older generations of Indigenous activists who they consider too dependent on these institutions.
19. Iñigo Carrera, "Sujetos productivos," 229–31.
20. Benedict de Spinoza, *Ethics* (Penguin Classics, 1996), 11–76.
21. Renisa Mawani, *Colonial Proximities: Crossracial Encounters and Juridical Truths in British Columbia, 1871–1921* (UBC Press, 2009), 1–34.
22. Ana Vivaldi, "Indigeneidades urbanas: Formaciones espacializadas de raza y experiencia Toba (Qom) en Buenos Aires," *Quid 16: Revista del Área de Estudios Urbanos*, no. 11 (2019): 151–74.
23. For more on Indigenous fetishism with official documents, including ID cards, see Gastón Gordillo, "The Crucible of Citizenship: ID-Paper Fetishism in the Argentinean Chaco," *American Ethnologist* 33, no. 2 (2006): 162–76.
24. María Cristina Cravino, *Las villas de la ciudad: Mercado e informalidad urbana* (Universidad Nacional de General Sarmiento, 2006), 53.
25. Gordillo, "The Crucible of Citizenship."
26. Carrasco, *Los derechos*, 25–48.
27. Showing the different relation with institutions that Fernando has, in contrast to Martín, he once told me: "We spent a long time talking about the people who do not have an ID card. Some children never had one issued! But I say what did the parents do? They had to bring their birth certificate

with them." His perspective shapes him as proper citizen who understands his rights. He implied, following government logic, that people in the barrio were responsible for their lack of ID, and ultimately their own exclusion from civil rights.

28. Canelo, *Fronteras internas*, 1–45.
29. Javier Auyero, *Patients of the State: The Politics of Waiting in Argentina* (Duke University Press, 2012), 23–36.
30. Comaroff and Comaroff, *Ethnicity, Inc.*, 6–22.
31. As discussed in Chapter 1, the expectation of finding a community is not only a romantic idea of middle-class groups, but also a legal requirement for creating an Indigenous association, registered in INAI, and having a legal figure is a requirement for receiving lands. James Brow, "Notes on Community, Hegemony, and the Uses of the Past," *Anthropological Quarterly* (1990): 1–6.
32. Li, *The Will to Improve*, 1–60.
33. Gordillo, *Places and Academic Disputes*, 447–65.
34. Gordillo, *The Savage Outside*, 241–67.
35. Cristian Vitale, "Dale aborigen," *Página 12*, May 21, 2006, http://www.pagina12.com.ar/diario/suplementos/no/12-2239-2006-05-21.html. Translated by Daniel Low.
36. Gordillo, *The Savage Outside*, 241–67.
37. Fassin, "Heart of Humaneness," 269–94; Ticktin, "Transnational Humanitarianism," 273–89.

CHAPTER 5

1. With a group of colleagues, we wrote a collective reply to this news. See Grupo de antropologos de la Facultad de Filosofia y Letras (UBA), "Narrar el hambre," *Página 12*, October 13, 2007, http://www.pagina12.com.ar/diario/suplementos/futuro/13-1798-2007-10-16.html.
2. Deleuze and Guattari, *A Thousand Plateaus*, 502.
3. Deleuze and Guattari, *A Thousand Plateaus*, 502–4.
4. I use the concepts of (de)territorialization as an organization of the activity and a definition of a space. While the concept has not originated in Indigenous scholarship, the recent discussion about Indigenous territorialities as grounded normativity operating outside notions of boundary and unified total jurisdiction resonates strongly. Glen Coulthard and Leanne Betasamosake Simpson, "Grounded Normativity / Place-Based Solidarity," *American Quarterly* 68, no. 2 (2016): 249–55. The concept of grounded normativity, however, does not enable me to particularly describe Qom practices of connection across space to their full extent.

5. See Kathi Wilson and Evelyn J. Peters, "'You Can Make a Place for It': Remapping Urban First Nations Spaces of Identity," *Environment and Planning D: Society and Space* 23, no. 3 (2005): 395–413; Renya K. Ramirez, *Native Hubs: Culture, Community, and Belonging in Silicon Valley and Beyond* (Duke University Press, 2007), 58–83.
6. Guha, *Elementary Aspects*, 220–332.
7. The notion of assemblage has been used in anthropology mostly to refer to transnational and global dynamics, such as the compelling work of Aihwa Ong, who understands neoliberalism as an assemblage of heterogeneous work and economic relations constituting one complex system. See Aihwa Ong, *Neoliberalism as Exception: Mutations in Citizenship and Sovereignty* (Duke University Press, 2006), 75–96.
8. One of the best-documented examples of this are *balikbayan* boxes—consumer goods from the Global North sent to the Philippines. Fritzie de Mata, "Zeugmatic Formations: Balikbayan Boxes and the Filipino Diaspora," in *Geo-Spatiality in Asian and Oceanic Literature and Culture*, ed. Shiuhhuah Serena Chou et al., Geocriticism and Spatial Literary Studies (Springer International, 2022).
9. Gago, *Neoliberalism from Below*, 153–178; Mandrile, "El corredor de remesas," 11–28.
10. Stuart A. Rockefeller, *Starting from Quirpini: The Travels and Places of a Bolivian People* (Indiana University Press, 2010), 221–50.
11. Héctor Parra García, "Ensamblajes transnacionales de la colectividad boliviana en Buenos Aires," *Diálogo Andino*, no. 66 (2021): 337–49.
12. Deleuze and Guattari, *A Thousand Plateaus*, 109.
13. Sending back remittances is uncommon, as most urban families are in a very precarious situation. When people are paid, they quickly spend most of the money immediately on food or on phone credit. There is an indirect form of cash circulation when a family pays for the bus ticket for a relative in the Chaco to come and visit. But in general, the central relation is the circulation of objects rather than money.
14. Gago, *Neoliberalism from Below*, 1–28.
15. Salamanca and Tola make a relevant analysis of the pressures to share. Carlos Salamanca and Florencia C. Tola, "La brujería como discurso político entre los tobas del Chaco argentino," *Desacatos* 9 (2002): 96–116.
16. Karen Adkins, *Gossip, Epistemology, and Power: Knowledge Underground* (Springer International, 2017), 1–50.
17. Marilyn Strathern, "Cutting the Network," *Journal of the Royal Anthropological Institute* 2, no. 3 (1996): 517–35.

18. Miller, *The Argentine Toba Evangelical*, 149–59.
19. See Miller, *The Argentine Toba Evangelical*, 149–59; Ceriani Cernadas, "Evangelio, política y memoria en los Qom (Toba) del Chaco argentino," *Nuevo Mundo Mundos Nuevos*, https://nuevomundo.revues.org/61083.
20. A gigantic informal-economy clothing fair where people who work in sweatshops sell brand clothing they have produced. See Gago, *Neoliberalism from Below*, 108–53.
21. Gendarmería is the national force securing borders and routes; the gendarmes have a reputation for being uncorrupted.
22. When the officer left, women commented that she was a good officer because she was taking care of women.
23. Deleuze and Guattari, *A Thousand Plateaus*, 351–423.
24. Ana Vivaldi, "Stuck on a Muddy Road: Frictions of Mobility Amongst Urban Qom in Northern Argentina," *Identities* 18, no. 6 (2011): 599–619; Anna Lowenhaupt Tsing, *Friction: An Ethnography of Global Connection* (Princeton University Press, 2005), 1–75.
25. Beasley-Murray, *Posthegemony*, 217, 234.
26. The church was created in the 1950s, and the first request of registry as a recognized "religion" was in 1957, with the aid of Mennonite missionaries.
27. There is no official number, but some people calculated that over forty full buses had arrived, which, plus the local population and the people arriving on their own, meant it was probably an encounter of over 1,500 people. The word used to refer to this meeting is *encuentro*, literally, "encounter," yet the best parallel in English is *revival*. I use this notion to make it clearer for the reader, although it is not the ethnographic category.
28. Citro, *Cuerpos significantes*, 133.
29. Pablo Wright, "Toba Pentecostalism Revisited," *Social Compass* 39, no. 3 (1992): 355–75.
30. The intensity seemed to have a role keeping both people and churches together against dissolution and competition. By "intensity," I mean the degree of transformation of capacities.
31. Citro has pointed to the way the church services in eastern Chaco are a place of socialization of youth. She shows how, especially through dance, young men and women look to find a partner. Citro, *Cuerpos significantes*, 243–97.
32. Miller, *Los tobas argentinos*, 21–50.
33. Hall, "Negotiating Caribbean Identities," 3–14.
34. Stuart Hall, "Race, Articulation, and Societies Structured in Dominance," in *Black British Cultural Studies: A Reader* (University of Chicago Press 1996), 14–58.

35. In my other trips with people from the barrio, the church enabled our mobility too. For example, during Martín's long visit to his relatives in Castelli, we stayed with his relatives, who were also preachers.
36. The trip back was also marked by an unexpected tragedy. An eight-year-old girl who had remained in Buenos Aires was begging for food on the streets when she was run over by a bus. People got the news through text messages. During our trip back, many people were crying and took turns to pray for the girl.
37. This is a pseudonym. I attended a meeting of the land association on an earlier trip and its members explicitly requested that I restrict my work to the families who had invited me. I was unable to build a deeper relationship, and they were suspicious I wanted to extract a deep history of the communities without their permission. I respect the request here.
38. *El monte* is a relative category expressing degrees of a place's rurality. In earlier work, I found that Qom people living in the city talk about rural villages indistinctly as *monte*, but when I traveled to these rural villages, I found that the places where the houses and farms are located are distinguished from the wilder areas of forest, marshlands, and riverside that constitute the *monte* of that location. See Ana Vivaldi, "'If I Have a Job in the City, I'll Go to the Bush on Weekends': Place Production Among Qom People in Northern Argentina" (MA thesis, University of British Columbia, 2007), https://open.library.ubc.ca/cIRcle/collections/ubctheses/831/items/1.0100666.
39. Carrasco and Briones, *La tierra*, 91–148.
40. Massey, *For Space*, 8.
41. Massey, *For Space*, 9.
42. This was also a good option for the lands: Gregorio explained that it was hard to find people from the town wanting to move to those lands, as there were no services there.
43. Massey, *For Space*, 8–12.
44. Santos, *The Nature of Space*, 34–53; Liisa Malkki, "National Geographic: The Rooting of Peoples and the Territorialization of National Identity Among Scholars and Refugees," *Cultural Anthropology* 7, no. 1 (1992): 24–44.
45. Ong, *Neoliberalism as Exception*, 75–96.
46. Santos, "The Return of the Territory," 25–31. Analyzing the territory emerging from an assemblage closely follows Santos's challenge to avoid misrecognition of the territory as only what is subordinated to state juridico-legal order, when that is only one of the possible effects of disputes over space. This is where Santos, coming from the analysis of territory, meets assemblage theories, which share an emphasis on activity as defining territoriality.
47. Guha, *Elementary Aspects*, 278–333.

CONCLUSION

1. Tola, *Yo no estoy solo en mi cuerpo*, 151–73.
2. Massey, *For Space*, 130.
3. Santos, "The Return of the Territory," 25–31.
4. Raúl Mandrini, *Los araucanos de las pampas en el siglo XIX* (Centro Editor de América Latina, 1984).
5. Alberto and Elena, *Rethinking Race*, 1–22.
6. Identidad Marrón et al., *Marrones escriben*, 5–57.
7. Wade and Moreno-Figueroa, "Alternative Grammars of Anti-Racism," 20–50.
8. Donald S. Moore, *Suffering for Territory: Race, Place, and Power in Zimbabwe* (Duke University Press, 2005), 35–128.
9. Santos, "The Return of the Territory"; Massey, *For Space*; Beasley-Murray, *Posthegemony*.

BIBLIOGRAPHY

Adamovsky, Ezequiel. "El color de la nación argentina: Conflictos y negociaciones por la definición de un ethnos nacional, de la crisis al bicentenario" (The color of the Argentine nation: Conflicts and negotiations for the definition of a national ethnos, from the crisis to the bicentenary). *Jahrbuch für Geschichte Lateinamerikas (Colonia)* 49 (2012): 343–64.

Adamovsky, Ezequiel. *El gaucho indómito de Martín Fierro a Perón: El emblema imposible de una nación desgarrada* (The indomitable gaucho from Martín Fierro to Perón: The impossible emblem of a torn nation). Siglo XXI, 2019.

Adamovsky, Ezequiel. *Historia de la clase media argentina: Apogeo y decadencia de una ilusión, 1919–2003* (History of the Argentine middle class: The rise and fall of an illusion, 1919–2003). Planeta, 2009.

Adamovsky, Ezequiel. *Historia de las clases populares en la Argentina: Desde 1880 hasta 2003* (History of the popular classes in Argentina: From 1880 to 2003). Penguin Random House, 2012.

Adkins, Karen. *Gossip, Epistemology, and Power: Knowledge Underground*. Springer International, 2017.

Agamben, Giorgio. *Homo Sacer.* Stanford University Press, 1998.

Aguiló, Ignacio. *The Darkening Nation: Race, Neoliberalism and Crisis in Argentina*. University of Wales Press, 2018.

Aguiló, Ignacio, and Ana Vivaldi. "Race and the Shantytown in a Race-Less Country: Negros Villeros, Whiteness and Urban Space in Argentina." *Latin American and Caribbean Ethnic Studies* (2023): 551–73.

Alarcón, Cristian. "El barrio fuerte" (The strong neighborhood). *La Prensa Gráfica*, 2009. http://www.laprensagrafica.com/revistas/septimo-sentido/14390-el-barrio-fuerte.

Alarcón, Cristian. *Cuando me muera, quiero que me toquen cumbia: Vidas de pibes chorros* (When I die, I want you to play me cumbia: Lives of the *pibes chorros*). Norma, 2003.

Alberto, Paulina L., and Eduardo Elena, eds. *Rethinking Race in Modern Argentina*. Cambridge University Press, 2015.

Albó, Xavier. "El Alto, la vorágine de una ciudad única" (El Alto: The vortex of a unique city). *Journal of Latin American Anthropology* 11, no. 2 (2006): 329–50.

Álvarez, Miriam, and Laura Kropff Causa. "La diáspora puelche en la obra de teatro Tayiñ Kuify Kvpan" (The Puelche diaspora in the theater play *Tayiñ Kuify Kvpan*). *Cadernos de Arte e Antropologia* 11, no. 1 (April 2022): 48–65.

Anderson, Judith M. "Will the Real Negros Please Stand Up? Understanding Black Identity Politics in Buenos Aires, Argentina." *Transforming Anthropology* 23, no. 2 (2015): 69–78.

Andrews, George Reid. *The Afro-Argentines of Buenos Aires, 1800–1900*. University of Wisconsin Press, 1980.

Appelbaum, Nancy P., Walter D. Mignolo, Irene Silverblatt, and Sonia Saldívar-Hull. *Muddied Waters: Race, Region, and Local History in Colombia, 1846–1948*. Duke University Press, 2003.

Arístegui, Inés, Virginia Zalazar, and Fundación Huésped. *Informe Técnico Ley de Identidad de Género y acceso al cuidado de la Salud de las personas trans en Argentina*." Fundación Huésped, April 2014.

Auyero, Javier. *Patients of the State: The Politics of Waiting in Argentina*. Duke University Press, 2012.

Auyero, Javier. *Poor People's Politics: Peronist Survival Networks and the Legacy of Evita*. Duke University Press, 2001.

Auyero, Javier, Philippe I. Bourgois, and Nancy Scheper-Hughes. *Violence at the Urban Margins*. Oxford University Press, 2015.

Auyero, Javier, and Débora Alejandra Swistun. *Flammable: Environmental Suffering in an Argentine Shantytown*. Oxford University Press, 2009.

Beasley-Murray, Jon. *Posthegemony: Political Theory and Latin America*. University of Minnesota Press, 2010.

Beverley, John. "The Im/possibility of Politics: Subalternity, Modernity, Hegemony." In *The Latin American Subaltern Studies Reader*, edited by Ileana Rodríguez. Duke University Press, 2001.

Bioy Casares, Adolfo, and Jorge Luis Borges. "La fiesta del Monstruo" (The monster's party). In *Nuevos cuentos de Bustos Domeq*. Emecé, 2004.

Blaustein, Eduardo. *Prohibido vivir aquí: La erradicación de villas durante la dictadura* (Prohibited from living here: The eradication of slums during the dictatorship). Punto de Encuentro, 2006.

Bourdieu, Pierre. *Outline of a Theory of Practice*. Cambridge University Press, 1977.

Bourgois, Philippe I. *In Search of Respect: Selling Crack in El Barrio*. Cambridge University Press, 1995.

Brablec, Dana. "Indigenising the City Together: Ethnic Place Production in Santiago de Chile." *Journal of Ethnic and Migration Studies* 49, no. 3 (2020): 1–17.

Braunstein, José, and Elmer Miller. "Ethnohistorical Introduction." In *Peoples of the Gran Chaco*, edited by Elmer Miller. Bergin & Garvey, 1999.

Briones, Claudia. *La alteridad del "Cuarto Mundo": Una deconstrucción antropológica de la diferencia* (The otherness of the "Fourth World": An anthropological deconstruction of difference). Ediciones del Sol, 1998.

Briones, Claudia. *Cartografías argentinas: Políticas indigenistas y formaciones provinciales de alteridad* (Argentine cartographies: Indigenous policies and provincial formations of otherness). Editorial Antropofagia/GEAPRONA, 2005.

Briones, Claudia. "Mestizaje y blanqueamiento como coordenadas de aboriginalidad y nación en Argentina" (Mestizaje and whitening as coordinates of aboriginality and nation in Argentina). *Runa* 23, no. 1 (2022): 61–88.

Brow, James. "Notes on Community, Hegemony, and the Uses of the Past." *Anthropological Quarterly* 63, no. 1 (1990): 1–6.

Bryce, Benjamin. "Paternal Communities: Social Welfare and Immigration in Argentina, 1880–1930." *Journal of Social History* 49, no. 1 (Fall 2015): 213–36. https://doi.org/10.1093/jsh/shu132.

Cadena, Marisol de la. *Race, Culture, Place: Indigenous Mestizos and the Politics of Representation in Cuzco, 1919–1991*. Duke University Press, 2000.

Cadena, Marisol de la, and Orin Starn. *Indigenous Experience Today*. Berg, 2007.

Caggiano, Sergio. *Lo que no entra en el crisol: Inmigración boliviana, comunicación intercultural y procesos identitarios* (What does not fit in the melting pot: Bolivian immigration, intercultural communication, and identity processes). Prometeo, 2005.

Caggiano, Sergio. "Racismo, fundamentalismo cultural y restricción de la ciudadanía: Formas de regulación social frente a inmigrantes en Argentina" (Racism, cultural fundamentalism, and restriction of citizenship: Forms of social regulation toward immigrants in Argentina). In *Las migraciones en América Latina: Políticas, culturas y estrategias*, edited by Susana Novick. Catálogos-CLACSO, 2008.

Caldeira, Teresa Pires do Rio. *City of Walls: Crime, Segregation, and Citizenship in São Paulo*. University of California Press, 2000.

Cameli, Eva. "Politicidad villera: El movimiento villero Peronista, 1973–1976" (*Villa* politics: The Peronist *Villero* Movement, 1973–1976). *Quid 16: Revista del Área de Estudios Urbanos* 7 (2017): 231–34.

Canelo, Brenda. *Fronteras internas: Migración y disputas espaciales en la Ciudad de Buenos Aires* (Internal borders: Migration and spatial disputes in the city of Buenos Aires). Antropofagia, 2013.

Cañuqueo, Lorena. "El territorio relevado, el territorio disputado: Apuntes sobre la implementación de Ley Nacional 26.160 en Río Negro, Argentina" (The assessed territory, the disputed territory: Notes on the implementation of National Law 26.160 in Río Negro, Argentina). *Revista de Geografía Norte Grande*, no. 62 (2015): 11–28.

Cañuqueo, Lorena, and Laura Kropff. "MapUrbe'zine: Los cuerpos de 'la lucha' en el circuito heavy-punk mapuche" (MapUrbe'zine: The bodies of 'the struggle' in the Mapuche heavy-punk circuit). *E-misférica* 4, no. 2 (2007). https://go.exlibris.link/tY9YgVyD.

Cardin, Lorena. "Entre realidades y simulacros: El proceso de relevamiento del territorio qom" (Between reality and simulacra: Surveying the territory). In *Campos de interlocución y políticas de reconocimiento indígena en Argentina*, ed. Morita Carrasco. Antropofagia, 2018.

Carrasco, Morita. *Los derechos de los pueblos indígenas en Argentina* (The rights of Indigenous Peoples in Argentina). International Work Group for Indigenous Affairs, Vinciguerra, 2000.

Carrasco, Morita, and Claudia Briones. *La tierra que nos quitaron* (The land that was taken away from us). International Work Group for Indigenous Affairs, 1996.

Carri, Albertina. *Los rubios: Cartografía de una película* (The blondes: Cartography of a film). Ediciones Gráficas Especiales, 2007.

Casagrande, Olivia. "Towards a Tuwün Wariache? Place-Making and Creative Acts of Traversing in the Mapuche City." *Journal of the Royal Anthropological Institute* 27, no. 4 (2021): 949–75.

Cernadas, César Ceriani. "Fronteras, espacios y peligros en una misión evangélica indígena en el Chaco Argentino (1935–1962)" (Borders, spaces, and dangers in an Indigenous evangelical misión station in the Argentine Chaco, 1935–1962). *Boletín Americanista*, no. 67 (2014): 143–62.

Chase-Sardi, Miguel, Alejandra Siffredi, and Edgardo J. Cordeu. *El gateo de los nuestros: Narrativa erótica indígena del Gran Chaco* (Our crawling: Indigenous erotic narrative of the Gran Chaco). Ediciones del Sol, 1992.

Citro, Silvia. *Cuerpos significantes: Travesías de una etnografía dialéctica* (Significant bodies: journeys of a dialectical ethnography). Biblos, 2009.

Clifford, James. *Returns: Becoming Indigenous in the Twenty-First Century*. Harvard University Press, 2013.

Comaroff, John L., and Jean Comaroff. *Ethnicity, Inc.* University of Chicago Press, 2009.

Conklin, Beth A. "Body Paint, Feathers and VCRs: Aesthetics and Authenticity in Amazonian Activism." *American Ethnologist* 24, no. 4 (1997): 711–37.

Coordinadora Contra la Represión Policial e Institucional. "Archivo de casos 2014." 2014. http://correpi.lahaine.org/?p=1342.

Cordeu, Edgardo J., and Alejandra Siffredi. *De la algarroba al algodón: Movimiento mesiánico de los guaycurú* (From carob to cotton: The messianic movement of the Guaycurú People). Juárez Editor, 1971.

Coulthard, Glen Sean. *Red Skin, White Masks: Rejecting the Colonial Politics of Recognition*. University of Minnesota Press, 2014.

Coulthard, Glen, and Leanne Betasamosake Simpson. "Grounded Normativity / Place-Based Solidarity." *American Quarterly* 68, no. 2 (2016): 249–55.

Cravino, María Cristina. *Construyendo barrios: Transformaciones socioterritoriales a partir de los programas federales de vivienda en el Área Metropolitana de Buenos Aires (2004–2009)* (Building neighborhoods: Socio-territorial transformations from Federal Housing Programs in the Metropolitan Area of Buenos Aires, 2004–2009). CICCUS and Universidad Nacional de General Sarmiento, 2012.

Cravino, María Cristina. *Los mil barrios (in)formales: Aportes para la construcción de un observatorio de hábitat popular del Área Metropolitana de Buenos Aires* (The thousand (in)formal neighborhoods: Contributions for the construction of a popular habitat observatory in the Metropolitan Area of Buenos Aires). Universidad Nacional de General Sarmiento, 2008.

Cravino, María Cristina. *Las villas de la ciudad: Mercado e informalidad urbana* (The slums of the city: Market and urban informality). Universidad Nacional de General Sarmiento, 2006.

Cusicanqui, Silvia Rivera. "Ch'ixinakax Utxiwa: A Reflection on the Practices and Discourses of Decolonization." *South Atlantic Quarterly* 111, no. 1 (2012): 95–109.

Da Silva, Denise Ferreira. *Unpayable Debt*. Sternberg Press, 2022.

Deleuze, Gilles, and Félix Guattari. *A Thousand Plateaus: Capitalism and Schizophrenia*. University of Minnesota Press, 1987.

Deloria, Philip Joseph. *Indians in Unexpected Places*. University Press of Kansas, 2004.

Edwards, Erika Denise. *Hiding in Plain Sight: Black Women, the Law, and the Making of a White Argentine Republic*. University of Alabama Press, 2020.

Elena, Eduardo. *Dignifying Argentina: Peronism, Citizenship, and Mass Consumption*. University of Pittsburgh Press, 2011.

Engelman, Juan Manuel. "Etnización de políticas públicas al sur del Área Metropolitana de Buenos Aires, Argentina" (Ethnicization of public policies south of the Metropolitan Area of Buenos Aires, Argentina). *Anales de Antropología* 53, no. 1 (2019): 121–31.

Engelman, Juan Manuel. "Indigenous Population in the Cities: Visibility and Ethno-Political Organization in the Metropolitan Area of Buenos Aires, Argentina." *Journal of Historical Anthropology and Anthropological Sciences* (January 2018): 44–49.

Engelman, Juan Manuel. "Migración y acceso a la tierra urbana en la década de 1990: El caso de la comunidad indígena toba-qom 'Yape' de Bernal Oeste, Provincia de Buenos Aires" (Migration and access to urban land in the 1990s: The case of the Toba-Qom 'Yape' Indigenous community in Bernal Oeste, province of Buenos Aires). *Andes* 32, no. 1 (2021): https://www.redalyc.org/journal/127/12767786006/html/#fn6.

Escolar, Diego. "Represión y represión: Militarización de la seguridad interior, prácticas de la memoria e imágen institucional en la Gendarmería Nacional Argentina" (Repression and repression: Militarization of internal security, memory practices, and institutional image in the Argentine National Guard). In *Memorias militares sobre la represión en el Cono Sur: Visiones en disputa en dictadura y democracia*, edited by Felipe Agüero and Eric Hershberg. Siglo XXI, 2005.

Fanon, Frantz. *The Wretched of the Earth*. Translated by Richard Philcox. Grove Press, 1963.

Fassin, Didier. "Heart of Humaneness: The Moral Economy of Humanitarian Intervention." In *Contemporary States of Emergency: The Politics of Military and Humanitarian Interventions,* edited by Didier Fassin and Mariela Pandolfi. Zone Books, 2010.

Fassin, Didier, and Mariella Pandolfi. *Contemporary States of Emergency: The Politics of Military and Humanitarian Interventions*. Zone Books, 2010.

Faustino Sarmiento, Domingo. *Facundo, civilización y barbarie: Vida de Juan Facundo Quiroga* (Facundo, civilization and barbarism: The life of Juan Facundo Quiroga). Editorial Porrúa, 1966.

Ferguson, James, and Akhil Gupta. "Spatializing States: Toward an Ethnography of Neoliberal Governmentality." *American Ethnologist* 29, no. 4 (2002): 981–1002.

Fernández, Fabiana A., and Matías A. Stival. "Políticas, sentidos y vulnerabilidad sociocultural asociados al VIH-Sida en las poblaciones qom de Rosario, Argentina" (Politics, meanings and sociocultural vulnerability associated to the HIV-AIDS in the Qom people in Rosario, Argentina). *Desacatos* 35 (2011): 29–40.

Fischer, Brodwyn M. Introduction to *Cities from Scratch: Poverty and Informality in Urban Latin America*. Duke University Press, 2014.

Foucault, Michel. *Society Must Be Defended: Lectures at the Collège de France, 1975–76*. Edited by Mauro Bertani and François Ewald. Picador, 2003.

Foucault, Michel. "The Subject and Power." *Critical Inquiry* 8, no. 4 (1982): 777–95.

Frigerio, Alejandro. "'Negros' y 'blancos' en Buenos Aires: Repensando nuestras categorías raciales" ("Blacks" and "whites" in Buenos Aires: Rethinking our racial categories). *Temas de Patrimonio Cultural* 16 (2006): 77–98.

Gago, Verónica. *Neoliberalism from Below: Popular Pragmatics and Baroque Economies*. Duke University Press, 2017.

Garaño, Santiago. "Entre el cuartel y el monte: Soldados, militantes y militares durante el operativo independencia (Tucumán, 1975–1977)" (Between the barracks and the bush: Soldiers, activists, and military during the Independence Operation, Tucumán, 1975–1977). PhD diss., University of Buenos Aires, 2012.

Gavazzo, Natalia. "Jóvenes migrantes e hijos de inmigrantes latinoamericanos en Buenos Aires: Una generación en movimiento" (Young migrants and children of Latin American immigrants in Buenos Aires: A generation in motion). *Confluenze: Rivista di Studi Iberoamericani* 10, no. 1 (2018): 131–65. https://doi.org/10.6092/issn.2036-0967/8298.

Gavazzo, Natalia, and Débora Gerbaudo Suárez. "Desigualdades generacionales y prácticas políticas en las juventudes migrantes paraguayas en Buenos Aires" (Generational inequalities and political practices among Paraguayan migrant youth in Buenos Aires). *Migraciones: Publicación del Instituto Universitario de Estudios sobre Migraciones*, no. 48 (April 2020): 133–60. https://doi.org/10.14422/mig.i48y2020.006.

Geler, Lea. "African Descent and Whiteness in Buenos Aires: Impossible Mestizajes in the White Capital City." In *Rethinking Race in Modern Argentina*, edited by Paulina Alberto and Eduardo Elena. Cambridge University Press, 2016. https://doi.org/10.1017/CBO9781316228050.010.

Geler, Lea. *Andares negros, caminos blancos: Afroporteños, Estado y nación: Argentina a fines del siglo XIX* (Black walks, white roads: Afro-porteños, state, and nation: Argentina at the end of the nineteenth century). Prohistoria, 2010.

Geler, Lea. "Categorías raciales en Buenos Aires: Negritud, blanquitud, afrodescendencia y mestizaje en la blanca ciudad capital" (Racial categories in Buenos Aires: Blackness, whiteness, Afro-descendence, and mestizaje in the white capital city). *Runa* 37, no. 1 (2016): 71–87.

Geler, Lea, Carmen Yannone, and Alejandra Egido. "Afro-Argentines of Buenos Aires in the 20th Century: The Suburbanization Process." *Quinto Sol* 24, no. 3 (2020): 90–116.

Gilroy, Paul. *Postcolonial Melancholia*. Columbia University Press, 2005.

Goldberg, David Theo. *Racist Culture: Philosophy and the Politics of Meaning*. Blackwell, 1993.

Goldstein, Daniel M. *Owners of the Sidewalk: Security and Survival in the Informal City*. Global Insecurities. Duke University Press, 2016.

Gómez, Mariana. *Guerreras y tímidas doncellas del Pilcomayo: Las mujeres tobas (qom) del oeste de Formosa*" (Warriors and shy ladies of the Pilcomayo river: Qom women in western Formosa). Biblos, 2016.

González, Melitón. *El Gran Chaco argentino* (The Argentine Great Chaco). Comp. Sud-Americ. de Billetes de Banco, 1890.

Gordillo, Gastón. "The Crucible of Citizenship: ID-Paper Fetishism in the Argentinean Chaco." *American Ethnologist* 33, no. 2 (2006): 162–76.

Gordillo, Gastón. *Landscapes of Devils: Tensions of Place and Memory in the Argentinean Chaco*. Duke University Press, 2004.

Gordillo, Gastón. "Longing for Elsewhere: Guaraní Reterritorializations." *Comparative Studies in Society and History* 53, no. 4 (2011): 855–81.

Gordillo, Gastón. "Places and Academic Disputes: The Argentine Gran Chaco." In *A Companion to Latin American Anthropology*, edited by Deborah Poole. Blackwell, 2008.

Gordillo, Gastón. "The Savage Outside of White Argentina." In *Rethinking Race in Modern Argentina*, edited by Paulina Alberto and Eduardo Elena. Cambridge University Press, 2016.

Gordillo, Gastón, and Silvia María Hirsch. *Movilizaciones indígenas e identidades en disputa en la Argentina*. La Crujía-FLACSO, 2010.

Gorelik, Adrian. "Buenos Aires Is (Latin) America Too." In *City/Art: The Urban Scene in Latin America*, edited by Rebecca E. Biron. Duke University Press, 2009.

Gott, Richard. "Latin America as a White Settler Society." *Bulletin of Latin American Research* 26, no. 2 (2007): 269–89.

Gramsci, Antonio. *Prison Notebooks*, vol. 1. Columbia University Press, 2011.

Gregory, Derek. "The Everywhere War." *Geographical Journal* 177, no. 3 (2011): 238–50.

Grimson, Alejandro. *Racialidad, etnicidad y clase en los orígenes del peronismo, Argentina 1945* (Race, Ethnicity, and Class in the Origins of Peronism, Argentina 1945). Kompetenznetz Lateinamerika, 2016.

Grossberg, Lawrence. "Identity and Cultural Studies: Is that All There is?" In *Questions of Cultural Identity*, edited by Stuart Hall and Paul du Gay. Sage, 1996.

Grossberg, Lawrence. *We Gotta Get Out of This Place: Popular Conservatism and Postmodern Culture*. Routledge, 1992.

Guha, Ranajit. *Elementary Aspects of Peasant Insurgency in Colonial India*. Oxford University Press, 1983.

Guha, Ranajit, and Gayatri Chakravorty Spivak. *Selected Subaltern Studies*. Oxford University Press, 1988.

Hale, Charles R. "Does Multiculturalism Menace? Governance, Cultural Rights and the Politics of Identity in Guatemala." *Journal of Latin American Studies* 34, no. 3 (2002): 485–524.

Hale, Charles R. "Neoliberal Multiculturalism." *PoLAR: Political and Legal Anthropology Review* 28, no. 1 (2005): 10–19.

Hale, Charles R. "When I Hear the Word Culture . . ." *Cultural Studies* 32, no. 3 (2018): 497–509.

Hall, Stuart. "Negotiating Caribbean Identities." *New Left Review* 209 (1995): 3–14.

Hall, Stuart. "Race, Articulation, and Societies Structured in Dominance." In *Black British Cultural Studies: A Reader*, edited by Houston A. Baker, Manthia Diawara, and Ruth H Lindeborg. University of Chicago Press, 1996.

Hartman, Saidiya V. *Wayward Lives, Beautiful Experiments: Intimate Histories of Social Upheaval*. W.W. Norton, 2019.

Harvey, David. *Justice, Nature and the Geography of Difference*. Wiley-Blackwell, 1996.

Hetch, Ana Carolina. *"Todavía no se hallaron hablar en idioma": Procesos de socialización lingüística de los niños en el barrio Qom* ("They are not yet comfortable speaking in the language": Linguistic socialization processes of children in a Qom neighborhood). Lincom Europa, 2010.

Horevitz, Elizabeth. "Understanding the Anthropology of Immigration and Migration," *Journal of Human Behavior in the Social Environment* 19, no. 6 (2009): 745–58.

Horn, Philipp. *Indigenous Rights to the City Ethnicity and Urban Planning in Bolivia and Ecuador*. Routledge, 2019.

Identidad Marrón, Ana Vivaldi, and Pablo Cossio. *Marrones escriben: Perspectivas antirracistas desde el sur global* (Marrones write: Anti-racist perspectives from the Global South). Identidad Marrón—Culturas de Anti Racismo en América Latina. University of Manchester, 2021.

INDEC. "INDEC Censo 2001 datos por provincia." 2005. http://www.indec.gov.ar/micro_sitios/webcenso/provincias_2/provincias.asp.

INDEC. "WebINDEC - Población / poblaciones específicas / pueblos originarios." 2011. https://sitioanterior.indec.gob.ar/nivel4_default.asp?id_tema_1=2&id_tema_2=21&id_tema_3=99.

Ingold, Tim. *Being Alive: Essays on Movement, Knowledge and Description*. Routledge, 2011.

Iñigo Carrera, Nicolás. *La colonización del Chaco* (The colonization of the Chaco). Centro Editor de América Latina, 1983.

Iñigo Carrera, Nicolás. *Violence as an Economic Force: The Process of Proletarianisation among the Indigenous People of the Argentinian Chaco, 1884–1930*. IWGIA, 1982.

Iñigo Carrera, Valeria. "Sujetos productivos, sujetos políticos, sujetos indígenas: Las formas de su objetivación mercantil entre los tobas del este de Formosa" (Productive subjects, political subjects, Indigenous subjects: Mercantile objectification of the Toba People of eastern Formosa). *Cuadernos de Antropología Social*, no. 32 (2010): 229–31.

Isla, Alejandro. *En los márgenes de la ley: Inseguridad y violencia en el Cono Sur* (On the margins of the law: Insecurity and violence in the Southern Cone). Paidós, 2007.

Isla, Alejandro, and Daniel Míguez. *Heridas urbanas: Violencia delictiva y transformaciones sociales en los noventa* (Urban wounds: Criminal violence and social transformations in the 1990s). Editorial de las Ciencias-FLACSO, 2003.

James, Daniel. *Resistance and Integration: Peronism and the Argentine Working Class, 1946–1976*. Cambridge University Press, 1988.

Keith, Michael. *After the Cosmopolitan? Multicultural Cities and the Future of Racism*. Routledge, 2005.

Kessler, Gabriel. "Las consecuencias de la estigmatización territorial: Reflexiones a partir de un caso particular" (The consequences of territorial stigmatization: Reflections based on a specific case). *Espacios en Blanco: Serie Indagaciones* 22, no. 1 (2012): 165–97.

Kessler, Gabriel. "¿Exclusión social y desigualdad? Nociones útiles para pensar la estructura social argentina?" (Social exclusion and inequality? Useful notions for understanding the social structure of Argentina?) *Lavboratorio*, no. 28 (2018).

Kessler, Gabriel. *El sentimiento de inseguridad: Sociología del temor al delito* (The sense of insecurity: The sociology of the fear of crime). Siglo XXI, 2009.

Ko, Chisu Teresa. "From Whiteness to Diversity: Crossing the Racial Threshold in Bicentennial Argentina." *Ethnic and Racial Studies* 37, no. 14 (2013): 2529–46.

Ko, Chisu Teresa. "Making Identities Visible and Invisible: The Uses of Race in Argentine National Identity." PhD diss., Columbia University, 2009.

Kropff, Laura. "Debates About Politics Among Young Mapuche in Argentina." *Revista Latinoamericana de Ciencias Sociales, Niñez y Juventud* 9, no. 1 (2011): 83–99.

Kropff, Laura, Julieta Wallace, Pilar Pérez, and Lorena Cañuqueo. *La tierra de los otros: La dimensión territorial del genocidio indígena en Río Negro y sus efectos en el presente* (The land of others: The territorial dimension of Indigenous genocide in Río Negro and its effects today). Editorial UNRN, 2019.

Kulick, Don. *Travesti: Sex, Gender, and Culture among Brazilian Transgendered Prostitutes*. University of Chicago Press, 1998.

Latour, Bruno. *Reassembling the Social: An Introduction to Actor-Network-Theory*. Oxford University Press, 2005.

Lawrence, Bonita. *"Real" Indians and Others Mixed-Blood Urban Native Peoples and Indigenous Nationhood*. University of Nebraska Press, 2004.

Lazar, Sian. *El Alto, Rebel City: Self and Citizenship in Andean Bolivia*. Duke University Press, 2008.

Lazzari, Axel. "Autonomy in Apparitions: Phantom Indian, Selves, and Freedom." PhD diss., Columbia University, 2010. http://gradworks.umi.com/34/47/3447981.html.

Lazzari, Axel, and Diana Lenton. "Araucanization, Nation: A Century Inscribing Indians in the Pampas." In *Contemporary Perspectives on the Native Peoples of Pampa, Patagonia, and Tierra del Fuego: Living on the Edge*, edited by Claudia Briones and José Luis Lanata. Bloomsbury Publishing USA, 2002.

Lazzari, Axel, and Diana Lenton. "The Indian and 'Politics': Transgressive Indigeneities in Political Activism Before and After State Terrorism in Argentina." *Journal of Intercultural Studies* 40, no. 6 (2019): 681–99.

Lefebvre, Henri. *The Production of Space*. Wiley-Blackwell, 1991.

Lenton, Diana. "Argentina's Constituent Genocide: Challenging the Hegemonic National Narrative and Laying the Foundation for Reparations to Indigenous Peoples." *Armenian Review* 53, no. 14 (2012): 63–84.

Lenton, Diana. "The Malón de la Paz of 1946: Indigenous Descamisados at the Dawn of Peronism." In *The New Cultural History of Peronism*, edited by Matthew B. Karush and Oscar Chamosa. Duke University Press, 2020.

Li, Tania. "Articulating Indigenous Identity in Indonesia: Resource Politics and the Tribal Slot." *Comparative Studies in Society and History* 42, no. 1 (2000): 149–79.

Li, Tania. *The Will to Improve: Governmentality, Development, and the Practice of Politics*. Duke University Press, 2007.

Lobo, Susan, and Kurt Peters. *American Indians and the Urban Experience*. Altamira Press, 2001.

Ludlow, Francis, Lauren Baker, Samara Brock, Chris Hebdon, and Michael Dove. "The Double Binds of Indigeneity and Indigenous Resistance." *Humanities* 5, no. 3 (2016): 53.

Malkki, Liisa. "National Geographic: The Rooting of Peoples and the Territorialization of National Identity Among Scholars and Refugees." *Cultural Anthropology* 7, no. 1 (1992): 24–44.

Mandrile, Matteo. *El corredor de remesas sur-sur Argentina-Bolivia* (The remittances corridor south-south Argentina to Bolivia). International Organization for Migration, 2014. http://hdl.handle.net/20.500.11788/1403.

Mandrini, Raúl. *Los araucanos de las pampas en el siglo XIX* (The Araucanians of the Pampas in the nineteenth century). Centro Editor de América Latina, 1984.

Mari, Óscar Ernesto. "La transición entre dos ciclos y sus efectos sociales en un territorio argentino: Conflictos de convivencia en el Chaco ante una nueva etapa colonizadora (1920–1940)" (The transition between two cycles and its social effects in an Argentine territory: Conflicts of coexistence in the Chaco during a new colonization phase, 1920–1940). *Revista de Geografía Norte Grande*, no. 42 (2009): 21–40.

Mariotti, Daniela, María de Estrada, and Andrés Jorge. "Fronteras en tensión" (Borders in tension). *Revista Eletrônica Associação dos Geógrafos Brasileiros Secao Três Lagoas*, no. 12 (2010): 7–37.

Marx, Karl. *Capital: A Critique of Political Economy*. Translated by Ben Fowkes and David Fernbach. Penguin/New Left Review, 1981.

Massey, Doreen B. *For Space*. Sage, 2005.

Massidda, Adriana, Eva Cameli, and Valeria Snitcofsky. "'Villas miseria' en Buenos Aires hacia mediados del siglo XX: Tensiones políticas y primeras conceptualizaciones estatales" (*Villas miseria* in Buenos Aires in the mid-20th Century: Political tensions and initial state conceptualization). *EURE* 49, no. 147 (2023): 1–21.

Mata, Fritzie A. de. "Zeugmatic Formations: Balikbayan Boxes and the Filipino Diaspora." In *Geo-Spatiality in Asian and Oceanic Literature and Culture*, edited by Shiuhhuah Serena Chou, Soyoung Kim, and Rob Sean Wilson. Geocriticism and Spatial Literary Studies. Springer International, 2022.

Mauss, Marcel. "Techniques of the Body." *Economy and Society* 2, no. 1 (1973): 70–88.

Mawani, Renisa. *Colonial Proximities: Crossracial Encounters and Juridical Truths in British Columbia, 1871–1921*. UBC Press, 2009.

McNelly, Angus. "Baroque Modernity in Latin America: Situating Indigeneity, Urban Indigeneity and the Popular Economy." *Bulletin of Latin American Research* 41, no. 1 (2022): 6–20.

Messineo, Cristina. "Del Gran Chaco al Gran Buenos Aires: Programa participativo de capacitación y fortalecimiento de la lengua y la cultura qom en una comunidad indígena Urbana" (From the Gran Chaco to Greater Buenos Aires: Participatory training and strengthening program for the Qom language and culture in an urban Indigenous community). *Primer Congreso sobre Lenguas Indígenas de Latinoamérica*, Austin, Texas, 2003.

Messineo, Cristina, Ana Dell'Arciprete, Paola Cuneo, and Ana Carolina Hetch. "Lingüística y etnografía: Un proyecto de investigación colaborativa en la comunidad qom" (Linguistics and ethnography: A collaborative research project in a Qom community). *Signo & Seña* 17 (2007): 229–45.

Mignolo, Walter. *The Darker Side of the Renaissance: Literacy, Territoriality, and Colonization*. University of Michigan Press, 1995.

Míguez, Daniel. *Los pibes chorros: Estigma y marginación* (Los pibes chorros: Stigma and marginalization). Capital Intelectual, 2004.

Miller, Elmer S. "The Argentine Toba Evangelical Religious Service." *Ethnology* 10, no. 2 (1971): 149–59.

Miller, Elmer S. *Los qoms argentinos: Armonía y disonancia en una sociedad* (The Argentine Qoms: Harmony and dissonance in a society). Siglo XXI Editores, 1979.

Moore, Donald S. *Suffering for Territory: Race, Place, and Power in Zimbabwe*. Duke University Press, 2005.

Muehlmann, Shaylih. *Where the River Ends: Contested Indigeneity in the Mexican Colorado Delta*. Duke University Press, 2013.

Nacuzzi, Lidia R. "Los grupos nómades de la Patagonia y el Chaco en el siglo XVIII: Identidades, espacios, movimientos y recursos económicos ante la situación de contacto. Una reflexión comparativa" (The nomadic groups of Patagonia and the Chaco in the eighteenth century: Identities, spaces, movements, and economic resources in the context of contact. A comparative reflection). *Chungará (Arica)* 39, no. 2 (2007): 221–34.

Ong, Aihwa. *Neoliberalism as Exception: Mutations in Citizenship and Sovereignty*. Duke University Press, 2006.

Palermo, M. A. "Reflexiones sobre el llamado complejo ecuestre en la Argentina" (Reflections on the so-called equestrian complex in Argentina). *Runa* 16 (1986): 157–78.

Parra García, Héctor. "Ensamblajes transnacionales de la colectividad boliviana en Buenos Aires" (Transnational assemblages of the Bolivian community in Buenos Aires). *Diálogo Andino*, no. 66 (2021): 337–49.

Pérez, Pilar. "Historia y silencio: La conquista del desierto como genocidio no-narrado" (History and silence: The Conquest of the Desert as an unnarrated genocide). *Corpus* 1, no. 2 (2011). http://corpusarchivos.revues.org/1157.

Petrie, Daniel. *Fort Apache, the Bronx*. Producers Circle, 1981.

Postero, Nancy. *The Indigenous State: Race, Politics, and Performance in Plurinational Bolivia*. University of California Press, 2017.

Povinelli, Elizabeth A. *The Cunning of Recognition: Indigenous Alterities and the Making of Australian Multiculturalism*. Duke University Press, 2002.

Pratt, Mary Louise. *Imperial Eyes: Travel Writing and Transculturation*. Routledge, 1992.

Quevedo, Cecilia. "Espacialización, alterización y bienestar en el barrio qom de la ciudad de Resistencia, Argentina" (Spatialization, othering, and well-being in the Qom neighborhood of the city of Resistencia, Argentina). *Pluriversidad*, no. 6 (2020): 85–103.

Quijano, Aníbal. "Coloniality of Power and Eurocentrism in Latin America." *International Sociology* 15, no. 2 (2000): 215–32.

Raibmon, Paige Sylvia. *Authentic Indians: Episodes of Encounter from the Late-Nineteenth-Century Northwest Coast*. Duke University Press, 2005.

Ramirez, Renya K. *Native Hubs: Culture, Community, and Belonging in Silicon Valley and Beyond*. Duke University Press, 2007.

Ramos, Alcida Rita. *Indigenism: Ethnic Politics in Brazil*. University of Wisconsin Press, 1998.

Ramos, Alcida Rita. "16. The Commodification of the Indian." In *Human Impacts on Amazonia*, edited by Darrell A. Posey and Michael J. Balick. Columbia University Press, 2006.

Ratier, Hugo E. *El cabecita negra* (The black-headed person). Centro Editor de América Latina, 1972.

Ratier, Hugo E. *Villeros y villas miseria* (Shantytowns dwellers and shantytowns). Centro Editor de América Latina, 1971.

Rich, Adrienne. *Compulsory Heterosexuality and Lesbian Existence*. Onlywomen Press, 1980.

Rockefeller, Stuart A. *Starting from Quirpini: The Travels and Places of a Bolivian People*. Indiana University Press, 2010.

Rodríguez, Ileana, and María Milagros López. *The Latin American Subaltern Studies Reader*. Duke University Press, 2001.

Rosaldo, Michelle Zimbalist, Louise Lamphere, and Joan Bamberger. *Woman, Culture, and Society*. Stanford University Press, 1974.

Salamanca, Carlos. "Deslizándose en las fisuras de la utopía: Los Qom en las fronteras del estado nación argentino" (Sliding through the cracks of utopia: The Qom at the borders of the Argentine nation-state). *Corpus* 5, no. 1 (2015). http://corpusarchivos.revues.org/1422.

Salamanca, Carlos. "Revisitando Napalpí: Por una antropología dialógica de la acción social y la violencia" (Revisiting Napalpí: For a dialogical anthropology of social action and violence). *Runa* 31, no. 1 (2009): 67–87.

Salamanca, Carlos, and Florencia C. Tola. "La brujería como discurso político entre los tobas del Chaco argentino." *Desacatos* 9 (2002): 96–116.

Salazar, Noel B., and Alan Smart. "Anthropological Takes on (Im)Mobility." *Identities* 18, no. 6 (2011): i–ix.

Saldanha, Arun. *Psychedelic White: Goa Trance and the Viscosity of Race*. University of Minnesota Press, 2007.

Salvatore, Ricardo D. "The Unsettling Location of a Settler Nation: Argentina, from Settler Economy to Failed Developing Nation." *South Atlantic Quarterly* 107, no. 4 (2008): 755–89.

Salvatore, Ricardo D. *Wandering Paysanos State Order and Subaltern Experience in Buenos Aires During the Rosas Era*. Duke University Press, 2003.

Santos, Milton. *The Nature of Space*. Duke University Press, 2021.

Santos, Milton. "The Return of the Territory." In *Milton Santos: A Pioneer in Critical Geography from the Global South*. Springer International, 2017.

Sarmiento, Jacqueline. "Indias urbanas en el Buenos Aires tardocolonial: Familia y grupos domésticos" (Urban Indigenous women in late colonial Buenos Aires: Family and domestic groups). *Anuario del Instituto de Historia Argentina*, no. 11 (2011): 27–41.

Sassone, Susana María. "Migración, territorio e identidad cultural: Construcción de lugares bolivianos en la Ciudad de Buenos Aires" (Migration, territory and cultural identity: Construction of Bolivian Places in the city of Buenos Aires). *Población de Buenos Aires* 4, no. 6 (2007).

Sciortino, Silvana, and Mariana Gómez. "Mujeres indígenas, derechos colectivos y violencia de género: Intervenciones en un debate que inicia" (Indigenous women, collective rights, and gender violence: Interventions in a debate that begins). *Revista de la Carrera de Sociología* 5, no. 5 (2015): 37–63.

Segato, Rita Laura. *La nación y sus otros: Raza, etnicidad y diversidad religiosa en tiempos de políticas de la identidad* (The nation and its others: Race, ethnicity, and religious diversity in times of identity politics). Prometeo, 2007.

Segato, Rita Laura. "The New Forms of War and Women's Bodies." *Sociedade e Estado* 29, no. 2 (2014): 341–71.

Segura, Ramiro. "Elementos para una crítica de la noción de segregación residencial socio-económica: Desigualdades, desplazamientos e interacciones en la periferia de La Plata" (Elements for a critique of the notion of socio-economic residential segregation: Inequalities, displacements, and interactions in the periphery of La Plata). *Quid 16*, no. 2 (2012): 106–32.

Segura, Ramiro. "Segregación residencial, fronteras urbanas y movilidad territorial. Un acercamiento etnográfico" (Residential segregation, urban borders, and territorial mobility: An ethnographic approach). *Cuadernos del IDES*, no. 9 (2006): 3–24.

Sexton, Jared. "The Vel of Slavery: Tracking the Figure of the Unsovereign." *Critical Sociology* 42, nos. 4–5 (2016): 583–97.

Sheller, Mimi, and John Urry. "The New Mobilities Paradigm." *Environment and Planning* 38, no. 2 (2006): 207–26.

Simone, AbdouMaliq. *The Surrounds: Urban Life Within and Beyond Capture*. Duke University Press, 2022.

Simpson, Audra. *Mohawk Interruptus Political Life Across the Borders of Settler States*. Duke University Press, 2014.

Solimano, Andres. "Globalizacion y migracion internacional: La experiencia latinoamericana" (Globalization and international migration: The Latin American experience). *Revista de la CEPAL*, no. 80 (2003): 55–72.

Spennemann, Ingrid. "Migración y proceso político identitario: La comunidad indígena Qom de la provincia de Buenos Aires" (Migration and political identity process: The Qom Indigenous community in the province of Buenos Aires). PhD diss., Universidad de Buenos Aires, 2006.

Spinoza, Benedict de. *Ethics*. Penguin, 1996.

Spivak, Gayatri Chakravorty. "Can the Subaltern Speak?" In: *Marxism and the Interpretation of Culture*. University of Illinois Press, 1988.

Stephen, Lynn. *Transborder Lives: Indigenous Oaxacans in Mexico, California, and Oregon*. Duke University Press, 2007.

Strathern, Marilyn. "Cutting the Network." *Journal of the Royal Anthropological Institute* 2, no. 3 (1996): 517–35.

Svampa, Maristella. *Los que ganaron: La vida en los countries y barrios privados* (Those who won: Life in "countries" and gated communities). Editorial Biblos, 2001.

Svampa, Maristella. *La sociedad excluyente: La Argentina bajo el signo del neoliberalismo* (The excluding society: Argentina under the sign of neoliberalism). Taurus, 2005.

Svampa, Maristella, and Sebastián Pereyra. *Entre la ruta y el barrio: La experiencia de las organizaciones piqueteras* (Between the road and the neighborhood: The experience of the Piquetero organizations). Biblos, 2003.

Sztulwark, Diego. *La ofensiva sensible: Neoliberalismo, populismo y el reverso de lo político* (The sensitive offensive: Neoliberalism, populism, and the reversal of politics). Caja Negra, 2019.

Tamagno, Liliana E. *Nam qom huetáa na doqshi l'ma: Los qoms en la casa del hombre blanco: Identidad, memoria y utopía* (Nam Qom huetáa na doqshi l'ma: The Qoms in the house of the white man: identity, memory, and utopia). Ediciones Al Margen, 2001.

Taussig, Michael T. *Shamanism, Colonialism, and the Wild Man: A Study in Terror and Healing*. University of Chicago Press, 1986.

Taylor, Lucy. "Four Foundations of Settler Colonial Theory: Four Insights from Argentina." *Settler Colonial Studies* 11, no. 3 (2020): 344–65.

Ticktin, Miriam. "Transnational Humanitarianism." *Annual Review of Anthropology* 43, no. 1 (2014): 273–89.

Tola, Florencia C. "Constitución de la persona sexuada entre los qom qom, del Chaco argentino" (Constitution of the sexual person among the Qom of the Argentine Chaco). *Pueblos y Fronteras* 4, no. 1 (2007): 1–24.

Tola, Florencia C. *Yo no estoy solo en mi cuerpo: Cuerpos-personas múltiples entre los Qoms del Chaco argentino* (I am not alone in my body: Multiple bodies-personhood among the Qoms of Argentine Chaco). Antropofagia, 2012.

Trouillot, Michel-Rolph. "Anthropology and the Savage Slot: The Poetics and Politics of Otherness." In *Global Transformations: Anthropology and the Modern World*, edited by Michel-Rolph Trouillot, 7–28. Palgrave Macmillan, 2003.

Tsing, Anna Lowenhaupt. *Friction: An Ethnography of Global Connection.* Princeton University Press, 2005.

Tsing, Anna Lowenhaupt. "Indigenous Voice." In *Indigenous Experience Today*, edited by Marisol de la Cadena and Orin Starn. Berg, 2007.

Urry, John. *Mobilities.* Polity, 2007.

Vázquez, Héctor, and Graciela Rodríguez. "Socio-Ethnic Interaction and Identity Formation Among the Toba in Rosario." In *Beyond Multiculturalism: Views from Anthropology*. Ashgate Publishing, 2009.

Virilio, Paul. *Speed and Politics: An Essay on Dromology*. Columbia University Press, 1986.

Vivaldi, Ana. "'If I Have a Job in the City, I'll Go to the Bush on Weekends': Place Production Among Qom People in Northern Argentina." MA thesis, University of British Columbia, 2007. https://open.library.ubc.ca/cIRcle/collections/ubctheses/831/items/1.0100666.

Vivaldi, Ana. "Indigeneidades urbanas: Formaciones espacializadas de raza y experiencia toba (qom) en Buenos Aires" (Urban indigenities: Spatial racial formations and Toba [Qom] experience in Buenos Aires). *Quid 16*, no. 11 (2019): 151–74.

Vivaldi, Ana. "Stuck on a Muddy Road: Frictions of Mobility Amongst Urban Qom in Northern Argentina." *Identities* 18, no. 6 (2011): 599–619.

Vivaldi, Ana, and Rafael Wainer. "Más acá de la representación: Imágenes de 'Cuerpos del hambre' en el Chaco, producción afectiva de públicos y biopoder." Presentation, Asociación Latinoamericana de Sociología, Buenos Aires, 2009.

Voirol, Jérémie. "Assembling 'Indigeneity' Through Musical Practices: Translocal Circulations, 'Tradition,' and Place in Otavalo (Ecuadorian Andes)." *Popular Music* 40, no. 3 (2021): 428–49.

Wacquant, Loïc J. D. *Urban Outcasts: A Comparative Sociology of Advanced Marginality*. Polity, 2008.

Wade, Peter. "Blackness, Indigeneity, Multiculturalism and Genomics in Brazil, Colombia and Mexico." *Journal of Latin American Studies* 45, no. 2 (2013): 205–33.

Wade, Peter. "Rethinking Mestizaje: Ideology and Lived Experience." *Journal of Latin American Studies* 37, no. 2 (2005): 239–57.

Wade, Peter, and Monica Moreno-Figueroa. "Alternative Grammars of Anti-Racism in Latin America." *Interface: A Journal for and about Social Movements* 13, no. 2 (2022): 20–50.

Warren, Sarah D. "Indigenous in the City: The Politics of Urban Mapuche Identity in Chile." *Ethnic and Racial Studies* 40, no. 4 (2017): 694–712.

Warren, Sarah D. "Territorial Dreaming: Youth Mapping the Mapuche Cross-Border Nation." *Latin American and Caribbean Ethnic Studies* 14, no. 2 (2019): 116–37.

Weber, Max. "The Nation State and Economic Policy." In *Max Weber: Political Writings*, edited and translated by Peter Lassman and Ronald Speirs. Cambridge University Press, 2004.

Weiss, Laura, Juan Engelman, and Sebastián Valverde. "Pueblos indígenas urbanos en Argentina: Un estado de la cuestión" (Urban Indigenous Peoples in Argentina: A state of the art). *Revista Pilquen* 16, no. 1 (2013): 2–17.

Wilson, Kathi and Evelyn J. Peters. "'You Can Make a Place for It': Remapping Urban First Nations Spaces of Identity." *Environment and Planning / Society and Space* 23, no. 3 (2005): 395–413.

Wolfe, Patrick. *Traces of History: Elementary Structures of Race*. Verso, 2016.

Wright, Pablo. "Colonización del espacio, la palabra y el cuerpo en el Chaco argentino" (Colonization of space, word, and body in the Argentine Chaco). *Horizontes Antropológicos* 9, no. 19 (2003): 137–52.

Wright, Pablo. "Histories of Buenos Aires." in *Peoples of the Gran Chaco*, edited by Elmer S. Miller. Greenwood Publishing, 1999.

Wright, Pablo. "Ser católico y ser evangelio: Tiempo, historia y existencia en la religión Qom" (Being Catholic and Being Evangelical: Time, History, and Existence in Qom Religion). *Revista Anthropológicas* 13, no. 2 (2011): 61–81.

Wright, Pablo. *Ser-en-el-sueño: Crónicas de historia y vida Qom* (Being-in-the-dream: Chronicles of Qom history and life). Biblos, 2008.

Wright, Pablo. "Toba Pentecostalism Revisited." *Social Compass* 39, no. 3 (1992): 355–75.

Zajac, Joaquín. "Los centinelas del cinturón sur: La actividad policial de la Gendarmería Nacional Argentina en los barrios del sur de la CABA" (The sentinels of the southern belt: The police activity of the Argentine National Gendarmerie in the southern neighborhoods of Buenos Aires). *I Jornadas de Estudios Sociales Sobre Delito, Violencia y Policía*, nos. 20–21 (April 2017).

Zajac, Joaquín. "Tapando baches, apagando incendios: Las prácticas de prevención e investigación de delitos de la Gendarmería Nacional Argentina en los barrios del sur de la CABA" (Patching holes, putting out fires: The preventive and investigative practices of the Argentine National Gendarmerie in the neighborhoods of southern Buenos Aires). *Sociales en Debate* no. 11 (2016). https://publicaciones.sociales.uba.ar/index.php/socialesendebate/article/view/3257.

INDEX

aboriginality, 105–6, 188–89, 191–98, 227. *See also* Indigeneity
affect
  affective mobilities, 21–27, 39–48, 50–53, 71
  politics and, 64, 67–72, 93–100, 124
  racialized encounters and, 119–23, 142, 144, 154
  shaping life in common, 134, 160, 164–65, 190
Afro-Argentines, 3–5, 14, 57–61, 77
anthropologists
  collaborative methodology, 2, 20
  Qom views of, 142, 193
anti-racism. *See* racialization and race
Área Metropolitana de Buenos Aires (AMBA)
  location of Barrio Qom, 8–10, 17
  racialized space, 100–102
  urban complexity, 5, 10, 73, 96–99
Argentine state
  bicentennial anniversary, 1–3, 22, 196
  whitening project, 15, 123, 195
assemblages / Indigenous subaltern assemblages
  heterogeneous connections of, 40–41, 169, 177, 182–83
  Indigenous territoriality shaped by, 150–56, 162–63, 168
  mobilization of resources through, 13, 147–51, 156
  politics of indigeneity, 176–79, 183–85, 191–93
  remaking space, 135, 180–83
  theory of, 3–13
authenticity, Indigenous
  co-construction of, 91–94, 127
  as criteria for recognition, 83–105, 94, 111–25, 135, 187–90
  and neoliberal multiculturalism, 107–8, 114
  urban Qom struggle for, 91, 107–14
  youth and, 60, 106–7

Barrio Qom in the Area Metropolitana de Buenos Aires (AMBA)
  Chaco and, 114
  contrasted with *villas*, 8, 10, 81–88
  creation of, 8, 21, 87–89, 92
  legal recognition of, 90–108
Beasley-Murray, Jon, 40, 61
Bermejito, Chaco, 18, 169–71

cabecita negra, 15, 61
Cañuqueo, Lorena, 13
Castelli, Chaco, 148, 152–56

Chaco region
Evangelical missionaries in, 156–58
land displacement and labor exploitation in, 28–31, 160
Qom communities in, 60, 87–110, 126, 148–52
citizenship rights
access to documentation, 136–37
denial of, 14, 138
Ciudad de Buenos Aires (CABA)
center of European project, 4, 15, 141–43
as culturally plural/diverse, 91–99
racial control over, 61, 100, 144–45
coloniality of power, 14, 57–58, 60, 106
comisión vecinal, 9, 44, 108, 156
Conurbano. *See* Área Metropolitana de Buenos Aires (AMBA)
cotton industry, 23, 28, 30–31
Coulthard, Glen, 13, 113
cultural work
authenticity and, 91, 112
economic function, 90–92, 148–49
handicraft production and, 96, 148–52
Cusicanqui Rivera, Silvia, 106

Deleuze, Gilles, and Félix Guattari
assemblage concept, 5, 12
on territoriality, 146–48, 152
diaspora, Indigenous, 5–7, 52, 147, 191

encounters, spatiality of
generating conviviality, 21, 57, 71–73, 153, 192
humanitarianism as, 17, 93–94, 118–122
evictions from *villas*, 83–84
expropriation of Qom's land, 26–31, 57

Fuerte Apache / barrio Ejército de los Andes, 18, 57, 74–82

Gago, Verónica, 13, 154
gender
difference, 20–25
mobilities and, 30, 38–39, 51
mujeres fuertes (strong women), 41–45
Gordillo, Gastón, 64–67, 144
gossip, 38, 47–49, 155
Greater Buenos Aires Area (GBA, within the AMBA) 68, 89, 158

Hall, Stuart, 40, 165–66
humanitarianism
access to city and institutions, 9, 118, 133–37
frictions of, 122–24, 131–32, 144
as racialized relation, 119–21, 126, 143

Iglesia Unida and Qom evangelical churches
mobility connections and, 10, 14, 96, 156–57, 160–61
reconnecting assemblages, 163–68, 179
tension with *la joda*, 165–67
Indigeneity
Marrón identity, 90, 104, 189
and national identity, 1–3
negros and, 61–62, 83–86
Qom self-identification, 5, 60, 85–86, 110, 112, 125
racialized, 14–21, 56–66, 69–77, 86–98, 144, 187
urban, 10, 16–21, 58, 128–37, 146–47, 191

Indigenous legislation, 31, 64, 170–74, 183
  constitutional recognition of 1994, 18–20, 31–36, 102–8
  Law 23.302, 95
  National Institute for Indigenous Affairs (INAI) role, 18–21, 90–95
Indigenous people
  as border migrants, 5, 14, 104
  in Buenos Aires, 83–90, 102, 113–19
  erasure from the city, 3–4, 22, 61
  as rural visitors, 1–3, 126–27
Indigenous politics
  affect and, 40, 71–72, 134
  leaders, 41, 91–94, 109, 133, 156
  organization and activism, 27–32, 94, 108–13, 134, 142, 193
  of recognition, 60, 84, 94, 107–10, 114, 118, 123
  state and, 82–83, 101–9, 112–14, 118–19, 182–88
  subalternity and, 14, 124, 191

kinship
  connecting Indigenous subaltern assemblages, 178–79
  matrilocal tendency, 44
  mobilizing resources, 13, 151
  organizing force for Qom life, 12, 163, 168–69
  orphans / lack of kin, 25, 41, 45–48
  political alliances and, 12, 156

land claims
  in Chaco, 31, 52, 173, 183
  to create Barrios Qom, 88–89, 94, 103–8, 124–28
  as historical reparation, 103, 105, 108–9

Latin America
  cities, 62–63, 82, 97
  Indigenous rights, 10–11, 14–15
  mestizo identities, 57–60
  neoliberal multiculturalism in, 40, 106
  racialization in, 57, 82
Lefebvre, Henri, 72–75, 99

Mapuche People, 7–8, 16, 89, 103–5, 115, 127–28
Marrón identity, and anti-racist activism, 61, 90, 101–4, 189
Massey, Doreen, 17, 56, 72, 177, 180–87
  multiplicity notion of, 92, 177–78, 180–87, 192
middle class, urban
  as allies, 22, 94, 123–24, 142
  humanitarianism and, 84, 94, 118, 123, 144
  villeros negros and, 15, 67, 119
  as white European, 15, 22, 67, 123
military
  militarization of shantytowns, 80–83
  military draft (*colimba*) 41, 49–51
  regulating Qom's mobility, 18, 158–60
mobilities
  affective, 25–26, 40, 51–53, 134
  concept, 17, 20, 25–27, 152–53, 188
  politics of, 18, 39–41, 132, 144–45
  youth, 35, 48
multiculturalism
  and Indigenous recognition, 101–6, 189

neoliberal, 106–7
Napalpí massacre (1924), 30
negros (Argentine racial category)
  Argentine racial formation and, 3, 15, 56–59, 60, 67, 83–85

negros (Argentine racial category) (*continued*):
connection to *villeros*, 21, 60, 77, 83–85
policing, 3, 75, 83, 100
neighborhood commission, 9, 44, 108, 156
nongovernmental organizations (NGOs)
collaboration with Qom, 119–22, 131–34, 140–44
role in land negotiation/support, 31, 94, 109

orphans, 25, 41, 45–48. *See also* kinship

Peronism
anti-Peronism, 120–23
historical context, 20–21, 61–62
Qom participation in, 63–68, 69–71
piqueteros, 3, 134
Povinelli, Elizabeth, 106–7, 113
Puente Transbordador Nicolás Avellaneda (bridge) 185, *186*

Qom Barrio Buenos Aires. *See* Barrio Qom in Area Metropolitana de Buenos Aires (AMBA)
Qom identity, 40, 166, 182
Qom/Toba people, 5–6, 14, 19–20, 52–53

racialization and race
anti-racism, 7, 83, 189–90
Indigenous, 14, 59–60, 77, 85–86, 125
Afro, 14–15, 59, 61
in urban space, 56–57, 61, 72, 80–85, 100, 189
recognition. *See under* Indigenous politics
research ethics / politics, 2, 9, 20, 119, 138, 142, 189
Santos, Milton, 27, 182–83, 192, 197
settler colonialism, 26–31, 57
shantytowns. *See villas*
Simone, AbdouMaliq, 101
space
concept, 5–10, 28, 99, 144–45, 180–82, 192
horizontal, 96–99, 101, 187, 193
multiplicity of, 6, 17, 72, 177, 187
production of, 21, 89–92, 97–99, 187–88, 191
racial organization of, 15, 57, 100, 119
See also territory/territoriality
subalternity and subaltern
assemblages, 13–14, 22, 58, 148, 183, 191–92
Indigeneity and, 14, 119, 191
villas as, 15, 84–85
surrounds, 101

territory / territoriality
beyond bounded spaces, 148–52, 192
Indigenous, 5, 20, 147–48, 182–83
Toba ethnonym, 5

unions, 9, 47, 71–72
urban Indigeneity. *See* Indigeneity
urban inequalities, 4, 56–57, 97, 102
urban Latin America, 57–58, 62–63, 66, 82, 97–98
urban segregation
racial, 12, 66–70, 82, 89, 96, 134
spatial divisions creating, 20, 56–59, 62–63

villas
conviviality in, 56–57, 72
policing of, 21, 74, 83
Qom experience in, 54–57, 62–71, 77–79, 81–83, 90
villeros
Peronism and, 21, 67, 71
racialization of, 56–57, 84, 119

whiteness
modernization as, 15, 119, 123, 134, 145 (*See also* humanitarianism)
white European citizenship project, 1, 4, 15, 61

youth and children
education of, 22, 132, 162
mobility as coming-of-age, 35–48, 167
tensions around identity of, 9, 35, 107–10, 137

www.ingramcontent.com/pod-product-compliance
Lightning Source LLC
LaVergne TN
LVHW091125080826
845145LV00008B/2041

* 9 7 8 0 8 2 6 5 0 8 3 5 5 *